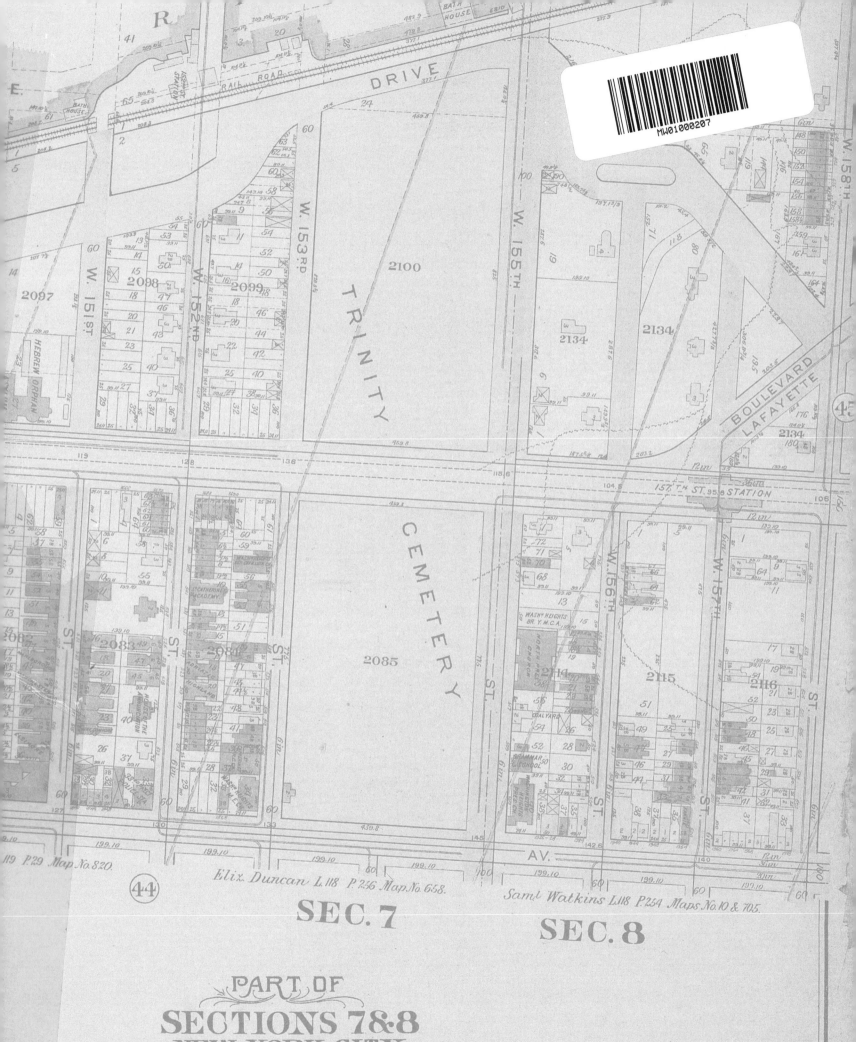

DRIVE

TRINITY

2100

CEMETERY

2085

SEC. 7

SEC. 8

PART OF

# SECTIONS 7&8
## NEW YORK CITY

Scale 150 feet to the inch.

# HARLEM
## LOST AND FOUND

# HARLEM
## LOST AND FOUND

An Architectural and Social History, 1765–1915

MICHAEL HENRY ADAMS
PHOTOGRAPHS BY PAUL ROCHELEAU

PREFACE BY ROBERT A. M. STERN
FOREWORD BY LOWERY STOKES SIMS

THE MONACELLI PRESS

The author and the publisher acknowledge with gratitude
the generous contributions of the Museum of the City of
New York and the New-York Historical Society.

Page 1: Dr. J. Gardner Smith on West 150th Street
at St. Nicholas Place, 1892

Page 2: Theodore Minot Clark, 729–731 St. Nicholas
Avenue, 1886

First published in the United States of America in 2002 by
The Monacelli Press, Inc.
902 Broadway, New York, New York 10010.

Copyright © 2002 The Monacelli Press, Inc.
Text copyright © 2002 Michael Henry Adams

Library of Congress Cataloging-in-Publication Data
Adams, Michael Henry.
Harlem, lost and found : an architectural and social history,
1765–1915 / Michael Henry Adams ; photography by
Paul Rocheleau ; preface by Robert A. M. Stern ; foreword
by Lowery Stokes Sims.
p.   cm.
Includes bibliographical references and index.
ISBN 1-58093-070-0
1. Harlem (New York, N.Y.)—Buildings, structures, etc.
2. Architecture—New York (State)—New York. 3. New
York (N.Y.)—Buildings, structures, etc. 4. Harlem (New
York, N.Y.)—Social life and customs. I. Rocheleau, Paul.
II. Title.
NA735.N5 A33 2002
974.7'1—dc21                    2002005823

Printed and bound in Italy

Designed by Abigail Sturges

# CONTENTS

I dedicate this work to some of Harlem's human landmarks—both those who, though *lost*, continue to inspire and those who, still to be *found*, enrich the scene:

Joan Shepard, Monica Smith, Jean Williams Wade, Bayard Rustin, Jonathan Bryce, David Wilson, Jervis Anderson, Freddie Hamilton, Raven Chanticleer, Markiver Grissom, Christopher Dixon, Kevin Lamont Dickey, Brian Leonard Philip, Maurice Anderson, Corey O'Brien, Cedrick Mickles, Jerome Stark

Josephine Ebaugh Jones, Martha Chandler Dolly, Isabel Washington Powell, Carol Thomas, Sophie Johnson, Mrs. Frederick O'Neal, Marvin P. Smith, David Fontaine, Grafton S. Trew, Raul Abdul, Marguerite Marshall and Warren Blake, Delilah Jackson, Dorothea Towles Church, Olive Adams

*It would seem to be a spiritual necessity for a man to deny and destroy what his father and grandfather had achieved in order to affirm himself . . . with even the process of ultimate rediscovery fortifying the egotism of the fourth generation which recognizes and corrects the prejudiced and shortsighted judgments of its immediate progenitors.*

—Bainbridge Bunting, *Houses of Boston's Back Bay*

# ACKNOWLEDGMENTS

For a writer the greatest difficulty is to begin. My first thanks go to those instrumental in prodding me to start: Suzanne Slesin, Carolyn Cassady Kent, Mrs. John B. Dempsey, Randolph Black, Claudette Law, Anne Bridges Bradley, April Tyler, Lana Turner, Jean-Claude Baker, Shirley Driks, Erik Dawon Fields, Shellie D. Williams, Ruth Messinger, Sybil Bruel, Peter Dixon, Dotson Webster, John Franklin Miller, and Peter Hellman. I also thank my agent, Caroline Press, for safely leading me to the inestimable publisher Gianfranco Monacelli. The invaluable editors who transformed my labyrinthine effort into a readable narrative were Barbara Einzig and Andrea Monfried, ably assisted by proofreader Elizabeth Burpee. How fortunate I was to be able to work with the brilliant designer Abigail Sturges. For guiding me through the thickets of word processing, many thanks must go to Maynard Cassady Kent.

Generous and invaluable financial assistance came first from Chicago's Graham Foundation for Advanced Studies in the Fine Arts, to which I was kindly directed by Mrs. John T. McCutcheon Jr. The Graham Foundation's director, Richard Solomon, and administrator, Patricia Snyder, were extremely helpful. Timely assistance was also provided by Victoria Newhouse of the Architectural History Foundation, and recurring help was offered by my friend Walter Naegle of the Bayard Rustin Fund. A Rosenwald Fellowship, granted under the auspices of the New-York Historical Society, similarly proved beneficial.

Perhaps even more gratifying than these institutional awards was the generous encouragement of several dear individuals, including Christabel Gough; Ellyn Shannon and her entire family; Zita deShaughnessy; Yuien Chin; the late Ormond deKay and the late Nicholas King; exemplary hosts Hal Bromm, Doneley Meris, Margaret Scott Hammond, Mrs. deCorsey Fales, Ann and Dale Dobson, and Valerie Jo Bradley; Anthony Q. Crusor; Ronald Mack; Ron Lester; Crispin Blake McRea; and Kevin Wolfe. Contributors who funded the acquisition of period illustrations are Joan and Charles Adams Platt, Patricia Jones, Roberta Todd, Lisa Rankin, J. S. Ellenberger, Michele Marsh, Agnes Louard, Diane and Alix Michel, Juliet G. Irvine, Sylvia Waters, Sylvia Shorto, Sylvia Tyler, Ibrahim Hussain, Delores Schultz, Peter Mahler, Larry Ortiz, Leigh and Lynden Miller, the Hon. Deborah A. James, the Reverend Robert and Mrs. Castle, the Reverend Canon Frederick Williams, Barry Bergdoll, William Ryall, Ronald Melichar, Christopher Walter London, Barbara Lowell, Peggy Shephard, Charles Lovejoy, Beth Venn and Thomas Draplin, Margaret Anderson, Nina Siegal, Eleanor Eastman, Robert Van Lierop, Katherine Williams, Jethro M. Hurt, Thomas Britt, Mario Buatta, Clive Aslet, Bobby Short, Barbara J. Shannon, Rosamond Shannon, Malcolme Decker, Raymond Saroff, Beverly Hall-Lawrence, Don Harvey, Sherman E. Lee, Mrs. William P. Kannel, Dorothy Shinn, Tracie Rozhon, Deidre Scott, Yanick Rice Lamb, Norma Jean Darden, the Hon. William Perkins, the Hon. Keith Wright, Gwendolyn Giles-Madden, George Goodwill, Francis Redhead, Warner Johnson, Alexa and Bethany Donaphin, Grace Williams, Randy and Elois Dupree, Abigail McGrath, Klara Silverstein, Dr. Thelma Adair and Dr. Jeanne Adair, and Denise Shaw. For inspiration I thank Ania Dolly, Tahbo Geister, Brandon Parham, Taylor Monique Range, and Victor Alexander Evans.

McKim, Mead & White, 203–269 West
139th Street (Strivers' Row), 1891

Imperative to the depiction of Harlem lost are previously unpublished—for the most part—vintage photographs from sources including Culver Pictures, where I was heroically assisted by Harriet Culver and Eva Tucholka; the Museum of the City of New York, where it is especially important to acknowledge the tireless help of Eileen Morales, Kathleen Benson, and Marguerite Lavin; the New-York Historical Society, where thanks must be extended to Betsy Gotbaum, Stuart Desmond, and Nicole Wells; the New York Genealogical and Biographical Society, where executive director William Potter Johns provided essential assistance; the Frick Art Reference Library, where I must thank Elisabeth Duffy; and the Municipal Archives, where I was helped by Kenneth Cobb. Gil Amiaga and Andrew Alpern were also important sources of historic photographs.

I owe an enormous debt of gratitude to three world-renowned scholars who took the time not only to read this book in manuscript form but to enhance it with commentary of their own: Lowery Stokes Sims, Robin Middleton, and Robert A. M. Stern. Other scholars whose works informed my own include James T. Maher, David Levering Lewis, George Chauncy, Steven Watson, David Garrard Lowe, Thomas Mellins, Thomas Wirth, Thomas Fisher, Christopher Gray, Carson Anthony Anderson, A'Lelia Bundles, Hilton Kramer, Jay Shockley, Mildred Schmertz, Andrew S. Dolkart, and Gretchen S. Sorin. Most important, I thank Paul Rocheleau for his sensitive, collaborative interpretation of Harlem. His photographs adroitly convey the timeless beauty of this special place. I further thank anyone I have unintentionally omitted.

Finally, I offer abiding thanks to my family: my sisters, Deborah Louise Parham, Athena Marie Littlepage, Valerie Lynn Adams, and Tracey Alexandria Smith; my stepmother, Sheila Adams; and my patient parents, Willie Dean Hollinger Adams and Alexander Leroy Adams Jr.

# PREFACE

This is a fine book, long overdue, which unites social history and architectural history—a rare and most welcome combination. Harlem as it now exists was largely built from the 1880s through the early 1900s to meet the housing requirements of Manhattan's expanding white population. Since World War I it has been home to a substantial portion of New York's African-American population. But as Michael Adams intimates, good architecture is essentially color-blind: the historic architecture of Harlem has served its changing population remarkably well, despite the complex issues of racial strife and poverty that have come very close to breaking it apart. Virtually overwhelmed by a vicious cycle of overcrowding, relentless subdivision, neglect, and often abandonment, Harlem has not only survived but is now regaining its position as an important center in the city's economy and cultural life—to which this book is brilliantly timed.

Adams's book not only brings a fresh perspective to Harlem's evolution but provides a wealth of fascinating historical detail, about both important buildings and also the architects, developers, and patrons who helped create this exceptional slice of urbanism. But Adams does not neglect the frequently overlooked, everyday masterpieces that do so much to shape the character of the area. Moreover, his scholarship is wonderfully reinforced by remarkable, in many cases unknown historic photographs, and by Paul Rocheleau's color photography, which is perhaps nowhere more powerful than when it offers rare glimpses inside many buildings only recently restored.

Adams is a historian with a mission: his book is surely and properly admonitory to those in the preservation community who have been slow to officially recognize the area's landmarks. It is not as a scold, however, but as a guide that Adams makes his greatest contribution. With this book, scholars and travelers can no longer ignore Harlem's architecture and urbanism. Most of all, seasoned New Yorkers can no longer plead ignorance of Manhattan's brilliant uptown. We owe Michael Adams a debt of gratitude for "finding" Harlem for us all.

ROBERT A. M. STERN

11

# FOREWORD

My mother grew up in Harlem during the Depression. She married my father right after World War II, and they immediately decamped to Washington, where he pursued a second degree in architecture and where I was born. When my father began work at an architectural firm in New York City, we moved for a time into the Harlem River Houses. This was where my brother and sister were born. By the mid-1950s, however, we decamped again and joined the new suburban migration, settling into a newly built house, euphemistically marketed as "colonial." We thought we had made it.

"Harlem" and "architecture," therefore, have been a part of my life—although not necessarily as part of a unified concept, as in "Harlem architecture" or "architecture in Harlem." Indeed, while I often drew and drafted next to my father, and read his architecture history books as he studied for his architectural license, I was estranged from the concept of Harlem. By the 1950s and 1960s, it had been firmly planted in my head that Harlem was a place where you were from, and where you visited friends and relatives who were not so lucky as to have moved away. So on occasion we tentatively returned to visit a great-aunt and -uncle and some cousins.

At college in the later 1960s and 1970s, I began to learn about and appreciate the rich cultural history of Harlem in the burgeoning concentrations in black history and culture that were coming into formation in various colleges and universities. It was a time when I first met people of my generation or slightly older who were moving to Harlem and renovating brownstones—like Sam and Carolyn Brown Anderson—and through them met long-time Harlem residents. And in the 1970s and 1980s, as the regentrification process gained momentum, my visits to Harlem became more frequent, particularly as I became involved in the Studio Museum in Harlem, which opened its doors at its first location on Fifth Avenue and 125th Street in 1968. I report on this because, in light of the red-hot interest in Harlem real estate today and the related controversy engendered by the most recent gentrification of Harlem, it is important to note that the early prime movers were for the most part African-American.

I became director of the Studio Museum in January 2000, and after that it seemed that Harlem exploded as the most topical of media subjects. With every passing day, the lines in the battle over who owns Harlem, who should live in Harlem, who embodies Harlem, are more firmly drawn on the sidewalks. There is where this wonderfully written narrative by Michael Adams comes in. Drawing on earlier studies, Adams provides a richly textured picture of the characters and inhabitants of Harlem, the rich, the poor, the famous, the infamous, the white, the Native American, the black. It is through the lives of individuals and the ambitions of individuals that it is possible to see how Harlem grew, was built, and was settled, and how in the end the architecture has prevailed and somehow preserved that rich history to influence the present.

Adams writes of Harlem's initial status as a country outpost for downtown New York City— a perception that still exists in the minds of many. He recalls the Native Americans, who were the first encountered by the Dutch, and describes their vaulted longhouses, which soon disappeared from the Manhattan landscape. This reminded me of the slave quarters that have disappeared from southern plantations, thus offering a skewed notion of the who, the what, and the when of American culture. Whether intentionally or not, these consequences both obliterate the contributions of supplanted and enslaved peoples and perpetuate an exclusively bricks-and-mortar notion of architecture.

As difficult as it is to think of Manhattan ever being the site of farming, Adams describes the homesteads of the Dutch settlers and establishes precedents for transplanting or adapting, which often resulted in architectural anomalies. Soon came the English and Dutch bearers of the names of places and locales that persist today: Dyckman, York, Beekman, Riker, and others. The story of the fortunes built by Philipses, the Morrises, and the Jumels and the mansions that were erected to declare those fortunes is recounted, as is the interest in expressing Enlightenment concepts through the adaptation of European models, such as those of the Italian architect Andrea Palladio. Adams treats Madam Jumel's role in Napoleonic political intrigues as well as the way that houses and estates pass from one hand to another as the consequence of an individual's or family's rise or fall. He discusses how residents dealt with health crises—the bane of urban life—and how neighborhoods gave way to new economic realities.

It is at the end of the nineteenth century that the story of architecture in Harlem heats up. Multiple-unit apartment houses that preceded the notion of "housing projects" appeared first for the wealthier class and then accommodated the shift in demographics made possible by the introduction of easier, faster transportation and the attraction of Harlem's proximity to employment centers. The subsequent development of parks—such as Mount Morris—and other recreational centers in Harlem could only follow. Adams recalls the architects—now largely unknown—who engineered this urban environment and predicated how people live and situate themselves in Harlem today. Many architects and critics, including Charles Eastlake and Montgomery Schuyler, persisted in the notion of using architecture to counter what Adams calls the "dehumanizing effects of burgeoning industrialization." Post-Victorian backlash, a more economic mix of dwellings at the beginning of the twentieth century, the influential presences of colleges, schools, and houses of worship—like St. Philip's, which led the way for African-American relocation to Harlem—all are discussed in Adams's text. He also records the contributions of a new generation of African-Americans in forming the Harlem urbanscape, from A'Lelia Walker in the 1920s to contemporary preservationists such as Martha Chandler Dolly, artist Grace Williams, and architect Alexa Donaphin. It is in their hands and those of countless others—African, European, and Asian American—that the future greatness of Harlem lies. By presenting its rich architectural heritage, Michael Adams provides a context within which Harlem's history may be appreciated and preserved for the future.

LOWERY STOKES SIMS

# INTRODUCTION

Harlem, where I live, is iconic, mythic, larger than life, known throughout the world. It is the home of jazz and black culture. It is feared as an impoverished, crime-ridden ghetto. However paradoxical Harlem's plight, there is one aspect in which it is undeniably rich: Harlem holds one of America's most comprehensive collections of intact late-nineteenth- and early-twentieth-century buildings. An opulent architectural legacy at a human scale, the structures do not obscure the sky. Together with the community's favorable location and rapid transit network, they form the basis of a burgeoning neo–Harlem Renaissance. At the outset of the twenty-first century, Harlem is attracting scores of new inhabitants, national retail chains, and eager and expectant European and Asian tourists, by the busload, on the hour.

17 East 128th Street (now Angelita Ortega and Pauline Fernandez house), 1864

How different today's Harlem is from the various and divergent Harlems of yesteryear. Like so much in American history, the earliest local settlements—indigenous and Dutch—have vanished with barely a visible trace. But all other periods of building between 1765 and 1915 are represented in today's Harlem, in one way or another, by extant buildings. Much of Harlem's architecture is valued not for qualities of uniqueness or of grandeur but for the way that the streetscape encapsulates historic experience. Most of the buildings in Harlem from this 150-year epoch imitate or derive from grander work in downtown New York or from well-known monuments of European design. Such models in turn were based on architecture conceived in the Middle Ages or in ancient times. Thus the buildings of Harlem are like the image produced by two facing mirrors: a reflection of a reflection of a reflection.

It is possible to time travel in Harlem simply by turning the corner from Seventh Avenue onto West 132nd Street, unexpectedly coming upon William Renwick's St. Aloysius's Roman Catholic Church of 1904. With scarlet doors and polychromed terra cotta, it so convincingly evokes Italy's late medieval churches that the effect, though delightful, can be somewhat disorienting. A similar sense of disjunction may occur while viewing Arnold Brunner's Temple Israel of 1907 at 201 Lenox Avenue, which might easily be mistaken for a bank or courthouse; it is rather a synagogue built by newly prosperous European immigrants who had moved to Harlem from the Lower East Side. Inspired by recently discovered archaeological evidence in the Holy Land, they harked back to Jerusalem's classical Second Temple, built during the Roman occupation. The impact of Gothic cathedrals and Greco-Roman temples was ubiquitous in yesterday's Harlem; strictly modern styles of building were generally resisted.

Certainly all this took place long ago. Practicality—technology, utility, and economy—has become all important, while traditional decoration and precedent are considered irrelevant. What, then, is the point of examining in such detail a community's architectural heritage that, however extensive, cannot be said to contain path-breaking buildings?

The history of Harlem is related as much through social convention as through stylistic expression. For instance, there is no better method to learn about the true life of A'Lelia Walker, Harlem's leading party girl of the 1920s, than by visiting her home at 80 Edgecombe Avenue, designed by

15

Gronenberg & Leuchtag and completed in 1915. Accounts of her pampered existence abound in contemporary newspapers and in the memoirs of the guests who flocked to her entertainments. Paul Frankel, one of the city's leading modernist decorators, designed her hideaway. But nothing in the enthusiastic commentary recounting champagne soirees honoring the crown prince of Sweden and various silent movie stars prepares a visitor for the place—a one-bedroom suite in an architecturally unexceptional walk-up apartment building. What other artifact could better demonstrate the disparity, even at the apex of society, between black and white New York during the 1920s?

Yet Harlem's historic buildings are by no means devoid of the creative impulse. On the contrary, the inventiveness, flair, and even wit exhibited by designers confronting a limited number of frequently repetitious building types are by any standard impressive. As they are today, most Harlemites of the past were ordinary people. Even when they were rich, they were not the wealthiest residents in the New York region. So it is worth noting that the buildings created for them were consistently realized at a high level of workmanship and design. Achievements of long-forgotten Harlem practitioners such as Henry Andersen or Neville & Bagge may be likened to those of such figures as onetime Harlemite Norman Rockwell or Maxfield Parrish; the aesthetic value of their work has often been downplayed because of their commercial success. While new scholarship and record sale prices have caused a reevaluation of the latter as accomplished painters, a similar movement on behalf of the former has not yet taken place.

This, then, is a goal of the present volume, which has been inspired by undertakings such as Robert A. M. Stern's pioneering New York series (with collaborators Thomas Mellins, David Fishman, Gregory Gilmartin, and John M. Massengale). Other writings that led me include Nathan Silver's *Lost New York*, Camilo José Vergara's *American Ruins*, and Andrew S. Dolkart and Gretchen S. Sorins's *Touring Historic Harlem*. Such endeavors lament what has been lost while extolling what remains; they have encouraged my drive to document and describe what still stands in Harlem, as has *The Destruction of the Country House,* by Roy Strong, Marcus Binney, and John Harris, which says so much about Britain's lost building heritage.

Because much of Harlem's architectural legacy has been destroyed, and because only 7 1/2 percent of the 12,000 protected landmarks of Manhattan are above 96th Street, I was at first tempted to make this a different kind of book. An encyclopedic survey of the sort exemplified by the late Bainbridge Bunting's unprecedented *Houses of Boston's Back Bay* offered a model of thoroughness. Yet as I continued with *Harlem, Lost and Found*, and especially as I started to collaborate with Paul Rocheleau, whose superb photographs have an uncanny ability to place the viewer on the spot, I envisioned a volume more in the spirit of James Mahers's exquisite, if too little known, *The Twilight of Splendor*. Accordingly, I have made every effort to place Harlem's architecture in a context of history and people, living and dead, not only builders and past residents but also those who preserve, cherish, and restore what has been built.

Much that is presented here is new. There was a great deal of material to consider, and behind nearly every fact included lies a host of stories untold. In some cases, memory or notation of sources has been less than perfect; any resultant errors are my own. Perhaps my unremitting labor of love and the compelling stories related will help to overcome any such faults. For *Harlem, Lost and Found* is intended above all to celebrate buildings that were meant to celebrate and to ennoble all—even ordinary people.

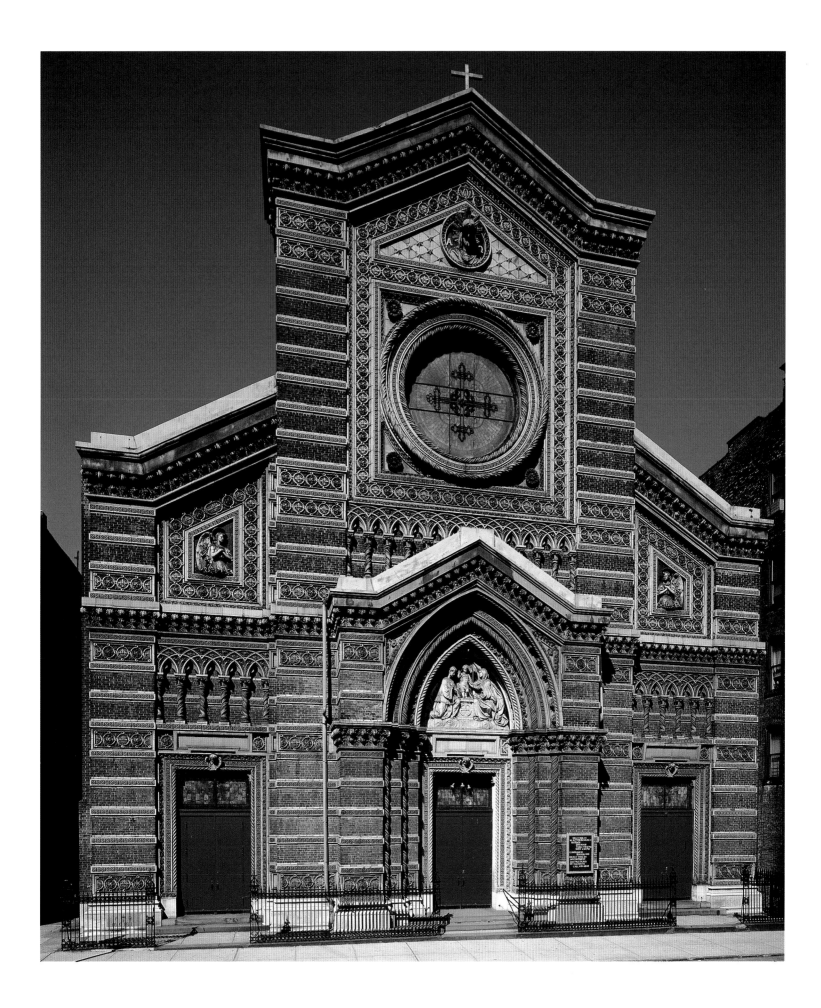

Harlem looking northwest from
East 115th Street and Pleasant Avenue,
c. 1891

Harlem looking west
from Mount Morris Park

St. Nicholas Place looking west
from West 150th Street, 1909

# CHAPTER ONE

# THE ORIGINS OF HARLEM

Morris-Jumel Mansion, St. Nicholas
Avenue and West 160th Street, 1765,
modified c. 1810. Shingled east side

A rchitectural historians have long noted that New York City, despite its
international consequence, has suffered from a small-town attitude. Historian
Charles Lockwood observed that when City Hall opened in 1812 (designed
by Joseph François Mangin with John McComb Jr., architect of one of Harlem's
most handsome and venerable structures, Hamilton Grange of 1802), white
marble was used to face the east, south, and west walls, but the north side was
brownstone, saving $15,000. Most city fathers felt this was a justifiable economy, since the city
lay some blocks to the south and marble facing on the north would have been "all out of sight to
all the world!" But this lack of vision is not entirely surprising: as historian Gilbert Osofsky has
noted, in the 1820s Harlem, to the north, consisted of ninety-one families and one church,
school, and library.

Throughout New York's and Harlem's booms and busts, underlying inhabitants' dreams and
dreams deferred, a pattern of rapid change has remained constant. Harlem's first prime building
period, corresponding to the establishment of steamboat and railway lines, occurred between
1830 and approximately 1860. Lockwood quotes from Philip Hone's 1839 journal: "The spirit
of pulling down and building up is abroad. The whole of New York is rebuilt about once in ten
years." In the 1860s the city's population expanded greatly and Harlem's followed suit; it was
annexed as far north as 155th Street in 1873, three years after authorities had filled in more than
one thousand acres of marshland. A second building bonanza began at this time and continued
intermittently until the first decade of the twentieth century. Because of a history of fortuitous
neglect, nowhere in the New York area can the cycle of economic success and distress be better
examined than in Harlem. Architectural historian Robert Stern has observed that Harlem, at least
in one respect, has always retained a provincial character. "Its tastes, architecturally, were
*retardataire*," he has written: many local developers, architects, and contractors tended to be
overly cautious. Frequently their application of alien new styles or untried ways of planning
exhibited a limited understanding at best. Having once learned to plan and build a structure that
appealed to the target market, they were reluctant to try anything new. Buildings formerly made

of wood and brick might suddenly be fabricated from brownstone, but the essentials of plan and mode remained, to a remarkable degree, the same as before. Similarly, the architects of many speculative row houses built at the end of the nineteenth century went on to design apartment houses with the same alliance to conservative and pragmatic adaptation.

Among the affluent, there was always greater leeway. Within bounds, the manner of dressing or living, and all expressions of taste, of a wealthy individual could reflect his or her personality. Nevertheless, even among the upper classes few architects were prepared to take aesthetic risks, and for the rich, poor, and in-between, style still mattered. In Harlem, the houses of the wealthy set the standard according to which other dwellings were formulated. If from the early 1700s through the 1860s the vast majority of America's mansions were designed in styles determined by classical European tradition, so were the vast majority of Harlem houses of all kinds and classes.

The variety this entails sometimes seems infinite. From 1830 to 1850, Harlem house builders took as their ideal template the severe temples of ancient Greece, a dominance called by historian David Garrard Lowe "the Greek Revival hegemony." The Grecian was succeeded by the Italianate, an adaptation of the villas of Renaissance Tuscany as popularized by Queen Victoria's retreat Osborne House. All the while, addressing a growing dissatisfaction with "cold, white, straight, and rule-bound classical design," the Gothic Revival hovered in the background. Because of its enduring identification with Christianity, many felt it to be a "morally superior mode."

Devotion to trends may be seen throughout the history of Harlem—as long as a certain stylistic iteration remained in vogue, it was an effective selling point, and Harlem builders' devotion was absolute. This adherence to what Lowe has colorfully described as a "kaleidoscopic plethora of sham Gothic castles, Egyptian Revival churches, octagonal Moresque pavilions and Italianate villas" has resulted in a Harlem streetscape richly stratified with layers of time past, as complex and satisfying as any that America or even Europe has to offer.

## The First Harlemites: Native Americans in Harlem

In 1906, at a time when apartment houses were rising all over Harlem, construction workers uncovered innumerable relics of earlier times. Some were almost missed: Reginald Pelham Bolton, a contemporary historian and amateur archaeologist, noted that what at first "appeared to be merely part of a boulder" was an exciting find: a "vase of very perfect form and design [that] had lain, quite undisturbed, for at least two, and perhaps more, centuries, while successive generations of farmers had tilled the soil or herded the cattle over its resting place, until the advance of the subway." A rough blue bead was found nearby, and there was speculation that it might be of the very sort for which the title to Native American homelands had been so cheaply bartered. In fact, Harlem's Native Americans had not been party to the famous transaction in 1626 in which, at the downtown site now known as Bowling Green, a confederation of tribes deeded all of Manhattan to Peter Minuit, director general of the Dutch West India Company, in exchange for approximately twenty-four dollars worth of goods and trinkets. Harlem's first people, members of the Weckquasgeek tribe that was part of the confederacy known as the Iroquois nation, were centered at modern-day Dobbs Ferry. Those specific to the Harlem area have come to be known as "Reckewa's people," after a chief present when the Dutch first arrived there.

The city that is now known as New York came into being because Europeans hoped to make great fortunes in the New World. Harlem was a key part of this effort. Holland's Dutch East India

Company, which had a lucrative monopoly in the Orient trading in spices, silks, and other luxury goods, had enriched many adventurers; the Dutch West India Company hoped for an equally remunerative Occidental venture. Outside of Scandinavia, Europe's vanishing woodlands were largely depleted of wildlife. The Europeans traded guns, whiskey, and inexpensive items for the Native Americans' fox, mink, sable, ermine, and beaver pelts. While the fur trade indeed proved profitable, the Dutch soon found an enterprise with a far greater return—the "triangular trade," which would transform New York into one of the greatest ports in the world as ships plied the waters between the coasts of western Africa, the Caribbean, and colonial America. Frederick Philipse and his son Adolph were among the instigators of this early form of global capitalism; they acquired land in the 1640s from the Weckquasgeek and Sint Sinks and built a formidable trading empire in the area, showing a genius for profiting from slaves (slavery remained legal in New York until 1830), rum, and wheat.

The royal charter granting the Dutch West India Company territorial authority encompassed the area that would eventually become New York and New Jersey. Those who acted under the auspices of this document disregarded any prior rights of the Native Americans. Settlers who moved northward over the island of Manhattan as early as 1636 took note of an Indian village just below the Mount Morris (Marcus Garvey) Park of today. Nearby, the Harlem River shared the name of this seasonally inhabited fishing station and planting field—Muscota, a word meaning "fields," "flats," and "a place where bulrushes grow." The stream that flowed into the Muscota was referred to as Reckewa's Creek and was later known as Harlem Creek or Montagne's Kill (Dutch for "small stream"). According to Gerard Koeppel's *Water for Gotham: A History*, it was the dividing line for tribal territories, and its regular flooding across Harlem's alluvial plain made for especially bountiful crops of corn. Dutch colonists were attracted by the fertility of this upriver portion of Manhattan and established the settlement known as Nieuw Haarlem.

Colonial accounts of the original inhabitants of Harlem range from the complimentary to the bewildered to the frankly unsympathetic. Reginald Bolton in his book about Washington Heights (known before about 1865 as Harlem Heights) cites a number of primary sources from the first half of the seventeenth century:

> They go, in deerskins loose, well-dressed—some in mantles of feathers, and some in skins of divers sorts of good furres. They have red copper tobacco pipes, and other things of copper they doe wear about their neckes . . .

> The barbarians are divided into many nations and languages, but differ little in manners . . . Their food is maze, crushed fine and baked in cakes; with fish, birds, and wild game. Their weapons are bows and arrows; their boats made from the truncks of trees, hollowed out by fire. Some lead a wandering life, others live in bark houses, their furniture mainly mats and wooden dishes, stone hatchets, and stone pipes for smoking tobacco . . .

> Their fare, or food, is poor and gross, for they drink water, having no other beverage; they eat the flesh of all sorts of game that the country supplies, even badgers, dogs, eagles and similar trash, which Christians in no way regard; these they cook and use uncleansed and undressed.

"Reckewa's people" lived in longhouses, vaulted dwellings formed of bent branches and strips of the slippery inner bark of elm trees, covered on the outside with sheets of bark that Bolton describes as having been "laced with cedar-roots and bark peelings." A fire in the center was

Manhattan Island before the Dutch

vented through a smoke hole. The architecture of the first inhabitants of Harlem left almost no trace; even shortly after these hunters and gatherers moved on, there would have been little sign of their early shelters.

## The Second Harlemites: Dutch Homesteads

Although initially the indigenous inhabitants of Harlem were friendly to the Dutch, when they saw they were being displaced they fought back. Land ownership was a concept alien to Native Americans, and they did not understand that accepting payment for their land implied that they would leave it. Harlem's first European farms were so repeatedly attacked that they were abandoned after only thirty years. But in 1658 the Dutch West India Company's new director general, Peter Stuyvesant, supported by the governing council, officially reconstituted the European village. The company was undoubtedly motivated by the need to establish some line of defense between hostile Indians to the north and the port city of New Amsterdam at the southern tip of Manhattan. Settlement in such an "outpost of civilization" was challenging, and settlers were found among the company's slaves, who were given freedom and land in exchange for taking up residence on this frontier. It is probable that these same African-Americans built the area's first highway, the Harlem Road, which connected the hamlet with New Amsterdam. The northern village was named after the town in Holland that shared a similar geographical relationship to the larger city of Amsterdam: the new and old towns were situated along a navigable river only ten miles apart.

Straight off their ships, Harlem's new Dutch settlers relied greatly on the expertise of the indigenous population in coping with their new environment. The first Dutch dwellings were improvised along the lines of Native American longhouses. But invaluable as these structures were for survival, they did not enable the Dutch to prove to themselves and to their new neighbors that they were still "civilized." Not long after they first arrived, the Dutch began building in a manner approximating the most basic form of shelter that they had left behind. While the buildings of New Amsterdam were primarily of brick, New Harlem's houses were constructed from fieldstone, wood, and shingles.

The Dyckman house, situated at what is now West 204th Street and Broadway, provides a model for the appearance of these early farmhouses. The building exhibits many of the features associated with the vernacular of Dutch Colonial farmhouses, with their gambrel and saltbox roofs. The original Dyckman house was built in 1700 but was burned by British troops during the Revolutionary War. The present house was built to take its place about 1798, and the fireplace mantels and other details are concessions to the Georgian taste current at the time. Yet the more rustic qualities of the original structure can still be observed.

Indeed, the Dyckman house looks like Harlem farmhouses that have not survived into the present day. While these modest structures were never regarded as architectural masterpieces, on the occasion of America's hundredth birthday two of them were venerated as relics of a proud past. Harlem's last true Dutch farmsteads were the so-called Stone House (c. 1710) at what is now St. Nicholas Avenue and West 152nd Street, which had originally belonged to Gerret Dyckman and was a familiar landmark into the 1870s, and the seventeenth-century house of Aron Bussing at the present Eighth Avenue and West 147th Street, which stood until 1910. A. B. Caldwell's 1882 history of Harlem cites another house from the colonial era, one belonging to Peter Benson, whose family, along with the Montagnes, Hoppers, and Raubs, was heir to a seventeenth-century land title. The Benson house, which survived until 1865, was distinguished by its typical Dutch fireplace. Purple, magnesium-glazed Delft tiles depicted biblical and mythological figures and reached almost to the beaded beams of the ceiling, offering a decorative counterpoint to the otherwise spare interior. A typical embellishment, reminiscent of East Indian and African customs, was the fine sprinkling of beach sand swept into waves or other curving patterns across newly scrubbed floorboards at least twice weekly.

Stone House, St. Nicholas Avenue and West 152nd Street, c. 1710

All three small houses, along with no more than a few dozen others, composed the Harlem of the early eighteenth century. All of these houses shared more or less identical plans, materials, and construction methods. The first floor's outer walls were made from coarse, dark gray mica schist, the bedrock of Manhattan that was excavated on site. At this time Harlem was densely forested, and half-timbering to save wood was hardly necessary. Yet the custom was so ingrained that the spaces between the heavy wood post-and-beam framework were filled with plastered basketwork covered with shingles or stones. The ends of gables and the roofs were covered with very long New Netherland shingles; eight- and even ten-inch exposures were common. Like the town houses of New Amsterdam, the chimneys of New Harlem were made from Dutch bricks that had been brought over as ships' ballast.

Engineering methods were unsophisticated, and thus the size of early dwellings was limited by the difficulties of raising the roof. This restriction was compensated for by extending the sloping roof beyond the exterior wall to provide cantilevered eaves often wide enough to shelter porches, many of which ran along the entire front and back of the house. Similarly, lean-to additions created the classic saltbox silhouette, in which one slope of the roof is closer to the ground than the other. Attic lofts, useful not only for storage but also as sleeping quarters for children, indentured servants, and slaves, were lit by shed-dormer windows, the tops of which ran parallel to the angle of the roof.

An even more economical means of creating a larger house was the gambrel roof, still found on many barns to this day. This was a gabled roof with doubled slopes, the lower typically angled about forty-five degrees and the upper about thirty degrees, with the upper generally far shorter than the lower. In many Dutch examples, both slopes were gently curved. The gambrel roof provided even greater headroom in the attic, allowing finished bedrooms to be situated there, and still required less material than a gabled roof.

Both types of Dutch Colonial farmhouses had a low ceiling of seven or eight feet, with small casement windows. The famous Dutch door, divided into upper and lower halves, allowed the house to be ventilated without letting livestock in or children out. It was generally made of oak and hung on stout wrought-iron strap-hinges.

Until late in the eighteenth century, all components in these buildings were handmade. These included costly glass, which was created by skilled craftsmen who, before roaring furnaces, manipulated molten bubbles of glass at the end of long tubes. Twirling the tubes deftly above the bright flames, the fabricators harnessed centrifugal force to form an unevenly flattened disk. From this disk, four feet in diameter at most, tables of crown glass were cut, yielding rectangular sheets. The curving pieces, particularly the "bull's eye" where the tube had been attached, had in Holland been regarded as little more than scraps. But the Dutch pioneers thriftily glazed their transoms with these small greenish squares, each swelling at the center toward a navel-like knob, unintentionally decorative. Precious flat windowpanes, cut into rectangles or diamonds, were protected by strong shutters, which also served as curtains or shades.

Fireplaces were the functional heart of these houses, providing light, warmth, and a place for many domestic activities. Soap and candles were made from tallow in large cauldrons that swung over the fire on heavy iron cranes. Other covered kettles with pointed feet were the original Dutch ovens. Another ingenious device of the period was a roasting spit that could be operated by family dogs running on a treadmill. Brick ovens, set into the chimney wall, were heated with coals.

## Mansions: From the English Period to 1915

British takeover of the New Netherland colony in 1664 caused New Amsterdam to become New York, but little changed in New Harlem. The township's boundaries endured and were codified by an English charter defining Harlem as lying north of a line extending from today's East 74th Street to the western end of 129th Street. Nevertheless, the English tried to give Harlem a new, distinctly English identity by christening the area "New Lancaster." (The Duke of Lancaster was the brother of the Duke of York.) This attempt was as unsuccessful as British efforts to establish Anglicanism in the face of Harlem's Dutch Reformed churches. However, the British influence was of great significance in architecture, as new colonists sought to recall the English houses they had left behind. These houses were larger and more classically correct than Dutch dwellings, with specialized rooms, higher ceilings, and more elaborate windows, staircases, and mantelpieces.

As time went on Harlem came to enjoy the presence of more imposing and magnificent structures where Dutch farmhouses had once stood. Historian James Riker has identified some of the leading residents from this time: Delanceys, Beekmans, Bleeckers, Rikers, Coldens, and Hamiltons. Eighteenth-century New Harlem was a prosperous and remarkably stable place, giving rise to the image of America's most optimistic dreams: the house set on a hill, distant from neighbors and grand in scale, distinguished by a soaring tower or a broad front portico with high white pillars.

Although many of the great estates were divided or sold in the early nineteenth century as the formerly fertile land gradually refused to yield sufficient returns, with the opening of the New York and Harlem Railroad in 1837 Harlem found new life: the neighborhood flourished as a scenic retreat for fashionable New Yorkers. Those who summered in Harlem were figures of considerable wealth and cultural importance, and were well acquainted with one another. John James Audubon, the famed naturalist who settled in 1840 on an estate that extended from West 155th to 158th Street between Amsterdam Avenue and the Hudson River, wrote, "I wonder that men can consent to swelter . . . their lives away amid those hot bricks and pestilent vapors, when the woods and fields are so near?" Yet in the aftermath of the Civil War, the beginnings of contemporary Harlem emerged; correspondingly, small farms and great estates alike disappeared, along with their hills, fields, and rushing streams, and feverish building commenced.

Despite Harlem's growth, as late as 1900 the past held some ground: some mansions still stood, including exceptional examples of the Federal, Greek Revival, Gothic Revival, Italianate, Second Empire, Eastlake, and Queen Anne styles. For the most part this architectural patrimony is lost to the present day. Extraordinary exceptions that have survived are the Morris-Jumel Mansion, Hamilton Grange, and the Bailey house, as well as the residences of the Benziger, Baiter, and Backer families. Each is an eloquent representative of its particular era and bears testimony to a vanished way of life, especially when viewed within the context of lost great houses, including the Watt-Pinckney Mansion, the Maunsell-Watkins and Bradhurst estates, the Mott Mansion, the Michael Sampter house, the George Richards house, the brownstone of Henry W. Genet, the Van Rensselaer estate, and the Madam C. J. Walker house.

## The Morris-Jumel Mansion (1765)

Manhattan's sole surviving colonial residence is today found near St. Nicholas Avenue, at the end of West 160th Street. Perched upon Harlem Heights's highest elevation, Mount Morris, the house is now set within a ten-acre city park and is bordered by Victorian row houses and apartment buildings of a later date. Originally it dominated the open countryside, occupying some 130 acres that spanned the Harlem and Hudson Rivers. It was the most imposing of houses built by the English colonists.

The property's historical background is rooted in the changing sources of industrial and commercial wealth in early America. The actual ground of the estate derived from the very early achievements of the Anglo-Dutch Philipse family, merchants who established a powerful colonial milling and trading complex at Yonkers, the Upper Mills of Philipsburg Manor. That site was constructed and operated by African slaves; the Philipse family house with its surrounding property has been restored as a working farm and mill, now open to the public.

Frederick Philipse's great-granddaughter was Mary Philipse, who was also related to the family of Elizabeth Hamilton (wife of Alexander), the Schuylers, and to many other prominent figures in the Anglo-Dutch elite of her day. At one time Mary was courted by George Washington, but she followed the wishes of her father and married Roger Morris, another military officer, in 1758.

The year before Colonel Morris completed building this prescient residence, he retired from the army and became a member of the King's Council, the body that governed New York. Not long after the mansion was finished, public agitation against the Crown, which would soon intensify to revolution, forced Morris to flee to England. Mary Morris and their young children returned to the relative safety of Philipsburg Manor, and in the politically turbulent times that followed the mansion they left behind passed through a number of transformations. With the victory of American forces at the Battle of Harlem Heights, Washington and his staff, including aide-de-camp Alexander Hamilton, established their headquarters there. But only a month later Hessian soldiers, fighting for England, made it their camp. In 1783, following the rousting of the British, it was sold by the new federal government's commissioner of forfeiture and served for some years as an inn.

The Morris Mansion had made a great impression on both Washington and Hamilton during their stay there, and they chose it as the site for a dinner in honor of the new president's cabinet on July 10, 1790. The house, by now an inn, was one of the most imposing in the area. Nearly unique when built, the layout had become quite typical of the houses of the wealthy at that time. Three large reception rooms and a butler's pantry flanked a wide central hallway, which led to a spacious drawing room on axis with the front door. The kitchen was relegated to the basement. (That this caused tepid food to be set on the table was considered less important than the elimination of cooking odors and an aesthetic of strict symmetry.) Each door and window was balanced by an identical counterpart.

The house was built at a time when the specialized dining room, used exclusively for meals, was just becoming common in grand houses. A serving pantry was also a novel development. Reached through a door placed beneath an elliptically arched recess to the right of the sideboard, the pantry was equally useful for cleaning and storing china and glassware. Nearby stairs went up to the bedrooms and down to the kitchen, while an outside door led to a barnyard with chickens, smokehouse, vegetable garden, dairy, orchard, and icehouse. This latter convenience, built of stone, kept cold beneath an insulating blanket of straw and sawdust blocks of ice that were harvested from the Hudson River with long ice saws.

Washington's party had driven the eleven miles north from New York in a ceremonious cavalcade, requiring almost every coach available at the time. The drawing room, normally used for conversation and card playing before and after dinner, was set up for this occasion as a

Morris-Jumel Mansion. Portico

banqueting hall. Following the dinner, punch and Madeira were served, and the arched entrance gallery served as a ballroom. Vice President John Adams and Secretary of State Thomas Jefferson were both present, along with Alexander Hamilton, secretary of the treasury, who was accompanied by his well-born wife, the former Elizabeth Schuyler.

The house's continuing influence on Washington and Hamilton is quite evident: both later incorporated several of its features into their own country retreats. Grandiose yet reserved, the mansion was at the forefront of taste among dwellings of its day, with a two-story, four-columned portico. The drawing room is octagonal, the first of its kind in America. Such trend-setting design was a product not only of the Philipse fortune but of the fact that Colonel Morris's father, also Roger Morris, had been an architect who was part of the circle of Richard Boyle, the third earl of Burlington and England's leading neo-Palladian. More important, his father's cousin was Robert Morris, an architect who wrote several extremely influential neo-Palladian volumes that were consulted as sources of architectural expertise during the second half of the eighteenth century.

Neo-Palladianism was an English theory of Italian architecture that with reverential caution imitated the simple, elegant, and monumental style of the sixteenth-century Venetian master Andrea Palladio. It rejected the exuberant English baroque prevalent at the start of the eighteenth century in favor of architectural rigor and purity. Robert Morris's desire for the propriety and regularity of classicism is evident in his titles: *An Essay in Defence of Ancient Architecture; or, A Parallel of the Ancient Buildings with the Modern: Shewing the Beauty and Harmony of the Former and Irregularity of the Latter* (1728), as well as *Lectures on Architecture, Consisting of Rules Founded upon Harmonick and Arithmetical Proportions in Buildings* (1734–36). *Select Architecture: Being Regular Designs of Plans and Elevations Well Suited to Both Town and Country*, which appeared in 1757, was even more influential in both America and England; Hamilton, Washington, and certainly Colonel Roger Morris must have had a copy of it in their libraries. In it, Morris extends the Palladian aesthetic from the vast and splendid palaces with which it had been associated, bringing its golden proportions and harmonies of scale and form to relatively simple structures.

In addition to these more democratic and positive aspects of the affinity for classicism, neo-Palladianism, with its references to ancient Roman art and civilization, may be seen as associated with the empire-building mentality then rife in England. Projecting images of imperial grandeur and authority, Greek and Roman architecture appealed to the British. Classical custom represented a rationale and justification for the eighteenth-century practice of slavery, for the rulers of these former highly vaunted civilizations had been slaveholders as well. While in the early eighteenth century the English were content to emulate Italian Renaissance evocations of Roman antiquity, as time went on they were more and more concerned with using actual archaeological sources for their re-creation of classical architecture.

While the Revolutionary War years slowed down the influence of this aesthetic, once neo-Palladianism took hold it was a critical element in the movement of American architecture toward ever more rational design. Moreover, *Select Architecture* includes one engraving (plate 5) that is no less than the Morris Mansion foretold—if Tuscan columns are substituted for Ionic, the parapet is eliminated, and wooden siding is exchanged for masonry. That icon of American architecture, the temple-fronted house with gigantic, two-story white columns, first occurs here. This observation is particularly important in consideration of the fact that during the nineteenth century the Morris Mansion was wrongly regarded as a rare example of Southern architecture in the North. In fact, it is the antebellum plantation house that took the same neo-Palladianism and its confident, simplified ornamentation as inspiration.

The Morris Mansion would have been understood by members of the contemporary British ruling class not as a nobleman's palace but as a comparatively new form, the villa. The greater informality of such dwellings made them far more suitable for conditions in America. Describing the difference between villas and ancestral country estates, Charles Middleton in 1795 explained:

> Villas may be considered under three descriptions: first, as the occasional and temporary retreats of nobility and persons of fortune from their town residence and must of course be in the vicinity of the metropolis; secondly, as country houses of wealthy citizens and persons in official station which also cannot be far removed from the capital . . . thirdly, the smaller kind of provincial edifices considered either as hunting seats or habitations of country gentlemen of moderate fortune. Elegance, compactness and convenience are the characteristics of such buildings in contradistinction to the magnificent and extensive range of country seats of our nobility and opulent gentry.

It is also interesting to consider how the Morris "villa" was related to the more typical colonial Georgian dwelling with its baroque or rococo detailing. Built only two years after the Morris Mansion (and demolished in 1892), John Edward Pryor's virtuoso Apthorpe house, at Broadway between West 91st and 92nd Streets, was as innovative an interpretation of the English baroque as the Morris Mansion was of neo-Palladianism. The robust appearance of the Apthorpe house, with scored wooden clapboards imitating stone masonry, contrasts with the severity of the Morris Mansion. The flush wooden boards of the latter were caulked and painted in order to create a far simpler, smoothly uninterrupted surface.

A century and a half after it was built, this purposefully plain aspect of the Morris Mansion was misinterpreted as evidence that the house was "built in a hurry," or was even unfinished, as if the builder lacked the time for decoration. Within the context of the period's more ostentatious architecture, the sight of this building must have been somewhat disconcerting. Originally the approach to the house was from the west, via an encircling gravel driveway, which revealed as a majestic surprise the previously obscured portico. This view was without doubt intended to impress. The prominent hipped roof is surmounted by a latticed railing that guards a lookout platform. Decorative touches, including the gracefully interlacing muntins of the dormer window, have far greater effect here than they would have in a more elaborate scheme. Nothing, not even the handsome octagonal panels of one of the two side entrances, appears without purpose or seriousness. Repetitive elements, such as the plain modillions along the cornice, serve to underscore the basic fenestration of the structure.

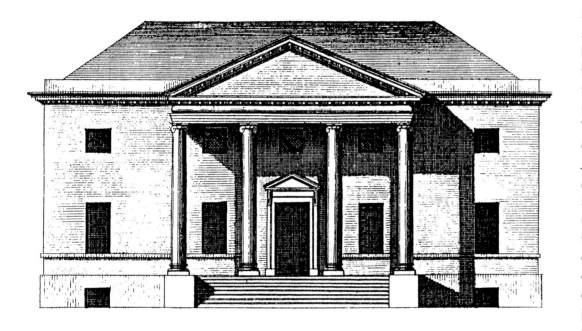

Robert Morris, *Select Architecture*, 1757. Plate 5

Similarly, the interiors are almost severe in their cool classicism. Boldly outlined round archways frame an enfilade that sweeps from the front door to the mantelpiece of the drawing room. These arches are vigorously overscaled but, compared to Jefferson's heftier versions at Monticello, rather tame. The surrounding woodwork is undecorated, apart from voussoirs flanking the "keystones," a detail that would become a distinguishing mark of American design. The staircase is placed just inside the first arch; its plain, cylindrical balusters and matching newel post again signal the Morris Mansion's overall restraint. In all principal rooms (in contrast to the slave quarters in the attic), the tone is set by wooden chimney pieces with crossetted architraves below plain torus moldings. Absolutely spartan, with no superfluous decoration, the revolutionary decor of the Morris Mansion is realized in an exacting manner unmatched by any other American house.

Indeed, the house may be favorably compared to neo-Palladianism's most elaborate monuments, such as Holkham Hall in North Norfolk, England, which had been completed in 1764 after a construction period of about thirty years. Despite the vast difference in scale and intention, Holkham and the Morris Mansion were indisputably connected by a common architectural lineage and vocabulary. Were the Morris Mansion to be translated into masonry but unaltered in any other way, it would have served perfectly well as the pavilioned wing of the larger house. Both Holkham and the Morris Mansion are linked by their spare, nearly frigid monumentality. At the Morris Mansion beveled wooden blocks nailed on at the corners to form quoins provide plastic emphasis to the otherwise stark exterior, just as at Holkham beveled blocks of brick—imitative of stone—create a rusticated ground floor.

On the northern side of the Morris Mansion, facing the barnyard and the worst weather, the carefully caulked wooden boards with sand mixed into the paint gave way to roughly adzed shingles. Economic and utilitarian, such shingles represented the last vestiges of New York's Dutch building heritage. The use of less expensive materials and sometimes more casual workmanship in parts of the house that would be seen primarily by servants or members of the family was not unusual during the eighteenth century. At countless country houses in both America and England, service courts, kitchen wings, and ancillary offices often appear quite crude when compared to the more refined and impressive front entrance.

The Morris Mansion represents a rare survival. It is a study in the juxtaposition of great refinement and rustic elements, particularly of interest in its techniques of construction. Behind the exterior board and between the structural timbers and the interior plaster is brick insulation, or nogging. This served to make the building cooler in summer and warmer in winter. An even more sensible explanation for in effect lining a timber-framed wooden building with brick walls can be found in a letter written by General Philip Schuyler to his son-in-law, Alexander Hamilton, in 1800. Hamilton was then in the process of building a summer house for his growing family less than a mile south of the Morris Mansion:

> If the house is boarded on the outside, and clap boards put on, and filled in with brick, I am persuaded no water will pass to the brick. If the clapboards are well painted, and filling in with brick will be little if any more expensive than lath and plaster, the former will prevent the nuisance occasioned by rats and mice, to which you will be eternally exposed if lath and plaster is made use of instead of brick.

Continuing, Schuyler discloses a process used to form rooms, the same as that employed at the Morris Mansion:

> The partitions between the apartments in the interior of the house, if made of joice and then lathed and plastered, also have vacancies for rats and mice. It is a little but not much more expensive to have the partitions of plank of 2 or 2 1/2 inches thick set vertically from floor to ceiling and joined together, but not planed, on these planks the lathes and plaster are to be put, thus a solid partition is formed.

A few years after the dinner given by President Washington, the house was sold. A contemporary newspaper advertisement provides a description of it at that time:

> February 23, 1793 TO BE SOLD
> Or leased for a term of years,
> That elegant, commodious and well-finished house, situated in Haerlem, on the road that leads from this city to Kingsbridge, near the 9-mile stone, adjoining the country seats of Dr. Bradhurst and J. Delancy, Esq. The orchard and garden is large, and contains a variety of the best fruit trees, enclosed by a pale fence—about ten or twelve acres of land is at present in the occupancy of Mr. John Mandeville. Possession, if required, will be given of part of the house and garden any time prior to the first of May . . . Any repairs that are wanting may be done by the tenant as may be agreed upon by the parties, and will be let to a private family only.

Some years later, on April 28, 1810, the mansion and surrounding thirty-six acres were acquired by Stephen Jumel, a French-born wine merchant, for 9,927 pounds, or $49,580, a fantastic sum at the time. Along with many of his compatriots, he had fled the Haitian revolution and settled in

New York, where he met and married Eliza Bowen of Providence, who flourished as a leading post-Revolutionary courtesan in New York. The marriage took place in 1804, prompted by Bowen's participation in a scene worthy of *Camille*. Taken fatally ill, Eliza had but one last request: to spend her final moments as a married woman. Shortly after her already grieving lover granted her wish, Eliza Bowen experienced a miraculous recovery and, to the shock of New York society, was "born again" as Madam Stephen Jumel.

With great expectations the Jumels undertook the rehabilitation of the mansion; according to Colonel Morris, it had not suffered as much as might have been expected, although there was extensive damage to the barns and outbuildings, as well as a nearly complete loss of every bit of timber on the farm. The Jumels reinstated on the property a superb fence with scalloped sections of graduated pickets set between piers topped with globe-shaped finials. This was erected all along the High Road (today Kingsbridge Road and St. Nicholas Avenue). Remarkably, the designer devised as part of the new fence a scaled-down version of Robert Adam's triumphal arched gateway at Syon House in Middlesex, England, including twin octagonal lodges.

Morris-Jumel Mansion. Fanlight and frieze of front door, modified c. 1810

OPPOSITE
Morris-Jumel Mansion. Interior view of front door, modified c. 1810

The identity of this able architect is unknown, but his expertise is attested to by the assured new front door, with a fanlight and leaded-glass sidelights inset with stained glass, the first known in an American dwelling. The decoration over this entrance was fresh and new, for instead of a half-circle fanlight, it is a half-oval. The ornamental frieze was also resourceful and engaging. Instead of what was standard at that time— triglyphs or a conventional egg-and-dart molding— it featured miniaturized Tuscan columns and Gothic fan vaulting.

For the most part, the Jumels preserved the interior of the house. An exception was the entrance to the drawing room, where paired, folding doors were installed along with a leaded, rectangular transom light. The outmoded wooden mantelpiece within was also exchanged for one with Ionic columns, contrasting Italian statuary, and yellow Siena marble.

Madam Jumel took great care to maintain the pretense that all changes were restorations, with the goal of re-creating the environment Washington had once savored. But she was hardly an antiquarian and in fact was proud of always employing the latest fashion. While New York society was then less rigidly structured than elite circles in Boston or Philadelphia, Eliza Jumel was shunned. Legend persists that not a single woman appeared at her housewarming party.

Undeterred, Madam Jumel's high spirits and equally high living—she always traveled in a brilliant yellow coach with four matched horses—continued apace. She visited Paris only a short time before Napoleon was banished, and is said to have offered the use of Stephen Jumel's yacht for his timely escape. Napoleon did provide her with several pieces of Imperial furniture, and many years later she was called upon in Harlem by Jérôme Bonaparte. There are other French elements in the Jumel decorations, including the drawing room's trompe l'oeil wallpaper in the style of Percier and Fontaine, Napoleon's designers. It represented stylized draperies hung between vertical borders of morning glories and horizontal bands boasting garlands of pearls and birds

drinking out of a fountain. A gilded bronze and cut-glass chandelier hanging in the same room was also French, as were Madam Jumel's mahogany bedroom furnishings, with chased gilt mounts or carved swans and dolphins. Although the design of the large parlor suite of sofas and chairs, ebonized with brass inlay, resembles that of French Empire furniture, it was made in New York.

Madam Jumel was sufficiently resourceful and alluring to have befriended both Emperor Napoleon I and his successor, King Louis XVIII. She was a personal guest at the king's coronation and later witnessed the crowning of his brother, Charles X. An active member of the congregation of Harlem's Episcopal Church of the Intercession, she eventually did find some acceptance among the local population, particularly by Lucy Audubon, the widow of the naturalist.

Only a few years after moving to Harlem Heights, Jumel conveyed the deed to his home and its expanded acreage to a trustee for his and his wife's joint benefit. By 1825, he conveyed his share to his wife, and three years later Madam Jumel directed that her estate be transferred to her adopted daughter, her niece Mary Jumel Bowen, as trustee. Madam Jumel remained its beneficiary, displaying a formidable business acumen. Jumel at the end of his life needed to spend more time in France, and his wife arrived back in New York in 1826 with his power of attorney. Having multiplied their investments and income, she retained this power upon Jumel's return.

After her husband was mortally injured in a carriage accident in 1832, Madam Jumel, reportedly the richest woman in America, made what appears to be the only serious miscalculation of her life. In 1833 she married Aaron Burr, the former vice president of the United States notorious for the killing of Alexander Hamilton in a duel, perhaps in an attempt to definitively transcend her outsider status. Only a few months' time saw Burr engaged in speculation with the wealth now at his disposal; when he attempted to sell her horses to pay a gambling debt, she sued for divorce, but Burr died in 1836, before a divorce decree could be granted.

A somewhat less significant misstep was the new balcony balustrade Madam Jumel installed over her front door in about 1856. Outlined with elegant pearl-like beading, the original balcony had most likely been constructed around 1815 and was provided with a delicate latticed railing. Cut by a mechanical jigsaw, the replacement railing—a Victorian design in the Italianate style—was totally at odds with both earlier Federal-style alterations and the original aesthetic of the Morris Mansion. It is extraordinary that this was the sole intervention at the Morris estate that in any way detracted from the historic site. At the time of Madam Jumel's death in 1865, Harlem's finest house stood as a monument not only to its previous inhabitants but to the entire eventful past and transforming fortunes of Harlem (see pages 96–98).

Morris-Jumel Mansion. Madam Jumel's bedroom

## The Watt-Pinckney Mansion (1796)

Superlative among the landmark buildings sacrificed to Harlem's relentless subdivision was the Watt-Pinckney Mansion. Built in 1796 by John Delancey, it stood on a low rise between what would become West 139th and 140th Streets. In the 1860s, when Seventh Avenue came north, the house was moved around the corner to West 140th Street, just west of Lenox Avenue. It must have been about that time that a high mansard roof and cupola were added to modernize the house, marring the architectural integrity of a mansion that had previously exemplified the Federal style.

Archibald D. Watt, a young and ambitious immigrant from Dundee, Scotland, acquired the house in 1826, along with the three-hundred-acre farm it stood upon, for $62,500. Eager to repeat the success of the new Erie Canal, he decided to build a ship canal from the Harlem River to the Hudson, following a creek and the Manhattanville Valley, which later became 125th Street. Although work was begun, it was never completed. Watt made a number of renovations to the Delancey house. So much of New York's early-nineteenth-century architecture has been wantonly eliminated that precise dating of Watt's renovations is not possible; a date between 1810 and 1830 may be ventured. It is therefore difficult to determine exactly which features of the house date to the original structure and which were introduced by Watt. The pilasters and corner quoins, flush boards of the facade, gracious entry with sidelights and semi-elliptical fanlight, and tetrastyle portico are all reminiscent of the nearby Morris Mansion. A certain delicacy with which these

Morris-Jumel Mansion. Parlor suite

features were handled by the unknown architect—the miniature arches used to ornament friezes in the hall, for instance—suggests the sensibility inherent in the Jumel alterations at the Morris Mansion. This resemblance may indicate a system of decoration unique to a specific designer or artisan or may instead signal a particular regionalist vogue.

Watt-Pinckney Mansion, West 140th Street, 1796. View in 1908

When Watt was caught short of funds by the crash of 1837, he was desperate. If relations had not been strained, he undoubtedly would have turned to his brother, James Watt, another Harlem enthusiast whose house, a square wooden building dating to about 1820, stood nearby between uncut Fifth and Sixth Avenues and West 109th and 112th Streets. As it was, his search for assistance led to his stepdaughter. Born in Maryland in 1810, the daughter of Colonel Joshua Ninan and Mary Pinckney, she had inherited enough property as a young girl to be able to loan $40,000 to her second father. It was secured by a mortgage on the extensive Watt acreage. This transaction made Mary G. Pinckney Harlem's greatest heiress. Ninety-eight at her death in 1908, she left a fortune in uptown real estate and a house that was worthy of being made a museum.

Some aspects of the interior of the house had been modernized by the mid-nineteenth century. In the parlor and the dining room, Italianate marble mantelpieces with round arches must have supplanted ones less pedestrian but at that time seen as old-fashioned; a complete matching set of rococo revival furniture with rosewood veneer, of the kind made famous by New York cabinetmaker John Henry Belter, replaced a Duncan Phyfe Empire suite veneered in mahogany. However, for the most part the house was the same as it had always been, even down to the family coach of the 1820s. Wall-to-wall carpets, vintage dolls in the nursery, and obsolete chamber stoves and brass warming pans in the bedrooms could be found as late as 1910.

Even in the 1960s some Harlem residents could still recall this local curiosity. A woman who grew up at the turn of the century in a West 139th Street tenement across the street from the Watt-Pinckney Mansion remembered

Watt-Pinckney Mansion. Hall in 1908

Watt-Pinckney Mansion. Staircase in 1908

Watt-Pinckney Mansion. Coach
(c. 1820) in 1908

Watt-Pinckney Mansion. Bedroom
in 1908

Archibald D. Watt (half-brother of Mary G. Pinckney) residence, West 141st Street, c. 1850. View in 1909

a farm that was a relic . . . probably the last of a very large estate . . . The Watt and Pinckney families sold off alternate blocks . . . and at the Lenox Avenue end, near which we lived, were the stables of Shetland ponies which one of the Pinckneys bred and raised for prizes . . . In the same block was a rather large truck garden . . . I'm sure that some of my own interests in plants and growing things came from . . . the early days opposite the Pinckney farm.

Around 1910 the house was converted into one of Harlem's first and most popular nightspots, the Lybia nightclub. It lingered in a shabby state until 1925, when it was torn down.

## Hamilton Grange (1802)

Alexander Hamilton's Grange was originally located on what is now the south side of West 143rd Street between Amsterdam and Convent Avenues but was moved in 1889 to its present location at 187 Convent Avenue between West 141st and 142nd Streets. The house is revelatory not so much as a reflection of Hamilton himself as of how he wished people to perceive him. His great preoccupation with correct form was very much a concern of his day. Hamilton and Thomas Jefferson were among the individuals who comprised an American aristocracy. Like many noblemen of the Old World, they lived in continual pursuit of fashion—and well beyond their incomes.

Their cultivation of a genteel way of life was in part motivated by a competitive sense of honor. Through grand gestures, they sought to impress each other and the European world with the new American standard of living. Even as down-to-earth a Yankee as John Adams purchased French furniture not merely to satisfy his own taste but for its status value. Unlike Europeans, such statesmen advanced a sense that American residential architecture could be both dignified and forward-looking without resorting to hundred-room houses furnished with tables costing as much as a new battleship. While in public life, all three of these men felt the need to project a gracious "national" image and to sustain a level of generous hospitality. For this purpose their stipends were shockingly inadequate; Hamilton's resignation as secretary of the treasury in 1795 was motivated as much by the desire to make more money in the private sector as by opposition to his policies.

His Federal-style country house, the Grange, was in its own way a creation as personal and filled with innovation and luxury as Thomas Jefferson's Monticello or George Washington's Mount Vernon. Like Monticello, the Grange was related closely to two contemporary residential forms that were intended for people who were of generous but not unlimited means: the English villa and the French pavilion. Perhaps for the first time in history, such buildings evince a quest for greater levels of comfort and convenience within beautifully designed and enviably appointed environments. Considerations such as privacy, hot food, non-smoking fireplaces, ample sunlight and warmth, the avoidance of pests, and even labor-efficient layouts and equipment were all given an emphasis equal to, or nearly equal to, traditional preoccupations with having a larger, lovelier, more up-to-date-looking house than anyone else. The new importance attached to these issues would itself become fashionable. Just as status had previously been derived from custom-made Chinese porcelain or French wallpaper, it was now dependent on, say, the possession of Count Rumford's new, more efficient stove. Such houses came to express their inhabitants' greater concern for family. The Grange is typical in this regard; to fully understand the building it is necessary to first consider the life of its builder.

Alexander Hamilton was born at St. Charles on the Caribbean island of Nevis in 1755. His father, an anchorless Scot, was the fourth son of Alexander Hamilton, Laird of Cambuskeith, who resided in Ayrshire at a house called the Grange. James Hamilton went to seek his fortune in the New World, and along the way formed a relationship with Rachel Fawcett Levine, a divorcée who under St. Croix law was ineligible for remarriage. The couple lived in a common-law arrangement for thirteen years; Alexander was the first of their two sons. Perennially unsuccessful, James Hamilton abandoned his family when Alexander was eleven. Two years later, Rachel died.

Even before the departure of his father, Hamilton had worked for Beekman and Cruger, a New York–based shipping firm with offices on St. Croix that was active in the triangular trade (of slaves, rum and sugar, and colonial products) between Europe, America, the West Indies, and Africa. Alexander's precocious business sense led to his rapid advancement and earned him a position of trust. However, even at fourteen he condemned "the groveling condition of a clerk and the like . . . and would willingly risk my life, though not my character, to exalt my station." He attracted the notice of Dr. Hugh Knox, a Presbyterian clergyman, who allowed him use of his library. In a short time, Hamilton's reputation as a scholar allowed Dr. Knox to subscribe a fund for his young friend's education on the mainland. Alexander Hamilton would leave his home in the tropics late in the summer of 1772, never to return.

Enrolling in King's College (today Columbia University), he finished in a year's time. Study of the law was postponed by the impending Revolution. As a very young officer in the American army, Hamilton performed valiantly in the battles of Harlem Heights, White Plains, Trenton, and Princeton. His record, as well as his persuasiveness and administrative skills, led to his post as secretary and aide-de-camp to George Washington, an association that was to be the turning point of his life.

In 1779 Major General Philip Schuyler was visited at camp by his daughter Elizabeth, and he introduced her to Hamilton. Concerning his future father-in-law, Hamilton wrote, "He is a gentleman of one of the best families of this country; of large fortune and no less personal and public consequence." Schuyler's mother was a Van Cortlandt, a leading New York family in the sugar business, and he had married into the rich and highly regarded Van Rensselaer family. Under the usual circumstances, a man of his station would have rejected out of hand the pursuit of his daughter by an unknown suitor of questionable origins, without connections or money. Hamilton's status as a Revolutionary, however, must have impressed him, and he wrote to Hamilton, "You cannot dear Sir be more happy with the connection you have made with my family than I am." Elizabeth Schuyler and Alexander Hamilton married in 1780.

Hamilton had distinguished himself at the front line and was to see action again at Yorktown. Yet the final battle of the war would turn out to be merely the beginning of Hamilton's combative political career. He was to go on as statesman and man of commerce—New York delegate to the Constitutional Convention, author of fifty-one Federalist papers, first secretary of the treasury, founder of New York's first commercial bank (the Bank of New York) and the New York *Evening Post,* brilliant counselor-at-law, and force behind the African Free School, which evolved into the city's public school system. It was an extraordinary trajectory, and it is against this background that an equally remarkable piece of architecture, the Grange, must be viewed.

During the summer of 1798, Alexander Hamilton went on a hunting trip with his friend John Baker, renting a house at Harlem Heights. Hamilton was so moved by Harlem's unspoiled beauty that he decided, then and there, to build a country villa, only inquiring afterward as to the availability of land in the vicinity. Wanting to make his wife happy may have emboldened him. Elizabeth Hamilton had known nothing but the very best: she had grown up at the Pastures on the Hudson at Albany, a large brick mansion. Health concerns also pushed Hamilton forward: neither sanitation nor water supply kept up with the tremendous expansion of the city of New York over the decades, and it is not surprising that leaving the city during the summer was considered a near-necessity by people of means. Departure to more salubrious environments offered protection from New York's periodic outbreaks of yellow fever and other diseases associated with coastal cities during warm weather. The concept of the Grange also carried a more symbolic meaning for Hamilton. It was a compelling emblem of aristocracy, a fine house at the center of a self-sufficient universe. It must have been a reassuring indication to him of how far he had risen in the world, a sign that he had triumphed over all he had worked so hard to overcome—the stigmas of poverty and of unmarried parents. Not surprisingly, the name of the place was an allusion to his forebears' estate. But it was to be a luxurious disappointment: the relatively small acreage acquired never managed either to sustain the Hamiltons or even to pay for itself. While her husband was away envisioning the Grange, Elizabeth and their five children visited her father in Albany. Later that same year, in the fall, she was back in New York and received a letter from her husband:

> I have formed a sweet project of which I will make you my confidant when I come to New York, and which I rely that you will cooperate with me cheerfully. You may guess and guess again. Your guessing will be in vain. But you will not be less pleased when you come to understand, and realize the secret.

Few individuals as overextended as Alexander Hamilton have ever been able to get further than dreaming of purchasing or building a house, if only because most bankers would refuse to provide them with a mortgage. Hamilton was not so constrained; he was well liked and widely acquainted, deeply involved in banking, and connected through his marriage to some of New York's wealthiest families. Between 1800 and 1803, Hamilton would purchase three adjacent land parcels in Harlem; totaling thirty-three acres, the estate was bordered by the Bloomingdale and Albany Post Roads.

To carry out his vision Hamilton chose John McComb Jr., the son of a builder who had left Ireland in 1732 for New York, where he established a substantial architectural and contracting practice. In general favoring English neoclassical design, the elder McComb was responsible for both the North Dutch Church (1769) and the New York Hospital (1775). He served in the Continental Army and in 1794 was appointed city surveyor. The son began his career at thirteen in his father's office; he was eventually sent to Europe to continue his architectural studies. When he returned in 1790, bringing back with him a library that included most of the major architectural texts then available, he established his own New York office. In 1802 he collaborated with a French-born architect, Joseph François Mangin, to win the competition for the design of New York's City Hall, which was built between 1802 and 1812. It is believed that the more experienced Mangin produced the facade, giving responsibility for the interiors to McComb. The sophistication of the City Hall interior is particularly notable in the exquisite central staircase (foreshadowed by Robert Adam at Home House in London), which leads to a balanced sequence of hierarchical spaces. Though rich in variety of forms, each room is carefully modulated, sustaining a harmonious relationship to the rest of the building, so that every element has its proper order. This same sensitivity was expressed in the planning of Hamilton's country house. It is quite likely that during McComb's stay in England he had visited villas near London. More than any other house of the Federal period built in greater New York, the Grange exemplified what Charles Middleton characterized as the house of "persons in official station" or "gentlemen of moderate fortune."

The "moderate fortune" was cleverly augmented; although Hamilton proudly refused cash assistance, he graciously accepted tens of thousands of dollars worth of supplies, materials, provisions, labor, and horses from his thoughtful father-in-law. After purchasing the first parcel of property, Hamilton and his family immediately occupied an existing farmhouse, made habitable by McComb. The site enjoyed panoramic views of the Harlem River. Meanwhile, without great sums or marble walls, McComb managed to create a notable building. Begun in 1801, the house was completed the following year. By this time Hamilton had retired from his cabinet post and was practicing law from an office on Wall Street adjoining his rented town house. When his family was at the Grange and he was confined by work in town, he would commute, sometimes five nights a week, by stage, which took about two hours in good weather.

While on business trips, Hamilton traveled most frequently in a light and speedy one-horse, four-wheeled phaeton, typical of the late eighteenth century, or in an even lighter, faster, two-wheeled carriage known as a chaise. He often wrote to correspondents along the way. In one such letter to fellow officer General Charles Cotesworth Pinckney of Charleston, he mused, "A garden as you know, is a very usual refuge of a disappointed politician. Accordingly, I have purchased a few acres about nine miles from town, have built a house, and am cultivating a garden." Well before construction had begun on the Grange, Hamilton seems to have set about collecting gardening advice from friends. He grew strawberries and asparagus for his table, with enough surplus to sell in the city for a small profit. He was pleased to affect the stance of a gentleman farmer and wrote constantly to his wife while away on extended trips, presenting multiple requests. Elizabeth Hamilton sometimes must have wished that her husband would tend to such matters himself:

> Claverack, New York, October, 14, 1803
> My Dear Eliza: I arrived this day, in about as good health as I left home though somewhat fatigued—There are some things necessary to be done which I ommitted mentioning to you. I wish the carpenter to make and insert two Chimnies for ventilating the Ice-House, each about two feet square & four feet long half above and half below the ground to have a cap on the top sloping downwards so as that the rain may not easily enter—The aperture for letting in and out the air to be about a foot and a half square in the side immediately below the cap (see figure on the other side). Let a separate compost bed be formed near the present one, to consist of 3 barrels full of the clay which I bought, 6 barrels of black moulds 2 waggon loads of the best clay on the Hill opposite the Quakers plain this side of Mr. Verplankes (the Gardener must go for it himself) and one waggon load of pure cowdung—Let these be well and repeatedly mixed and pounded together to be made-up hereafter for the Vines.

He goes on to mention planting apple trees, putting up a fence, "caulking piazzas," and caring for pigeons. As had been the case with her mother at the Pastures, the task of carefully superintending so many details fell largely to Elizabeth Hamilton.

Following the English romantic manner of gardening, popularized as much by the philosophy of Jean-Jacques Rousseau as by the influential British landscape architect "Capability" Brown, the Grange's landscape was treated as a naturalistic park. Not unlike the Morris Mansion, the house sat atop a broad plateau, near a clifftop. Carved by prehistoric glaciers, the grounds toward the Harlem River dropped off dramatically in a range of sheer ledges that Hamilton called his "terrace." Before the facade, which was oriented to the southeast, a gravel drive formed a *rond-point*, outlined with a ring of clipped boxwood and encircling a tree. During one of his prolonged absences, Hamilton wrote to his patient wife:

> If it can be done in time I shall be glad a space could be prepared in the center of the flower garden for planting a few tulips, lilies and hyacinths. The space should be a circle of which the diameter is eighteen feet and should be nine of each sort of flowers; but the Gardener will be well to consult as to the season they may be Arranged as thus.

This hurried note, probably written in the autumn, included a drawing illustrating Hamilton's intentions. One focal point that received his personal attention, however, was the planting of a grove of thirteen liquidambar (sweet gum) trees, purportedly brought as saplings from Mount Vernon. The grove was intended to represent the new United States "prospering together."

Guests arriving at the Grange were confronted by a structure quite disarming in the simplicity of its appearance. The entrance was on the narrow southeastern facade. A Doric frieze at the top of the house surmounted less exalted Tuscan porch columns with corresponding pilasters. The railings of the short flight of stairs were made of squared posts, perfectly plain. The house's southwestern and northeastern sides had full-length porches, which commanded picturesque river scenery. A number of architectural aspects of the house were historically significant, particularly the front entry, the upper window of which contained a leaded fan. According to architectural historian Fiske Kimball, this fan window, in combination with the rectangular transom and side lights, represents the first occurrence of that combined motif in New York and thus heralds the Greek revival style. Beneath the side porches were windows reaching the floor, with triple sashes that allowed access to the verandahs.

Reception rooms at the Grange—the parlor on the left and the dining room on the right—undoubtedly derived from Hamilton's memories of the Morris Mansion. Two octagonal rooms were joined by folding doors with inset mirrors; these were related to examples in Boston, Philadelphia, Charleston, and Savannah. Hamilton described how "delightfully . . . they catch reflections of the landscape." While he initially vetoed his architect and specified "unadorned" cornices throughout the interior, Hamilton later changed his mind, realizing that company rooms deserved an egg-and-dart molding. As at the Morris Mansion, beneath the more public area was an elevated and well-lighted basement containing the kitchen, offices, and servants' rooms. A second floor included five additional bedrooms.

The house became a busy hub of activity for New York society. The Hamiltons by now had seven children, and neighbors included Elizabeth Hamilton's cousin, the wife of the drug merchant Dr. Samuel Bradhurst. Among the family's intimates and frequent guests were such Revolutionary luminaries as Gouverneur Morris, Rufus King, Nicholas Fish, Dr. Samuel Bard, Dr. David Hosack, William Bayard, Timothy Pickering, and James Kent. Celebrities visiting New York were sure to be entertained at the Hamiltons' table, where they were attended by the Hamiltons' African slaves—preferred servants for the elite. Despite liberal abolitionist sentiments, according to historian Rob Weston, "Hamilton's ambitions to join the top ranks of urban society mandated his ownership of slaves."

Hamilton, whose care in matters of dressing led him to patronize French tailors, was equally refined in his regard for furnishings. He employed the era's leading cabinetmakers, including Adam Haines of Philadelphia, who supplied a large suite of mahogany Louis XVI–style furniture in the parlor. Although the house was intended as a summer residence, all the rooms had fireplaces, and McComb was instructed to select Italian marble mantelpieces (removed when the house was sold in 1834). While there are few accounts of the house's other appointments, Hamilton's reputation as a connoisseur is reflected in the correspondence of his sister-in-law, Angelica Church. While traveling in Europe she made various purchases for her sister. She wrote that she was sending a piano from London and went on to discuss the comparable merits of French versus English ceramics and to declare that "I know Hamilton likes the beautiful in every way, the beauties of nature and art are not lost on him."

This is well borne out by the Grange, a salient triumph of taste, no less indicative of its creators than ideally representative of its age. The area surrounding the estate remained a neighborhood of country houses for the affluent until the elevated railways were extended up Eighth and Ninth Avenues in the 1880s. In 1889 the house was given to St. Luke's Episcopal Church when the parish moved from Greenwich Village. Now a National Memorial, the old building is scheduled to be relocated yet again and restored.

51

## The Maunsell-Watkins and Bradhurst Estates

High, dry, and easy to reach, West Harlem had become one of elite New York's favorite places to spend the summer. Prior to the Revolutionary War, Colonel John Maunsell served in the British Army. In 1763 he married the wealthy widow of Captain Peter Wraxall, and three years later he purchased property situated just below the summer residence of his former comrade-in-arms Colonel Roger Morris, about three hundred feet east of today's Amsterdam Avenue, at West 148th Street. The new house they built was sided in wood, well made, and quite modest.

Hickson Field Mansion, Broadway and West 150th Street, c. 1842

Nearby at West 152nd Street and what would eventually be St. Nicholas Avenue, John Watkins, Mrs. Maunsell's nephew, bought the old Stone House. Watkins's wealthy aunt often lent him funds, and he was able to purchase nearly one hundred acres, so that the Watkins farm extended all the way to the Hudson. Anticipating the Revolution, John Maunsell sold part of his farm to Charles Atkin, a merchant from St. Croix. Atkin's heirs in turn sold it to a prominent shipper, druggist, and merchant, Dr. Samuel Bradhurst, in 1796. Newly named Pinehurst, the property was substantially added to, as was the old house, which in the process became a Federal-style mansion. It served as a roadside tavern and was not demolished until the 1890s. Some years afterward, the Pinehurst garden was wistfully recalled by a neighbor:

The long winding driveway . . . was shaded by large trees and a beautiful, well-kept, sloping lawn extended from the house . . .

The gardens were fine, there were many green- and hot-houses, and the surrounding grounds were beautifully kept. Across the Kingsbridge Road facing the Bradhurst house were fields belonging to that family, where the cows grazed, and I and two or three other friends were privileged to gather nuts off the trees that were there.

Mary Bradhurst, mistress of Pinehurst, was Mrs. Maunsell's niece. By 1820, she and her husband conveyed the two-hundred-acre estate to their son John Maunsell Bradhurst, who in 1845 deeded the property, in trust, to his daughter and her husband, Elizabeth and Hickson Field. West of her girlhood home, at West 150th Street and what is today Broadway, Mrs. Field built an elegant neoclassical mansion. After the draft riots of 1862, it functioned briefly as the Colored Orphan Asylum; in 1869 the structure was moved to avoid conflict with the cutting through of "the Boulevard"; and in 1892 John Duncan incorporated it into the Hebrew Sheltering Guardian Society (see pages 215, 216).

Following the Revolution, John Maunsell had successfully petitioned to regain title to the remainder of his farm, north of Pinehurst. He then sought to sell this land so that he could acquire a house in town but died before this aim could be accomplished. When Mrs. Maunsell died in 1815, the tract was divided between her nephew's three children: Dr. Samuel Watkins, Lydia Beekman, and Anna Dunkin.

## The Mott Mansion

According to building department records, the house at 2122 Fifth Avenue at 130th Street was designed by Andrew J. Garvey for Richard B. Connolly, otherwise known as "Slippery Dick." Connolly, the city comptroller, was a notoriously corrupt member of William M. "Boss" Tweed's Tammany Hall gang. Some sources estimate that Tweed and his associates stole as much as two hundred million dollars. Garvey himself had income of three million dollars between 1869 and 1870; the crusading *New York Times* deemed him "the prince of plasterers," citing the extraordinary amount of money received for work on city buildings, such as John Kellum's notorious nine-million-dollar New York County Courthouse, the cost of which exceeded by four times that of London's houses of Parliament. Connolly did in fact receive a substantial discount on the price of his mansion: it cost only $60,000, still expensive when it is considered that he never had the pleasure of living there. Once he discovered that the mayor, A. Oakey Hall, and Boss Tweed planned to shift all blame to him, he fled the country and died in comfortable exile in Marseilles in 1889. Tweed, however, spent a few nights in the house while planning his own flight to Spain, from whence he was extradited, eventually dying in prison in 1878.

Surviving photographs of the interior of this long-lost structure confirm that Garvey, while expensive, was an exceptional craftsman. The exterior of the solid suburban villa was red brick trimmed with brownstone, and its stylistic identity—Second Empire—relied heavily on the high, cast-iron-crested mansard roof. The impressive fence of shapely balusters surrounding the yard and the broad verandah's intricate railing and supports likely represent improvements introduced around the middle of the 1880s by owner Jordan L. Mott. At the time Mott's thriving foundry was expanding its operations with plants in New Jersey, and he left Mott Haven in the South Bronx, which he had established in 1850, for Harlem. An alderman active in the community, he was an avid collector of art, including works by Albert Bierstadt and Adolphe-William Bouguereau. There was ample room for the collection in the Mott Mansion; the couple's children were grown, but their daughter Marie chose to live in the house even after her marriage and was thus able to provide companionship for her father after he was widowed. It is ironic that her husband, Judge Charles Fraser MacLean, along with Samuel Tilden, was the man who had been most responsible for the fall of Connolly and the Tweed gang. Marie MacLean remained there, cosseted in Victorian opulence, as the neighborhood became a poor black enclave. In the early 1930s she engaged Seidman Photo Services to document the house, and she presented the portfolio of prints to the Museum of the City of New York in 1934. Only three years later, the house was demolished. The photographs record the magnificence of the black walnut parlor, the elaborate furnishings, the conservatory guarded by a bronze Amazon, the stenciled ceiling, and the parquetry floors strewn with oriental carpets.

Andrew J. Garvey, Mott Mansion, 2122 Fifth Avenue, 1871. Library in 1934

Mott Mansion. Drawing room in 1934

OPPOSITE
Mott Mansion. View in 1936

Michael Sampter house, Fifth Avenue
and 131st Street, c. 1870

OPPOSITE
Gage Inslee, 2044 Fifth Avenue, 1866;
Samuel A. Warner, Meeting House
of First Baptist Church of Harlem,
2050 Fifth Avenue, c. 1854; Rodgers
& Browne, George Richards house,
2056 Fifth Avenue, 1866

## Other Mansions in Harlem's Fifth Avenue Neighborhood (1866–71)

The house at the corner of Fifth Avenue and 131st Street was another fine example of the academic, Paris-inspired Second Empire style. Covered in clapboards above a high brownstone basement and surrounded by an elaborate wooden fence, it must have appeared the home of a rich lumber baron; it was in fact built around 1870 for Michael Sampter, a German Jew who had become a successful clothing merchant. In about 1937, the house was demolished to provide the northern half of a Harlem playground.

More Italianate in its curvilinear embellishments was the polychromed mansion, twenty-five feet wide and forty-two feet deep, of George Richards, at 2056 Fifth Avenue on the southwest corner of 127th Street. Built of wood in 1866, it was designed by Rodgers & Browne, a firm whose brownstone, brick, and clapboard Tuscan villas and row houses were common throughout New York. Richards's house, with bracketed eaves and curving mansard roof, would later serve as headquarters for the exclusive Irving Club. Founded in 1879, this association was known after 1881 as the Harlem Club. That year the group sponsored a design competition for a new clubhouse, to be built at 36 West 123rd Street at Lenox Avenue. This was won by Lamb & Rich, who submitted a hybridized design featuring Romanesque and Northern European Gothic elements beneath a high dormered roof of blackened tiles. Finances prevented its construction

Lamb & Rich, Harlem Club, 36 West 123rd Street, 1889; John E. Terhune, 246–248 Lenox Avenue, 1883

OPPOSITE
Gage Inslee, Henry W. Genet house (later John McLoughlin residence), 2041 Fifth Avenue, 1871

until 1889. Rather than admit Jewish members, the Harlem Club disbanded in 1907 and the clubhouse served as the Eastman Business School, which in its turn chose to relocate in 1930 rather than accept black students. Surviving as one of Father Devine's "peace missions," the building is now the Bethelite Community Baptist Church.

Well before 1907, the Richards house was demolished to make way for Finnish Hall, which served a community of immigrants that had been forming since the turn of the century. The same era witnessed the disappearance of two houses nearby that had been created by the architect Gage Inslee: a wooden house at the northwest corner of Fifth Avenue and 126th Street and the building across the street on the northeast corner. The latter had been the brownstone mansion of Harlem's own Prince Hal—Henry W. Genet, Esq. A colleague of Tweed and Connolly and a city building inspector, Genet had managed on a salary of less than three thousand dollars per year to erect a forty-three-by-sixty-foot house with balconies, multiple bays, and mansard roof. Completed in 1871, the house cost $42,000 and a year later was complemented by a $10,000 stable. From the mid-1880s until its demolition in 1907, it was owned by John McLoughlin, the well-known children's book publisher and woodcut engraver.

## The Van Rensselaer Estate (1885)

On April 3, 1869, the *New York Times* promoted a property located in Harlem Heights, an area that by this time was long associated with comfortable New Yorkers who had private incomes and old names:

> The whole is a beautiful plateau, level on the grade of the Grand Drive and the Avenue Saint Nicholas both of which intersect . . . The Outlook is Magnificent. Large portions of the island, Westchester County, and the Harlem River with their bridges, boulevards, groves and residences are spread out in full view . . . From its eastern edge the land slopes rapidly down to the level of that portion of the island lying between Washington Heights and Harlem and East Rivers, thus securing FOR ALL TIME unobstructed views of a most CHARMING LANDSCAPE the grade being 120 feet above tidewater . . . AVENUE ST. NICHOLAS. Being a diagonal, crossing all the parallel avenues north of the Park, is the shortest and most popular drive between the upper and lower portions of the city, by way of the Park. The grade and character of the land are such that building can begin immediately. CROTON WATER is to be supplied to the vicinity at once . . . Distance to the Eighth Avenue one block; to the Hudson River Railroad Station at 152nd Street, six minute walk.

Carl Pfeiffer, Van Rensselaer houses, 22–24 St. Nicholas Place, 1885

OPPOSITE
William Milne Grinnell, James Montieth houses, 14–16 St. Nicholas Place, 1883

This specific tract belonged to the grandson of Anna Dunkin (one of Mrs. Maunsell's two grandnieces), the Reverend Dr. Maunsell Van Rensselaer. One by one, the former great estates were coming onto the market for development. The gentry did not immediately move out, but people with unknown names and new fortunes began to arrive. The property became the site for a variety of architectural showplaces. In 1883 James Montieth, who had acquired most of the Van Rensselaer property, would spend $20,000 to build a pair of splendid shingled Queen Anne houses at 14–16 St. Nicholas Place. Designed to appear to be one "villa," they were the work of William Milne Grinnell, whose family had long lived in close-knit Audubon Park, an area that also had originally been a part of the Watkins farm.

Van Rensselaer had a great many connections to this landscape. He was able to recall his grandmother reminiscing about her Harlem childhood in the venerable Stone House, which was demolished only a year after he put his own property on the market. He remembered hearing that General Washington, a family friend, had dined there, and had taken special notice of the devotion of a particular slave, Jenny, who served the household. It is not surprising that, with such memories, Van Rensselaer did not leave, even after divesting himself of so much of his inheritance. He applied a portion of the proceeds of the land sale to building an extraordinary double house for himself and his son at 22–24 St. Nicholas Place (1885). This structure looked like a single, fantastic mansion. Built in the Queen Anne style of cherry-red brick, it was conceived by New York's premier exponent of the new mode, Carl Pfeiffer, and a rendering was published in *Building* in 1884. Superbly massed, with slender round towers, gables, porches, and attenuated chimneys, the Van Rensselaer houses set the tone for more modest residences in the area through the next decade.

Samuel Burrage Reed,
James Bailey house,
10 St. Nicholas Place,
1888

James Bailey house. First
and second floor plans

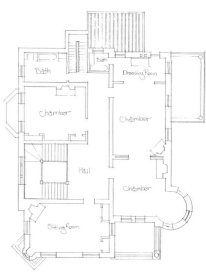

## The Bailey House (1888)

Number 10 St. Nicholas Place is one of New York's finest relics of Victorian bravura. Begun on February 24, 1886, and completed two years and four days later, this residence—replete with turrets, porches, balconies, and no fewer than sixty-six windows, three of which showed stained-glass allegories—was built for a personality equally unsubtle. James Anthony Bailey was a circus showman of consummate ability. He was born James McGinniss, the son of impoverished parents in Detroit. Neglected and uneducated, Bailey fulfilled many a boy's dream: he ran off to join the circus. Not yet sixteen at the start of the Civil War, he ably served with General Sherman's company. At the start of his rise in show business, Bailey made two momentous decisions. He changed his name to that of a "father figure" uncle, and he married Ruth Louisa McCaddon, the daughter of a hotel owner in Zanesville, Ohio. Beautiful and intelligent, she "excelled at learning and polite accomplishments," qualities that greatly appealed to Bailey. Self-conscious of perceived deficiencies, he respected education and knowledge in others. Ruth Bailey was devoted to her husband, always accompanying him, both in America and abroad, as he traveled with the circus.

A serious competitor of the legendary Phineas T. Barnum, Bailey quickly recognized that their individual talents were complementary, and the two master showmen decided to join forces in 1881. James Bailey's credo was "Give the people the best—spare no expense in doing it—and they'll reward you." He caused an international sensation immediately after his new alliance with Barnum when he purchased Jumbo the Elephant from the London Zoo for a record $10,000.

A possible motive for Bailey's choice of location was his nearby stable at 419 West 150th Street near Convent Avenue. (It now serves as a church.) At the time Bailey purchased the property, William Henry Vanderbilt and other New York sportsmen were accustomed to racing their spirited teams from Central Park along Kingsbridge Road to Harlem Heights and beyond. These activities helped bring about many changes in the neighborhood. Kingsbridge Road was newly graded, widened, and paved by 1890. The historic roadway was also renamed St. Nicholas Avenue, in honor of the patron saint of the New Netherlands. Intersecting the new avenue, the stretch of Ninth Avenue from West 150th to 155th Street was named St. Nicholas Place.

In 1897 the city and state legislature proposed the creation, at extraordinary expense, of a speedway to be reserved exclusively for the display and exercise of "fine horse-flesh." Completed by 1900, it began at West 155th Street and ran north along the Harlem River to Kingsbridge. (The speedway was renamed the Harlem River Drive in the 1930s, when it was reconfigured as a highway.) Designed by George Martin Huss and funded by Harlem's Hooper family, a quaint fountain at the entry to the drive—meant to refresh dogs, cats, horses, and humans—has been restored by the city.

Bailey, an avid sportsman, must have been delighted by the prospect of these improvements. The site he chose to build on provided a marvelous view onto all this activity. For $80,000 his architect, Samuel Burrage Reed, produced what was not unexpectedly an extravagant house. Reed unabashedly imitated the opulence of Fifth Avenue and also appears more specifically to have been drawing on a fanciful residence on the southeast corner of Lenox Avenue and West 119th Street, created by A. B. Jennings and completed for E. August Neresheimer in 1887. More accomplished as a designer, architect Jennings worked widely in Harlem, producing large row-house groups as well as mansions. One such commission was an ample house at 2042 Fifth Avenue, built in 1886 for Lucien Calvin Warner, president of the Warner Chemical Company and

James Bailey house

owner of a corset factory. This building is not as similar to Bailey's as the Neresheimer house, but the massing and porch details are familiar.

Samuel Burrage Reed was not an architect of superlative powers. His Bailey house is requisitely impressive—well planned and fashionably embellished. A boxed stoop with two changes of direction, almost like a small terrace, extends in front of the broad entrance porch. Walls of rugged gray Indiana limestone are neatly contained by smooth quoins. Emphasis is provided by means of carved ornamentation, such as an anonymous, quaintly flattened escutcheon above the entry arch.

This work resolutely expresses the Aesthetic Movement's eclecticism. Reed's liberal application of cunning devices to a long-familiar design, earnestly attempting something new, at least produced a decisive statement, exemplary of that epoch. In this regard he harmonized with his collaborator in charge of appointing the interiors. The decoration was based on the Bailey collection of treasures gathered around the world while touring with the circus. The task of creating a coherent aesthetic through an arrangement of this miscellany—real and mechanical songbirds, porcelains, a Dutch marquetry long-case clock, and more—fell to J. B. Tiffany and Company.

A. B. Jennings, Lucien Calvin Warner house, 2042 Fifth Avenue, 1886

Now, as in his lifetime, Joseph Burr Tiffany is not as widely known as his famous cousin, Louis Comfort Tiffany. Joseph Tiffany was born at Hudson, New York, and studied engineering at Cornell University. In 1884 he married Fanning Gere of Syracuse, New York, a step that perhaps gave him the confidence to strike out on his own. In 1887, a year after ground had been broken for the Bailey residence, the Joseph B. Tiffanys set up housekeeping on the extreme western end of 152nd Street, on the bank of the Hudson River. Louis Tiffany appears to have provided the inspiration for the formation of J. B. Tiffany and Company, "Specialist in Constructive and Decorative Fine Art," as stated by his entry in the New York City directory of 1888. Between 1886 and 1900 Joseph Tiffany completed at least a dozen commissions; while not at the vanguard of decorative innovation, they nonetheless pleased prominent patrons and comprised a variety of compelling spaces, replete with the taste for the exotic so characteristic of the era.

At the Bailey house such elements include massive amounts of contrasting French polished oak and ash woodwork and elaborate combination gas-electric light fittings. The salient elements, though, are innumerable stained-glass windows. Made in a mosaic technique by the Belcher Mosaic Glass Company, they were mass-produced in Irvington, New Jersey, by Henry F. Belcher. In 1884 he obtained a patent to manufacture "glass pictures." Belcher's technique of arranging individual bits of colored glass on a gummed sheet of asbestos and holding them together with an alloy of molten mercury poured between the pieces copied (with cheaper materials) that of Louis Tiffany. Examples of Belcher's craft occur in almost every room of the Bailey house, as well as in other houses decorated by J. B. Tiffany and Company. Particularly arresting is the abstracted sunrise in the hall, whose prismatic play of fluorescent color lends the staircase considerable grandeur. This is amplified by the enormous pier glass framed in ebony that graces the foot of the stair. For the visitor emerging from the bright white reception room into the hall's rich gloom, this illusion of a palatial double flight must have been dramatically effective.

65

In addition to sun rays refracted though clear cut-glass panels in the vestibule doors or filtered from the staircase window, the hall has additional light sources. The gas fireplace has a small stained-glass window, depicting an idealized landscape, set into the chimney breast. This favorite status symbol of technological prowess—a window over a fireplace—occurs in a larger format in the drawing room. Here, medieval huntsmen pursue deer. Atop the newel post, an elaborate lamp issued a flickering fishtailed flame within an etched-glass globe. Even more extraordinary is a tour-de-force, three-tiered gasolier and lantern that hangs in the stairwell. The splendor of the Bailey house proved so appealing that it was replicated in its entirety by Franklin Wickwire in Cortland, New York, in 1890. Wickwire came across the house while on his way to a business engagement and had to have it for his own.

## Mansions Versus Row Houses

As Harlem was transformed after the 1870s into a Manhattan suburb, the district became a kind of battleground. Following Bailey's and Van Rensselaer's examples, other wizards of high finance built showplaces on Edgecombe Avenue, St. Nicholas Avenue, and St. Nicholas Place. Others instead made plans to build row houses or even apartment buildings. Before surveying the transformation that followed, it is important to note several other buildings, the architectural context for buildings still standing in Harlem today.

Respectably reticent—were it not for its size and tiled roof—the Benziger house might well be passed by without much notice. Built in 1891 and located behind the Bailey house at 345 Edgecombe Avenue, the home of Nicholas and Agnes Benziger (and their seven children and four servants) must have obstructed the valley view somewhat. But the Benziger children delighted in their colorful neighbor's annual spring airing of animal skins and mounted trophies. A German immigrant, William Schickel, designed its interiors, now lost, featuring in the dining room stained-glass portraits of the children and a specially devised Swiss Gothic decor, planned by the architect as a reminder of his patron's homeland. Benziger was an early auto enthusiast, and the house also had one of Harlem's first private garages, a rare amenity always.

More in line with the exuberance established by the Bailey house is 6 St. Nicholas Place, designed in 1895 by Theodore G. Stein (who was soon to sell his architectural office to Emery Roth) and decorated by the Linspar Decorating Company. A cheerful combination of bright yellow Roman brick and buff terra-cotta detailing, this house is an essay in the Queen Anne "Flemish Renaissance" mode. Built for yeast magnate Jacob P. Baiter, a Harlem Club stalwart who engaged eight servants, it is a harbinger of the end of exclusivity. Although freestanding, it is built like a town house. Whatever the objections of those who could remember Harlem estates, change was coming, and soon the Baiter house would be surrounded by many other row houses. As the bewildered George A. Minafer duly notes in Booth Tarkington's *Magnificent Ambersons*,

> "Well, for instance, that house—well, it was built like a townhouse. It was like a house meant for a street in the city. What kind of a house was that for people of any taste to build out here in the country?"

> "But papa says it's built that way on purpose. There are a lot of other houses being built in this direction, and papa says the city's coming out this way; and in a year or two that house will be right in town."

William Schickel, Nicholas
Benziger house, 345
Edgecombe Avenue, 1891

Benziger house. Master
bedroom

In fact, it took very little time in Harlem for old-fashioned, spread-out country and suburban houses to appear totally obsolete. In 1912 the Baiter house and its ornate neighbor at 8 St. Nicholas Place—which had been designed by Richard S. Rosenstock for railroad czar John W. Fink and was completed in 1889—were acquired by Dr. Henry W. Lloyd. He joined the buildings to create a private sanatorium (designed by George Hardway and finished in 1915) "for Medical, Surgical, Maternity, and Convalescent Patients . . . with complete X-ray and pathological laboratories." The enterprise was successful, and within the next ten years Lloyd also obtained the Benziger house for use as a psychiatric facility.

Anticipating the trend toward greater density and consolidation, in 1883 Charles Fiske commissioned Charles W. Romeyn to build a residence at 2069 Fifth Avenue near 128th Street that introduced the Baiter model of the town house. Two years earlier, John Sherwood had engaged John E. Terhune to build a mansion on the northeast corner of Lenox Avenue and West 115th Street that was essentially disguised as two "ordinary" buildings. It had three stories, with basement and attic, and was large enough to display an extensive art collection. The mansard roof made the attic almost as high as an extra floor. Bay windows that projected continuously on several levels enlivened and urbanized its appearance. Sherwood was a pioneering Harlem investment banker and insurance executive who had built one of New York's first apartment houses in 1880. Terhune was also responsible for Sherwood's row-house development of 1883 a few blocks uptown at 240–248 Lenox Avenue. Even with such a sophisticated anticipation of trends, the Sherwood house was demolished in 1900 along with its more conventionally flamboyant neighbor, the Neresheimer house, to provide room for an apartment building.

The residence built in 1890 by Frank H. Smith for John Dwight (of Arm & Hammer) was to fare better. Located at 1 West 123rd Street, on the northwest corner of Mount Morris Park West, it was generous in proportion and divided into two almost equal sections—one bowed and the other square. At a distance it too appeared to be two standard-size row houses. Its light-colored masonry, iron balconies, and anthemion-crowned hood with coffered soffit and marble columns facilitated its later adaptation to institutional use. In the early 1920s it housed a doctor's practice, in the 1930s Harlem's W.P.A.-funded arts center, and in the 1950s the Ethiopian Hebrew Congregation. Other specially built mansions erected in 1890 include the Romanesque revival designs of Julius Frank at 131 West 122nd Street and of Cleverdon & Putzel at 227 Lenox Avenue for A. Hamilton Higgins. The former was of limestone while the latter—deemed by the *Real Estate Record and Builders' Guide* to be the costliest dwelling in Harlem—had a brownstone front that elicited the name "the Bronze Studio." This fashionable catering hall of the 1920s and 1930s was the venue where cabaret singer Jimmy Daniels would launch his celebrated career. Next door, 229 Lenox Avenue, designed by Clarence F. True and completed in 1899, provided an interesting contrast. A Beaux-Arts red brick and limestone house, it epitomized this style in Harlem.

**The End of the Private-House Era: The Backer and Walker Mansions**

The end of open space around houses in Harlem arrived with an intensity typical of New York, a city of extremes. Not only did mansions and broad gardens disappear, but toward the beginning of the twentieth century private houses of any size for the most part ceased to be built in Manhattan. This was true not only for the middle class in almost every neighborhood but for most wealthy citizens as well. During the nineteenth century, there had been numerous financial upsets. House building had slowed or stopped every time, but it always started up again when business improved. What was so different about the Panic of 1904–7? First, there had never been cars or fast electric trains before. Both were increasingly available to the very people Harlem developers hoped would buy their row houses. At the same time, more and more of the developers who once built row houses in Harlem turned to building bungalows in suburban communities elsewhere. Thereafter, as the population of the city at large and Harlem proper burgeoned, apartment houses came to replace the private house so dear to the Victorian era. In the city, even the well-to-do generally chose to live in apartments rather than houses, yielding—as prominent New Yorkers had from the very start—to fashion and practicality.

Harlem's last grand houses are in fact mansions built in the guise of these new building types. Fittingly, the identity of their architects is also indicative of the architectural history that would unfold as row houses and apartment buildings came to dominate the cityscape. In every neighborhood in metropolitan New York—Central Park West, Harlem, the Bronx—the majority of housing and commercial structures were not designed by such exalted firms as McKim, Mead & White or Carrère & Hastings, or by those who were serving very wealthy clients. Instead, lesser practitioners attempted to impart to their efforts for more modest clients the same elegance, ambience, and look that these leading firms advanced. Most designers of speculative projects were Jews or Roman Catholics, discriminated against and not allowed opportunities for more prestigious commissions. They had only occasionally trained at the elite Ecole des Beaux-Arts and were routinely denied membership in the city's leading professional associations. In every borough, the highly derivative buildings of such designers as Schwartz & Gross, Neville & Bagge, or John Hauser are in fact predominant. In this sense they may be called the men who built New York, defining in the imagination a precise vision of New York City. While the names of these architects are not familiar in the early twenty-first century, in Harlem's striving working-class and immigrant neighborhoods at the close of the nineteenth century they were proudly noted. However, black architects, extremely rare, had very few opportunities to practice even in an increasingly African-American but already densely developed Harlem.

George W. Backer's house at 51 Hamilton Terrace (1909) can be considered as a kind of deluxe private apartment house. It was the work of Schwartz & Gross, in its day the premier designer of apartment houses on both Central Park West and Park Avenue. The partnership was also responsible for some of Harlem's best-known apartment buildings, and this work on Hamilton Terrace entailed planning a hybrid form: a double-family house with a common entrance staircase and kitchen. There was a trend at this time away from an overly ornate aesthetic, and the house's design drew on an urban version of the earlier Federal mode suggested by Alexander Hamilton's residence. This is reflected in the brick walls and the arched parlor windows with iron railings. The limestone Tuscan-columned porch with a balcony above it, the colored glass in the doorway's fanlight, and the strip of sloping tiles above the cornice are suggestive of the Renaissance. Their presence is a reminder that Victorian-era architects often were unable to allow authenticity to restrain their John Ruskin–inspired exuberance.

The house was built by the Backer family, German-Jewish immigrants of the 1890s. George W. Backer began as a salesman of mantelpieces and became a contractor with a Madison Avenue office on Murray Hill. He is most remembered for Warren & Wetmore's Heckscher Building (built in 1921 and today known as the Crown Building). Some sections of 51 Hamilton Terrace measure twenty-five feet wide by eighty feet deep. There are four levels, including the basement, which contains a large billiard room and office, laundry, kitchen, storage rooms, bathroom, servants' rooms, and walk-in safe. A separate apartment at the top of the house was intended for Mrs. Backer's brother and his wife—a parlor and dining room, three bedrooms, and bath. No kitchen was provided, but in its place was a butler's pantry with warming oven and dumbwaiter to the basement. The restraint and refinement evident on the exterior are relaxed on the interior. The large and spare entrance hall leads to a drawing room with strikingly elaborate ornament: plaster cherubs, mirrors, and cut-glass light fixtures. At the core is the library, its fireplace—the site where the family most often gathered—embellished with a reproduction of an ancient Greek frieze. Just beyond is a spacious dining hall in Renaissance style, with oak panels and beams.

By the time the Backers left in 1913, they had seven children; five servants helped run the household. Although her family lived here only four years, daughter Rose Backer Heller at ninety-one still remembered her time there. She recalled that her father was "furious" that an apartment house was built next door; clearly what upset him most was that most of the apartments had no servants' rooms, an indication of the modest circumstances of the inhabitants. Mrs. Heller stated that her father was "very proud of our house; the architects were his friends. He always took special care to build finely crafted buildings." It is thus all the more unfortunate that in 2001 a large part of the elegant interiors was destroyed; the matchless original elements were thrown into a dumpster.

What may be considered Harlem's last mansion was, fittingly, the work of New York's first certified African-American architect, Vertner Woodson Tandy. Number 108–110 West 136th Street is one of only five houses known to have been designed by Tandy during a career that began in 1907. A graduate of Tuskegee Institute and Cornell University, he was born and raised in Lexington, Kentucky, where his father was a builder. In 1911 Tandy collaborated with another black architect, George W. Foster, in planning St. Philip's Church (Episcopal) at 214 West 134th Street between Seventh and Eighth Avenues.

Vertner Woodson Tandy, Madam C. J. Walker house, 108–110 West 136th Street, 1915. Madam Walker's car and driver

OPPOSITE
Madam C. J. Walker house

Tandy's patron represented a species even more rare than a black architect: the African-American woman millionaire. Born in 1867 in a Delta, Louisiana, log cabin to freed slaves, Sarah Breedlove Walker was by the age of twenty orphaned and widowed and had a small daughter. Race, gender, the death of her husband, and ill health never deterred her. From 1905 until her death in 1919 she worked ceaselessly, marketing her popular hair-care products and cosmetics to a market that had previously been all but ignored. Walker located her beauty-shop franchises all over the United States and in Central America and the Caribbean, and the techniques employed there allowed black women to enjoy the fashionable, Gibson girl–influenced hairstyles of the day.

Madam Walker's residence, a dignified brick and limestone design, was a remodeling of two existing houses behind a new facade; it resembles the Backer house in its hybrid form. Built in 1915, the structure was ahead of its time in combining a business with a residence, specifically a beauty salon and school on the ground floor and three stories of Madam Walker's residential space above. Both the business and the drawing room spaces were totally new, but the rest of the

Madam C. J. Walker house. Shop

mansion was an adaptation of the preexisting structure. The old-fashioned Victorian mantelpieces and architraves were retained, not removed. As at McKim, Mead & White's Clarence Mackay house (Harbor Hill) of 1902 or the same firm's Ogden Mills mansion of 1896, some decorative elements were painted white, inexpensively updating them. An assertion of both personal and group triumph, Tandy's design is indebted to the Percy R. Pyne house at 680 Park Avenue (now the Americas Society), which was designed by William Kendall of McKim, Mead & White in 1911. Tandy was also the architect for Madam Walker's Renaissance-style country house at Irvington, near the Rockefeller and Gould estates. Overlooking the Hudson, the house, built in 1916, was named the Villa Léwaro by Enrico Caruso. Both of Madam Walker's houses were decorated by the firm of Righter and Kolbe, also employed by members of the Vanderbilt family.

Against daunting odds, Madam Walker's accomplishments in business and as a person of color were broadcast by conspicuous edifices radically different from those inhabited by the majority of African-Americans. Clearly race proud, she took the time to seek out an African-American architect, and both of her houses were ingeniously distinctive in their affirmation of black excellence in an era when Harlem's average yearly wage was only eight hundred dollars. Seemingly ordinary when juxtaposed against the most palatial and sumptuous mansions built for the wealthiest whites from this time, they are nevertheless potent symbols of success. Madam Walker's city and country houses, intended to stand forever, may be viewed as allegories of the hope and aspirations of the new black community in Harlem. But all too quickly, 108–110 West 136th Street, functioning briefly after Madam Walker's death as the Harlem Renaissance's fabled "Dark Tower" meeting place, vanished. It was replaced, in 1942, by a public library.

Madam C. J. Walker house. Tea room

Madam C. J. Walker house. Daughter A'Lelia Walker's bedroom

# THE ROW HOUSE IN HARLEM

Hamilton Terrace looking south from
West 144th Street, 1909

East 116th Street looking west
from Pleasant Avenue, c. 1895

T he original inhabitants of Harlem's commodious and historic row houses were not wealthy. In fact, they were solid members of the middle class, secure and numerous enough to feel they warranted a certain degree of elegance. The row house had been established initially as part of the English architectural inheritance, and as Harlem grew and real-estate speculation became the order of the day, the dollar value of land became paramount in developers' eyes long before any actual profits had been realized. Row houses could potentially allow more families to live in the space traditionally required by a single household.

The first row houses were three or four stories, plus a basement and cellar. Initially they were made of wood, in the Greek Revival and Italianate styles, but after a decade or so were more often brick, with wooden cornices, brownstone trim, and louvered shutters painted green. During the earliest period of row-house construction, from around 1825 to approximately 1860, buildings were usually entered near the ground level. But as time went on, from about 1860 until the end of the row-house-building period around the turn of the century, access was primarily by means of an outdoor staircase twelve long steps from the sidewalk. The use of high stoops as protection against flooding was part of Harlem's architectural legacy from Dutch colonial times. Compact front and rear yards surrounded by whitewashed picket fences were common as well.

Harlem, because of its proximity to Manhattan jobs, was more convenient than New Jersey or Brooklyn, and for a while appeared destined to be the ideal commuter village. The pace of Manhattan's growth was such that Harlem shifted from country to suburban status quickly. Before the era of modern sanitation, air conditioning, and electric fans, summer's onset signaled that it was time for an annual, class-based exodus from urban environs. Residences in town were left shuttered—swaddled in sheets that were first laden with peppercorns and lavender sachets and then doused with camphor and patchouli—as their inhabitants left for cooler places. The fortunate few retreated to dynastic country houses, while others rented farmhouses, cottages, or cabins for the season. The Delaware Water Gap, the Catskills, the Poconos: the destination mattered less than the migration, an indication to the world of a certain prosperity.

This lifestyle was a somewhat reduced version of the standard that had originally been established by New York's venerable elite of Anglo-Dutch colonial lineage. Christened by Washington Irving the "Knickerbockers," this group was accustomed to fleeing the city proper in warm weather. Prior to New York's procurement of an adequate water supply, the motivation had often been to avoid serious health risks of exposure to cholera and other diseases, but after the building of the Croton Aqueduct, the well-off and well-bred continued to look abroad with idealistic motives. They were especially impressed and inspired by England's aristocratic society. As a result, New York houses, at least until sometime after the Civil War, imitated London's terraced rows: attached at the sides, nearly identical in appearance. Toward the end of the nineteenth century, the frenzy for building in Harlem reached its apex. In a period of roughly thirty years, from the 1870s through the first decade of the twentieth century, most of the housing stock was built by a limited number of specialized developers and architects. "Ready-made elements," introduced in the England of Robert Adam, were easily available in thriving metropolitan America, and the exteriors and layouts of houses were often built from pattern books that featured interchangeable elevations and plans. In 1903 architectural historians Harry W. Desmond and Herbert Croly noted that during the first three quarters of the nineteenth century the wealthy were not inclined to distinguish their dwellings from those of their poorer neighbors "except in size and sumptuousness." Economic factors only exaggerated this uniformity:

> Year after year, in order to meet the demands of the rapidly increasing population, rows upon rows of houses were built so rapidly and their character was so completely dominated by economic necessities that they became extraordinarily uniform in plan and appearance; the houses of the rich did not escape this influence any more than the houses of the poor.

As time went on, builders wondered if their customers could be satisfied with a row house less than twenty-five feet in width. Testing this thesis, they found that five houses each twenty feet in width fit nicely on just four lots and also that people would live in them quite happily. The cost initially struck renters and buyers, who were used to larger lodgings, as inexpensive. The occupants' savings were, of course, disproportionate to increased profits, and it was quickly discovered that four houses of somewhat more than eighteen feet in width could be squeezed onto three lots; three houses of sixteen feet eight inches onto just two; or five houses onto three—or even more.

Whether meaning to attract well-to-do buyers or less affluent renters, Harlem builders generally offered three options: renting by the month, leasing for a year or two, or acquiring the building outright. In the latter case, the builder aimed for a profit of about five percent—one reason why it was so tempting to crowd more and more houses onto fewer and fewer lots. Almost unheard of were long-term leases of fifty years or more, such as prevailed in London.

## The Subdividing of Harlem

Developers who acquired former farms or estates for subdivision made such improvements as laying out sewer lines and streets but seldom actually built houses themselves, leaving this job to speculative contractors. Some developers might indicate the type of building they wished to promote by constructing five to eight houses as models. However, Harlem's speculative house building gradually became an incestuous enterprise. Even when they were not directors for local banks, developers often financed contractors, and eventually contractor, architect, and developer were one and the same person. Contractors would put up between three and ten houses at one time, generally working from plans supplied by an architectural practice that specialized in such designs. In the 1870s and 1880s plans became increasingly varied and even individualized, but following the 1893 World's Columbian Exposition in Chicago houses again tended to be built in extremely uniform groups.

Period photographs capture a surreal landscape of such isolated structures in the middle of Harlem pastures dotted with squatters' shanties and untended livestock. Why, in a community so long retaining a rural character, at a moment when there was still an abundance of vacant and relatively inexpensive land, did developers build as if sites were scarce and costly? Why didn't more Harlemites elect to live in freestanding or semidetached houses with landscaped yards, along the lines of villas in the garden suburbs on London's outskirts? Wouldn't such a house better express its occupant's aesthetic sense, while better suiting a family's specific requirements? Increasingly, critic Montgomery Schuyler, his colleague Mariana Griswold Van Rensselaer, and a number of other critics disliked Harlem brownstones. "Harlem, speaking architecturally," wrote Schuyler, "and speaking generally, is one of the most depressing quarters of New York. There is in its streets the thoughtless and conventional repetition of intrinsically bad forms which makes up the bulk of the architecture of the island."

Schuyler recognized that much that is lamentable in New York's architectural history derives from the grid of avenues and streets that evenly divides the island of Manhattan. Ever since the days of the Dutch West India Company, New York and Harlem's operations have been closely intertwined with those of the state government, and it was the New York State legislature that authorized a plan for the city. The grid laid out in the Commissioners' Plan, approved in 1811, would become a critical document in the history of the city of New York. As the commissioners of streets and roads envisioned the northward spread of the city, they obliterated all natural features of the island—hills, nooks, springs—in favor of making room for what I. N. Phelps Stokes described as "right angled houses . . . the most cheap to build, and the most convenient to live in." Regimented avenues were traversed at right angles by numbered streets, and all land was divided into lots of twenty-five by one hundred feet. A proposed amendment for back alleyways for deliveries and rubbish removal (like those of Boston and Philadelphia) was ignored, underscoring the enormous power of the landlords' lobby. The commissioners in question were retired diplomat and senator Gouverneur Morris, lawyer John Rutherford, and state surveyor-general Simeon De Witt; the plan was drawn by surveyor John Randel Jr. and is sometimes known as the Randel Plan. Schuyler called it the work of "unconscious vandals," but novelist Edith Wharton, whose family was both friendly toward and related to the men in question, took a more sympathetic view, suggesting in *A Backward Glance* (1934) that theirs was "the prudent attitude of a society of prosperous business men who have no desire to row against the current." She goes on to describe a comically convoluted impulse toward conformity:

> The weakness of the social structure of my parents' day was a blind dread of innovation, an instinctive shrinking from responsibility . . . [A] group of New York gentlemen who were appointed to examine various plans for the proposed laying-out of the city, and whose private sympathies were notoriously anti-Jeffersonian and anti-democratic, decided against reproducing the beautiful system of squares and radiating avenues . . . designed for Washington, because it was thought "undemocratic" for citizens of the new republic to own building-plots which were not all of exactly the same shape, size—and value!

Charles Henry Hall house, Fifth to Sixth
Avenue, West 131st to 132nd Street,
c. 1810. View in 1886

## Transportation and Real Estate in Harlem

Regardless of the nature of the commissioners' political motives, Manhattan's lots of equal size
were not of equal value. It was only a matter of time before land speculators realized that the
Commissioners' Plan presented them with great opportunities when it came to the farms of Harlem.
If downtown property sold at a premium, in Harlem smaller builders and prospective householders
of limited means could find both affordable investments and housing. Some more prominent
operators quickly appreciated too that they might succeed in manipulating values upward. These
speculators imagined that if some form of mass transit could unite overcrowded, densely built-up
New York with scenic, healthy, and spacious Harlem, there would come a time when Harlem
property would be just as desirable, scarce, and expensive as parcels downtown.

It was a fortuitous coincidence that just as Harlem was poised to become a commuter suburb, the
steamboat and locomotive came to the fore. However, creation of the city's first railroad, the
Harlem line, was not simply left to chance. By "improving" Harlem, its promoters usually managed
to enhance their own circumstances. Typically, this involved buying up depleted, devalued
farmland. Charles Henry Hall, a bookkeeper for Thomas H. Smith & Sons, "the great India
merchants of the South," is a case in point. *The Old Merchants of New York* recounts that Hall
purchased land north of 125th Street from Fourth Avenue to Eighth Avenue for "nearly a mile . . .
in strips." Another history book praises Hall as "a public benefactor," particularly in his devotion
to securing "a good neighborhood for a town to come after him."

Hall's activities were not solely philanthropic. With his wife, Sarah, he had lived in some style at 576 Broadway, a large two-story double house leased from the Van Rensselaers, where he kept what were termed "the most superb stables ever erected." Each horse had its name painted over the stall. In the spring of 1829 Hall moved to Harlem. *A History of St. James Methodist Episcopal Church at Harlem, New York City* (1882) describes Hall's "new" Harlem home (which had been purchased from Gabriel Freeman on June 27, 1825) as a "widespread mansion" that "stood on a mound amidst charming fields and groves of trees that bordered a considerable pond of water artificially formed by Mr. Hall." The history concludes with an acknowledgment that Hall

> acquired much wealth, and foreseeing what this city would be . . . devised liberal things for the improvement of . . . the city at large . . . Being made alderman of the 12th ward, he had the taste and courage and influence to obtain the great work of re-grading the 3d Avenue through its six miles from 10th Street to Harlem Bridge, and the macadamizing of the carriage way from end to end, accomplishing this in the year 1832 . . . He also opened 129th Street from 3d to 8th Avenues, and had it paved in carriage way and . . . with the first sidewalks recovered from the general mud of Harlem.

Even more crucial was Hall's promotion of the Harlem railroad. This included his allowing passengers to use his garden for strolls and picnics. His generosity was justified by the fact that the railway's success tripled the value of Hall's holdings and brought on the area's first building boom.

## Manhattanville

Slightly earlier, on the West Side, Jacob Schieffelin and his brothers-in-law, John B. Lawrence and Thomas Buckley, were also hard at work on the development of Harlem. They acquired adjoining summer houses on estates that extended between today's West 125th and 145th Streets from Amsterdam Avenue to the Hudson River. Determined to make their property more valuable, in 1809 they established the village of Manhattanville in the low valley between the heights of Bloomingdale and Harlem, centered at what is now 125th Street.

Schieffelin had earlier been involved in land speculation in Canada. There, following his marriage to Hannah Lawrence, an early abolitionist and pacifist from a famous Quaker family, he worked for the British crown. In New York the couple wintered in a house on Pearl Street at Sloat Lane (Hanover Street); their summer house at Harlem, Rocca Hall, overlooked the Hudson between West 142nd and 144th Streets. Nearby Forest Hill was the property of Hannah Schieffelin's brother and included the property between modern Broadway and the Hudson from West 135th to 142nd Street.

At the very onset of the industrial revolution, the town's founders took advantage of the location of Manhattanville, which afforded cheap water transport, to create an industrial center that supplied the city with manufactured goods. Neither the founders nor Mayor Daniel F. Tiemann, whose paint and color works was for many years one of Manhattanville's largest concerns, seem to have shrunk from living just a stone's throw from industrial plants; soon livery stables, a tannery, a ribbon factory, at least two breweries, and a host of other businesses abounded.

As vigorously as Hall and other East Siders backed the Harlem Railroad, civic-minded residents of Manhattanville, including Schieffelin's sons, toiled on behalf of the Hudson River Railroad, which began operations only slightly later than the Harlem. The Hudson line carried scores of the moderately well-to-do, as well as the middle class.

## Minniesland

The Minniesland farm, between West 155th and 158th Streets from Amsterdam Avenue to the Hudson River, was purchased in 1840 by naturalist John James Audubon. Originally part of the Maunsell-Watkins estate, it was named in honor of Audubon's wife, Lucy ("Minnie" was a Scottish diminutive for mother). Here a guest of the Audubons, the noted portrait painter and inventor Samuel F. B. Morse, conducted his first underwater telegraphic experiments, sending signals to New Jersey. In the earliest days of their residence, the Audubons had as immediate neighbors only the Kingsland, Knapp, Monroe, and Jumel families, in addition to the households of their sons, Victor G. and John Woodhouse Audubon. Remembered by Dr. Thomas M. Brewer in 1880 for *Harper's Monthly*, Minniesland was idyllic. Brewer visited when Audubon was about sixty years old:

> It was truly a lovely spot on a wooded point running out into the river. [Audubon's] dwelling was a large old-fashioned wooden house, from the verandah of which was a fine view looking both up and down the stream, and around the dwelling were grouped several fine old forest trees. The grounds were well stocked with pets of various kinds, both birds and beasts, while his wild feathered favorites, hardly less confiding, had their nests over his very doorway. Through the ground ran a small rivulet over which was a picturesque wooden bridge.

At the time when the Audubon family began to sell parcels of the property to friends as building sites, the accepted architectural model for new houses was their own chaste Greek Revival structure, with a broad Tuscan columned porch and flush front siding. Audubon's home was virtually identical to the James F. Farrell house (c. 1849), which still stands in Brooklyn. Boulevard Lafayette was the most prestigious address in the area; it was crowned to the north, at today's Fort Washington Avenue and West 161st Street, by the grandiose, temple-fronted wood-frame mansion of Mayor Ambrose Kingsland (c. 1851) and, at today's 162nd Street north of Riverside Drive, by "merchant prince" Shepard Knapp's house, Melbourne (1851). Following the death of the elder Audubon in 1851, the remaining open space of the property was sold in 1864 to Jesse W. Benedict. The new owner also bought the naturalist's old house, to which he added a mansard roof. Subdivided, the acreage became plots for suburban houses.

## Carmansville

Some distance away, on West 185th Street, was the house of Richard Carman, a shrewd businessman who amassed his first fortune making boxboard. He is now almost completely forgotten, except for a playground bearing his name at West 152nd Street and Amsterdam Avenue. Carman arrived in Harlem slightly in advance of the Hudson River Railroad in 1850. At the time beautifully landscaped suburban churchyards, where Victorian ladies enjoyed excursions on the outskirts of town, picnicking among the departed, were a nationwide craze. When additional cemeteries were abruptly prohibited in the city of New York, Carman saw an opportunity. He sold a third of a parcel of land he had purchased from the Maunsell-Watkins estate, just south of the Audubon property, to New York's revered Trinity Church congregation, which intended to use it as a rural burial ground. The selling price was equal to what he had paid for the entire plot. In addition, Carman sold a few pieces of land to affluent people moving uptown. Yet Carman's main business was not in graveyards or properties for the rich but in building brick tenements with shops on the ground floor (located on today's Amsterdam Avenue) and renting them to merchants. He also built small wooden houses, both

Melbourne, Shepard Knapp residence
(later the Grand View Inn), West
162nd Street north of Riverside Drive,
1851

Mayor Ambrose Kingsland residence,
Fort Washington Avenue and West
161st Street, c. 1851

attached and freestanding, in the West 140s and West 150s and let them to laborers who grew produce for the city on truck farms that Carman owned. Other tenants were hands at local factories in both Carmansville and Manhattanville. Carmansville's fledgling manufactories included Dennis Harris's New Congress Sugar Refinery at West 159th Street and the Hudson River (1852).

## Audubon Park

Carman was among the promoters of railways in Harlem; he single-mindedly pursued a Hudson River Railroad stop at West 152nd Street. Assuming good weather, it became possible to reach downtown New York by train in half an hour. Another beneficiary of the Hudson line was Audubon Park, the property purchased by Jesse W. Benedict from the Audubon estate. The subdivision attracted genteel New Yorkers seeking a picturesque environment along lines of public transportation. In an attempt to preserve some semblance of the locale's scenic ambience, fences were restricted. Architecture, if not rustic, was decidedly suburban. As late as 1899, the *Real Estate Record and Builders' Guide* extolled the healthy atmosphere of the area:

> No better proof could be found of the natural attractiveness of Washington Heights as a place of residence than the crowds that flock to the plateau for a brief outing these hot summer holidays. Probably 50,000 people ride over the Amsterdam Avenue road [cable car, after 1885] . . . of a Sunday . . . The exhilarating air and prospect over the Palisades and Hudson act as a tonic on mind and muscle. In the heat of the day no cooler resting place can be found on Manhattan Island than Washington Heights.

There is no better description of Audubon Park's spacious retreats as they were from 1850 to 1870 than that of Booth Tarkington's fictional Midland City, from his trilogy *Growth:*

> At the beginning . . . most of the houses . . . were of a pleasant architecture. They lacked style but also lacked pretentiousness, and whatever does not pretend at all has style enough. They stood in commodious yards, well shaded by leftover forest trees, elm and walnut and beech, with here and there a line of tall sycamores where the land had been made by filling bayous from the creek. The house of a "prominent resident" . . . was built of brick upon a stone foundation, or of wood upon a brick foundation. Usually it had a "front porch" and a "back porch"; often a "side porch," too. There was a "front hall"; there was a "side hall"; and sometimes a "back hall." From the "front hall" opened three rooms, the "parlor," the "sitting-room," and the "library"; and the library could show warrant to its title—for some reason these people bought books. Commonly, the family sat more in the "library" than in the "sitting-room," while callers, when they came formally, were kept to the "parlor," a place of formidable polish and discomfort. The upholstery of the library furniture was a little shabby; but the hostile chairs and sofa of the "parlor" always looked new. For all the wear and tear they got they should have lasted a thousand years.

Sadly, for many land investors, this was a sorry state of affairs. Nothing would do, they felt, but to rush masses of people and profits up to the neighborhood that began to be known, after the Civil War, as Washington Heights. Would-be developers lamented in pamphlets that the area did not draw residents because it lacked a "line of railroad for rapid transit, by locomotive trains, from the Battery to Tarrytown, through Washington heights. The project has taken possession of the minds of capitalists and the public. The plan is to have a viaduct road for four tracks, from

William Almy Wheelock Mansion,
661 West 158th Street, 1865

the Battery, two to be devoted to local business and two for through trains." Although the viaduct
road was not forthcoming, by the late 1890s Harlem's ubiquitous speculative row houses had
taken firm hold. They signaled the end of the area's pastoral charm, as freestanding dwellings
became things of the past for all but the very rich. Audubon Park was swiftly becoming a
part of the city. An eagerly anticipated extension of Riverside Drive and the Broadway subway
(projected as early as 1888 and realized between 1904 and 1907) made land too valuable for
large residences on quarter-acre plots; several row houses could be accommodated on the same
parcel. Local examples were built with bow fronts larger than those of row houses downtown

87

Wheelock Mansion. View from library into dining room

and enhanced with balconies, from which occupants could catch the river breeze and enjoy the panorama of sunsets.

The roadway of the 1904 Riverside Drive extension was curved inward toward the east to avoid the remaining houses of Audubon Park, whose owners were initially reluctant to sell to the city. Laid out around an oval park with a white marble fountain, the road isolated these houses, which would gradually be replaced by apartment buildings. One of the last houses, which survived until 1938, was the mansion built in 1865 in the Second Empire style for William Almy Wheelock, a prominent banker and insurance executive.

## Mount Morris Park

Residential splendor endured next to Mount Morris Park, but in a less rustic fashion. The mass transit required to deliver large numbers of people to Harlem took more than the noblesse oblige of wealthy Harlem residents. It required political muscle, supplied with force by Tammany Hall, which had transformed from its 1790s origins as the Society of St. Tammany into a notorious, and notoriously corrupt, Democratic machine. By the 1860s, most of William M. "Boss" Tweed's unsavory cronies lived uptown. Buying up spent farmland and pungent tidal flats (which for years had been used as a dumping ground and shantytown), the Tweed gang set to work to increase the value of their holdings. They embezzled tens of millions of dollars in an era when a single dollar was a respectable daily wage. Marshes bought for a song were filled by the city to become building lots. Thoroughfares, budgeted at a certain amount, routinely overran the estimate by three times or more. But the Eighth Avenue elevated train, which reached West 129th Street in 1878, was the coup. In addition to making Harlem home to scores of new commuters—working people who both bought and rented houses—this train became a continual source of cash for Tammany Hall.

Landscaping for Mount Morris Park was long delayed, a pattern that seems to have become the norm in New York by the middle of the nineteenth century. It was supervised by the city's chief landscape gardener, Ignatz A. Pilat, identified by a contemporary as "a man of cultured taste who realized the artistic possibilities of this bold, land-covered hill." Pilat was also an acclaimed plantsman who would serve as an able associate of Frederick Law Olmsted during the creation of Central Park. In 1855 the Common Council invited estimates for an iron tower for fire sentinels at the summit of what was then termed Mount Morris Square. John Bogardus bid $5,750 against Julius Kroel's winning offer of $2,300. The function of the sentinel was all important. With so many wooden structures, Harlem was routinely plagued by fire. Like a ranger in a national forest, the watchman was continually on duty. Once a fire was spotted, he furiously tolled the bell (different peals indicated different neighborhoods) and used signal flags to alert the closest fire brigade. Under these circumstances, and with an inadequate water supply, firefighters must have often arrived to find a burned-out shell. Samuel Morse's telegraph was to put these towers, once located all over New York, out of business.

Long associated with prominent politicians, the region abutting the park declined only at the close of the nineteenth century. On Sunday, August 2, 1903, the *New York Herald* reminisced about

> the days when there inhabited it some of the leading lights of Tammany Hall, and when Mount Morris Park itself buzzed with political talk as the sachems gathered there on the benches in the cool evenings . . . The home of former Mayor Thomas F. Gilroy is at No. 7 West 121st Street. Former Postmaster Charles W. Dayton lives at No. 13 Mount Morris Park West, and at the northwest corner of 123rd Street and Mount Morris Park West is the $100,000 home of John Dwight. The houses bordering the park are mostly four-storey brownstone front dwellings, as somber and respectable as anything that the Fifth avenue section can show. They never lack tenants, but not so large a percentage of them is occupied by owners as was the case ten years ago. At that time $40,000 was not considered a high price to pay for a dwelling facing on Mount Morris Park. That figure today is very exceptional.

Julius B. Kroel, Mount Morris Park fire tower, 1855

Ignatz A. Pilat, Mount Morris Park (now Marcus Garvey Memorial Park), between 120th and 124th Streets, Madison Avenue and Mount Morris Park West, land purchased 1839

## The Hamilton Grange District

The fate of the Hamilton Grange estate may be read as a kind of parable of the speculative fever that took hold in New York toward the end of the nineteenth century. The estate, including the house, was purchased in 1879 for $312,500 by Anthony Mowbray, a contractor active in Lenox and Murray Hills. Mowbray conveyed it to William H. De Forest and his son William junior, who intended to develop the thirty-three acres that Hamilton had originally acquired from the Schieffelins and the Bradhursts. De Forest was a leading silk importer, representing A. Guinet and Company of Lyons, France. The trio divided the land into three hundred building lots, slated to sell for $5,000 each. The lot with Hamilton's house was sold to Amos Cotting, who took an interest in the historic value of the building, but he feared that his heirs were not particularly preservation-minded. As De Forest senior's West 57th Street mansion, brimming with antiques and curios, was published in George W. Sheldon's *Artistic Houses*, McComb's masterful house appeared to be headed for destruction.

Yet this building was the beneficiary of chance. In 1889 the rector of St. Luke's Episcopal Church on Hudson Street in lower Manhattan, the Reverend Isaac H. Tuttle, was seeking a building suitable for gathering a congregation for the new St. Luke's, slated for construction on Convent Avenue and West 141st Street. Some three hundred feet north of the new church site, at West 143rd Street, Tuttle noticed a large, old-fashioned frame dwelling of some elegance and discovered through inquiries that it had been built and occupied by Alexander Hamilton. He arranged to meet Amos Cotting, who welcomed the opportunity to pass the house on to people who knew its value; Cotting offered the house to the congregation as a gift.

Tuttle faced some opposition from his vestry and churchwardens, but he prevailed, citing not only the residency of the nation's first secretary of the treasury but also the hand-hewn white oak timbers. Moving the building down and across Convent Avenue onto the church's property was a considerable but by no means unusual feat at the time. Ratcheted off its original foundation with a tool resembling a car jack, the house was rolled on logs to its new location, pulled across frozen ground by several teams of horses. Construction of the church's own building was completed in 1892, and by 1908 the Board of Aldermen passed an ordinance to acquire the house and move it again, this time to St. Nicholas Park. Financing for the preservation of Hamilton Grange was not truly secured until J. P. Morgan Jr. and his brother-in-law, distinguished banker George Baker, Hamilton's descendant, became involved.

Meanwhile, the De Forests and the other owners proceeded with their plans, building picturesque row houses from 1886 to 1906. Houses were designed by Adolph Hoak, William E. Mowbray (son of Anthony Mowbray), William Ström, Robert Kelly, Henri Fouchaux, John Hauser, Neville & Bagge, and others. The development was detailed in the contemporary press:

> Mr. De Forest has carefully fenced in the thirteen well-known trees representing the thirteen original
> States, though unless purchased by the city, the Historical Society, or some kindred body, these
> remnants of times gone by will be swept away by the ruthless hand of the invading builder . . .
> Some fifty to sixty buildings are being erected on the property by three builders alone. W. E. Mowbray
> is putting up between twenty and thirty ornate houses, which are rapidly approaching completion;
> J. D. Butler is building about twenty more, and Harvey L. Page is going on with ten more, between
> 143rd and 144th streets, on 10th avenue. Other improvements are contemplated . . . The ground is
> destined to increase largely in value over its present worth. The sale is expected to attract the principal
> buyers in the city.

William E. Mowbray, 464 West 144th Street (now Alexa and Bethany Donaphin house), 1890. Rear facade with terra-cotta plaque

De Forest and his son developed the property until 1893, investing not only an extraordinary amount of time but as much money as they had originally paid for it. De Forest senior's expectations were high: he expected to recover not five but fifty percent over his outlay. Father and son, in developing the estate, intended to be noticed. Within the confines of the gridiron, no expense was spared to give this subdivision a semisuburban setting and ambience. Gardens with flowers, trees, and grass, originally unencumbered by fences, embower the houses, each of which is set a full fifteen feet from the sidewalk.

The earliest group of Hamilton Grange houses, at 455–467 West 144th Street, was completed by William E. Mowbray in 1888. Assuming the form of town houses built by wealthy Dutch burghers in the seventeenth century, they commemorated the area's rich heritage. Far more ambitious than the typical dwellings colonists erected in New Netherland, they nevertheless embodied Mowbray's vision of what colonists might have built had they been able—grand houses like those of the original Haarlem. These row houses were built in an era when, partly in reaction to widespread immigration, descendants of earlier "founding" immigrants were establishing the Holland Society, the Daughters of the American Revolution, the Social Register, and the Colonial Dames. Seen in this light, these houses were more than mere shelter. Ultimately, they were expressions of nostalgia for a time when Knickerbocker authority was absolute.

Set on a gentle slope, the Mowbray row is configured so that every chimney and gable contributes to a pyramidal composition. Part of the setback from the sidewalk is given over to a broad stone terrace. The houses vary a great deal individually, particularly considering that they were built on speculation. Stone bases alternate in color; some employ bits of schist rubble, removed during the

94

William E. Mowbray, 452–466 West 144th Street, 1890; William E. Mowbray, 455–467 West 144th Street, 1888. View in 1909

excavation of the cellars, while others feature the more usual sandstone. Where it occurs, carving is well executed, such as the dragons at 461 Hamilton Terrace. There are extraordinary examples of red and gold terra-cotta decoration, with garlands, lions' heads, and other elements effectively placed. Of special interest are two terra-cotta sunbursts with stuck-out tongues at 467 West 144th Street. Enduring bits of whimsy, elaborate plaques adorn even the backs of the houses. Despite such indulgences, fire codes are observed and easily maintained roofs are provided; and Harlem is the richer for, arguably, one of the country's most compelling groups of late-nineteenth-century dwellings.

Completed by William H. De Forest Jr. in 1890, after his father's death, to designs by Mowbray, the houses at 452–466 West 144th Street appear chaste in comparison to the earlier group, yet all eight are individually handled. The *Real Estate Record and Builders' Guide* of September 13, 1890, states that "it's evidently been a point with the improvers of Hamilton Grange that the old-time plain brown stone front should not find a place . . . Mr. De Forest has adopted the plan of having each front of a different design . . . they are of various colors." The same review describes the houses as Gothic, and indeed the Venetian Gothic associated with Ruskin does seem to assert itself here. The De Forests' related rows on opposite sides of West 144th Street, between Amsterdam and Convent Avenues, epitomize the late Victorian tendency to exploit modern materials and methods as a means of embellishing historical reality.

Unfortunately, the architectural ambitions of De Forest and his son were not supported by developments in the marketplace, which typically were inclined to reward more conventional investment. The De Forests' venture officially failed in 1888, a fact that is betrayed by certain

95

Gilbert Robinson Jr., 1–19 and 2–20
Sylvan Terrace, 1882

oddly resolved details of the houses: the jagged stone squiggles on number 457, the crude and uncarved corbels at the base of the facade's drip molds on number 464. In the end De Forest senior was driven to madness by the mental strain of the heavy financial burdens he had incurred, and his last years were spent chaotically, alternating between confinement in and escape from mental institutions. The Hamilton Grange development never fully recovered. Lots, restricted to row houses, stood empty for years, awaiting the extinction of the deed covenants. Yet in time the De Forest heirs were fortunate. When the estate was finally settled in 1895, thanks to the recovery of the real-estate market and to supplementary investments, they shared between them several million dollars. In this more ruthless era, failure for some was opportunity for others. The vulnerability of wealthy Protestant families affected by the Panic of 1904–7 allowed immigrant German families, primarily Jewish, and prospering Irish Catholics to gain entrée to the neighborhood.

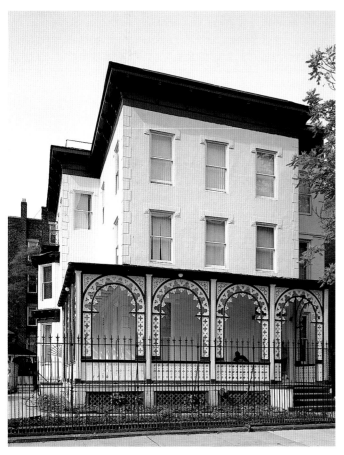

112 West 129th Street, c. 1870.
Porch built by Charles Buek, 1880–81

## The Row Houses of Sylvan Terrace

An equally complicated fate befell the large land holdings acquired by Eliza Bowen Jumel. All Madam Jumel's labor to amass an unrivaled fortune was destined to be challenged shortly after she was interred in 1865 in a hillside vault overlooking the Hudson at Trinity Cemetery. She had worked hard to establish an enviable estate and had adopted her niece and nephew as part of a careful plan. Yet shortly after her death, a man calling himself George Washington Bowen appeared and claimed to be her son. He stated that long before arriving in New York, Eliza Bowen of Providence gave birth to an only child. So intense was the class-based resentment that Jumel had inspired and so persuasively convincing was the charming young "heir" that it took seven years, from 1867 to 1874, to refute his claim. But if the true heir, niece Mary, now Mrs. Nelson Chase, was so guileless as to imagine her troubles over, she was to be sadly mistaken. Descendants of the second of her aunt's three husbands came forward, charging that through connivance their share in the estate had been usurped. Mary's husband was an attorney, but the claim was nonetheless deemed sufficiently valid by a jury, who forced the litigants to partition and share the extensive property. A marathon estate auction was held on November 14, 1882, and the old house itself was acquired by the Chases' son, William I. Chase.

In comparison to that mansion, the Italianate row houses of Sylvan Terrace are quite humble. The row flanks what was the carriage drive of the Morris-Jumel Mansion and ends along cobbled Jumel Terrace. Between 1891 and 1903, thirty-one more houses would appear on streets running through what was once Madam Jumel's garden.

With shiplap siding, bracketed eaves, and hooded stoops, the Sylvan Terrace row houses today constitute the most extensive surviving wooden-sided row in Manhattan and seem charmingly attractive, even quaint. Local legend claims that the houses were slave quarters, but these are far superior dwellings to any that were lived in by slaves, and their construction date of 1882 makes the story impossible. However, they were originally inexpensive and were rented to working-class tenants. Designed by Gilbert Robinson Jr., the group was offered for sale in the September 30, 1882, issue of *American Architect*:

97

Private Street: 20 two storey frame cottages, $30,000
James E. Ray owner, 322 E. 120th Street

Just one block long, the row is elevated above St. Nicholas Avenue, where West 161st Street is today. The houses are of steam-power-sawn lumber ornamented by fretted scrolls and turned joinery and cut by mechanized jigsaws and lathes. Such easily and swiftly erected houses were once quite common; Carmansville, just a few blocks south, abounded with them, as did Manhattanville. The Sylvan Terrace "cottages" are smaller, conventionalized, urban evocations of the more picturesque Tuscan villas built in the 1850s and 1860s, such as the Wheelock mansion of 1865, the longest-lived of the Audubon Park mansions, and 112 West 129th Street (c. 1870), with its superlative porch. These were the sorts of houses that wealthier Harlemites sometimes built and occupied between 1850 and 1875 instead of wooden, brick, or brownstone row houses. In contrast, the group by Robinson represents the most modest single-family house then available from an architect.

Each house has seven compact rooms that originally accommodated the typically large, servantless families of first- and second-generation immigrant laborers. In 1890 two occupants were patrolmen and one was a firefighter. Homer Gilles, at number 10, dealt in animal feed; his neighbor Thomas Ryerson, at number 17, was a grocer. One element that clearly identifies the ordinary circumstances of the original residents is the outside privy adjacent to each dwelling; the Croton Aqueduct had long made indoor toilets possible even for many laborers.

The humble interiors of the Sylvan Terrace row houses were scrupulously masked by attractive but forthright and unassuming facades. Handsome double doors, decorously shuttered windows, and discreet service entrances three steps below the stoops belie the mostly cramped conditions inside. Today it is difficult to imagine that originally not only bedrooms but also beds were shared in order to make space for the often indispensable boarder.

## The Harlem Brownstone Row House

The Sylvan Terrace houses were so generic and basic that they did not warrant the critical notice of Montgomery Schuyler or Mariana Griswold Van Rensselaer, who instead cast a cold glance on more upscale contemporary brownstone counterparts. Connoisseurs of architecture had little use for local brownstones, even when they were freestanding on Fifth Avenue corner lots and exhibited decided pretension, such as Henry W. Genet's exuberant Second Empire house of 1871 at 2041 Fifth Avenue. Brownstones in Harlem and elsewhere were considered by critics to be slightly less objectionable when freestanding than when placed together in long indistinguishable groups, block after block, street after street, mile after mile. Desmond and Croly wrote in *Stately Homes in America* that the attitude of New Yorkers toward their own use of New Jersey brownstone was one of "almost fatuous self-complacence." The passage included an even more stinging citation from the architect Russell Sturgis, who stated that all brownstone buildings "partook of the same spirit of dull, flat, dusk-brown monotony."

In Harlem, it could be argued, the situation was worsened by the various grades of brownstone, some more durable but all soft and brittle. If improperly laid up—with the natural layered bedding set vertically instead of on the horizontal—spalling and flaking were inevitable. The deliberate "stretching" of the stone by unscrupulous contractors or masons further aggravated the situation. While most disfigurement was caused by freezing and thawing cycles, comparable damage could

Lamb & Rich, 409–415 Lenox
Avenue, 1883

be precipitated by wind erosion. Such damage today obscures the exotic touches that enriched these buildings, such as the whimsical neo-Egyptian palm-leaf and lotus capitals on the columns supporting the porches of the brownstones designed by Charles H. Beer in 1886 at 260–274 Lenox Avenue. Other evidence of the harmful effects of wind erosion may be found in the iron railings at 4–10 West 122nd Street, designed by William B. Tuthill (best remembered as the architect of Carnegie Hall) in 1889: the original, columnar balusters long ago fell victim to such deterioration. Increasingly conscious of the inevitability of erosion, architects began employing cast-iron balustrades and cornices, which were painted brown to match the houses they graced. On the balustrades a sprinkling of sand added to the wet surface heightened the faux-brownstone effect.

Schuyler's criticism is linked to this lack of durability. He cites in the *Real Estate Record and Builders' Guide* of 1885 such problems as "the sinking of the foundations, the cracking of the walls, the leaking of the roofs, the warping and checking of the woodwork, and general caving in of plaster." In fact, he suggests that the collapse of the real-estate market was due to poor building practices, stating that the four-inch veneer of brownstone not only did not add to "the strength and carrying capacity" of the wall but actually was "a burden to it . . . Architecturally the whole thing was a false pretense that the material was more costly and the house more valuable than in fact it was."

Prior to 1893 or so, there was little attempt by architects to present the four-inch layer of brownstone, and later limestone, as anything other than what it was—a thin outer coating. However, builders began to employ quoins at the corners, to give the appearance of solid two-foot-wide blocks. In time, this small deception grew, and use of rusticated stone basements, with brick walls and stone-framed openings above, gave way to a uniform treatment of side and front. Since a corner house so appointed commanded twenty-five percent or more above the cost of an ordinary dwelling, the long side of houses began to be subjected to greater and greater aggrandizement. Viewed obliquely, these corner houses appeared to be freestanding mansions. Entirely stone clad, except at the rear, they boasted an array of turrets, towers, columned porches, and bay windows. All that remained to complete the illusion was the inevitable removal of the entrance from the narrow front to the imposing side.

The pronouncements of England's romantic, iconoclastic critics began to have an impact in Harlem. Concurrent with and sometimes an outgrowth of the Oxford Movement in the Anglican Church, the efforts of many of these design reformers took on the tone of a moral crusade to save humankind from the corrupting influences of bad taste. Undoubtedly John Ruskin, whose books on art and architecture were immensely popular at the time, was a catalyst for the reaction against brownstones. Dismayed by the dehumanizing effects of burgeoning industrialization, he was equally distressed by what he regarded as the inherent dishonesty of most Victorian design, with its imitation of materials and nature. An early preservationist, he also abhorred the Victorian tendency to destroy so much that was genuinely old in a misguided effort to improve upon the past, erasing, in the process, the transmuting effects of "tide and time." This last quality—the way in which mounting years imbue the human-made with an essential "life"—he much valued.

While more pragmatic, Charles Eastlake shared many of the same concerns as Ruskin. However, he welcomed modern machinery, which he thought might serve as a means of creating affordable and well-crafted buildings and furniture. Eastlake's designs, inspired by the medieval and marked by incised, rectilinear decoration, were meant to emphasize rather than hide the key role he envisioned for new technologies.

101

Cleverdon & Putzel, 13–15 West 122nd Street, 1888

Well versed in such teachings, Montgomery Schuyler was also a proponent of reform. For Harlem's longtime suburban setting, he advocated a distinctively suburban architecture. For example, he admired Charles Buek's restrained row on the south side of West 130th Street, numbers 8 to 62, built in 1883 as rental properties for the Astor estate. These were semidetached three-story dwellings with ample front gardens, and they originally rented for $1,100 per year. Moderately Italianate, they introduced striking broad front porches. Instead of the usual wooden, cast-iron, and galvanized-tin cornices, their friezes and cornices were made of brick.

Developer H. M. Blasdell's row of 1883—eight paired houses on the west side of Lenox Avenue between West 130th and 131st Streets—emulated the Astor houses in materials, layout, and porches. Yet the group, designed by Lamb & Rich, was far more elegant in appearance. Unfortunately, twelve additional houses planned by Blasdell for West 131st Street were never built, and by 1911 two of the Lenox Avenue group had already been demolished to make way for an apartment house. Lamb & Rich also designed a decorous brick Queen Anne–style row-house group at 481–493 West 145th Street (1884). Today, only number 481 survives.

## Innovation in Harlem

Buek's new approach to speculative row houses may have been welcome, but it was at best a tentative step. Many architects had long been content to build and live in houses that looked the same as one another. When a popular desire arose for something new, builders responded to meet the market, but their inclination, out of habit and experience, was nevertheless to resist change and to innovate as little as possible. Initially ignoring the whole issue of brownstone, they tried to address the attack on the "flattened appearance," "static lack of decorative interest," and "monotonous repetition" of their buildings, and set about making their facades more various and more ornamental. As a result, even more brownstone was employed for massive porches, elaborate stoops, and bay windows—all more heavily carved than ever before. Designing hundreds of speculative row-house groups in Harlem and on the Upper East and West Sides, commercial specialists Robert Cleverdon and Joseph Putzel also designed numerous loft and retail buildings. Representing a transition from the Italianate to the Queen Anne style, their brownstones at 7–21 West 122nd Street (1888) appear to display the era's reluctance to fully embrace the new, but a closer examination reveals otherwise. The columned door surrounds and porches are not unusual, but the way in which features are dispersed is decidedly new. Along with canted oriel windows, distributed in a similar alternating fashion, a sense of syncopation is established. However mild this innovation, there is no denying that it is different from countless row houses built in the area at roughly the same time.

The architects' treatment of decoration is somewhat eccentric. They seem to have derived particular pleasure from playing with scale. On the oriels, the incised anthemions are over-large, while the bases of the openings have strangely stunted colonnades. Introduced earlier in the 1880s, box stoops, with three changes of direction, sweeping steps, and scrolling parapets, are employed to ingenious effect.

## Artistic Building in Harlem: Picturesque Row Houses

In the January 16, 1885, *Real Estate Record and Builders' Guide*, retired city controller "Honest" John Kelly indicates full rental of his L-shaped row of fourteen red brick houses on the northwest

James Stroud, 881–887
St. Nicholas Avenue, 1883

James Stroud, 411–421 West
154th Street, 1883

corner of West 154th Street at St. Nicholas Avenue (1883). Designed by James Stroud, this imaginative group has everything any critic could have hoped for, including a sense of suburban charm presented with urban style. Each house exhibits a wealth of distinguishing elements, but all are subordinate to the whole. Lively and rhythmic, the houses command their position, set apart atop an angled grass embankment.

Unfortunately, "Honest" John's houses were not widely copied. But they did not go entirely unnoticed as an example of creative building. Covered in shingles, John H. Duncan's row houses

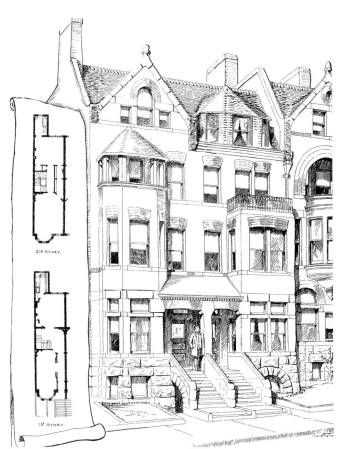

along the southern side of West 150th Street between Convent and Amsterdam Avenues represented another introduction of country sensibility to city houses. Built between 1882 and 1883, the row was punctuated by a tower at the easternmost corner. This group, with exaggerated gables and private recessed porches, is unique. It also represents a surprising departure for Duncan, who is most renowned as the author of Grant's Tomb.

Much of the same new spirit is expressed in H. L. Page and W. W. Kent's row of 1890 at 468–474 West 144th Street, in the Hamilton Grange subdivision. These houses far surpass former, less accomplished buildings that attempted a mix of neo-Romanesque and Queen Anne styles. In the combination of pressed red brick, brownstone, terra cotta, sheet metal, and wrought iron may be found the same restraint seen in the designers' handling of the facades and rooflines. Applied ornament is passed over in favor of carefully contrasted materials. Color, texture, and finish interplay, as do architectural elements, creating a satisfying unity of design.

Edward L. Angell's seven houses at 145–157 West 118th Street (1889) possess many of the same fine qualities, expressed through different means. His approach is more formal and profusely ornamented. Because the Queen Anne lineage includes Ruskin, among other eclectic sources, some openings have pointed Gothic arches. Parlor-floor oriel windows, stamped from copper, are fitted into semi-elliptical openings. The pediments' sweeping volutes, arabesques,

H. L. Page and W. W. Kent,
468–472 West 144th Street, 1890

OPPOSITE
Francis H. Kimball, 133–143 West
122nd Street, 1887

and garlands, as well as the facade's grotesque masks and sunflowers, find their source in the expansive iconography of the Aesthetic Movement.

All over Harlem, such elements were appropriated by builders barely aware of their stylistic significance. Francis H. Kimball, however, was entirely conscious of sources and implications. One of America's most talented architects, his career began when he was hired to act as supervising architect for new buildings at Trinity College in Hartford, Connecticut. The actual designer was the creative genius William Burgess, England's singular neo-Gothicist. He is best known for thorough (even heavy-handed) restorations of medieval monuments. However, his imaginative fantasies are so imbued with the spirit of the Age of Chivalry that it is difficult to begrudge his exuberance. Burgess's responsibilities as architect to the marquis of Bute kept him preoccupied in Wales and Scotland, so he needed a counterpart to oversee American operations, and Kimball was very fortunate to have been chosen. It was a time when many American architects were beginning to keep abreast of new design developments and trends, primarily through professional journals such as the *American Architect* or *Architecture and Building Magazine*. But Kimball, consulting and

actually working with Burgess and other influential designers in London, was on the cutting edge of the American interpretation of European advances. That he put his contacts and experience to good use is demonstrated by his extensive oeuvre. Kimball designed successfully in a wealth of divergent styles, producing such buildings as the neo-Moorish Casino Theatre (1881, razed 1930), the Gertrude Rhinelander Waldo residence on Madison Avenue (1898, now the Ralph Lauren flagship store), and the Montauk Club at Grand Army Plaza in Brooklyn (1891).

It is instructive that such a highly regarded, well-connected talent would design speculative houses. While others looked down on such "commercial" work, Kimball regarded his Harlem row houses as a fascinating design problem. The buildings he created at 133–143 West 122nd Street (1887) are astonishing. In less sure hands the brownstone lower stories would have seemed dour and old-fashioned. Similarly, the flame-colored brick and terra cotta of the upper stories might have been a lurid disaster. However, this masterful row is a veritable frieze encrusted with a panoply of ornate devices to delight the eye.

Kimball was among the earliest New York architects to use terra cotta, employed in Italy since antiquity and in England from the Renaissance onward. Terra-cotta architectural elements were made from clay fired in a kiln, just as much smaller bricks were. They were intricately embellished by one of two methods. Either the partly dried clay was sculptured with wood-carving chisels, creating "cut brick" ornaments, or more commonly, the clay was pressed into shape in hydraulic molds. The material had great potential for New York: it was durable and resistant to the city's sooty atmosphere, and it allowed for easily replicated precise detailing. Understandably it became very popular. The terra-cotta embellishments of 137 West 122nd Street, including assorted cherubs, garlands, and masks, are camouflaged by their color, which is close to that of the orange-red brick. The first owner of this house was Mrs. Charles D. Gambrill, the widow of the distinguished architect, onetime partner of H. H. Richardson and George B. Post, who, on a reduced income, moved here from a more valuable house in Brooklyn.

Inspired by the nation's hundredth birthday, American designers were beginning to study and examine early American architecture and furniture in a manner previously reserved for European prototypes. In 1877 young Stanford White undertook his famous sketching trip through New England with Charles Follen McKim, William Rutherford Mead, and William B. Bigelow. It was precisely during this period that Harlem's tumbling-down Dutch farmhouses and stately old mansions began to be documented in measured drawings and photographs. American architects studied European sources, too. Whereas McKim attended the world's most prestigious school of architecture—the Ecole des Beaux-Arts in Paris—White gained great aesthetic understanding from traveling across Europe on foot and by bicycle, sketchbook in hand.

If there is any one exterior feature that defines Harlem's late-nineteenth-century row house during this age of picturesque revivalism, it is the round tower or turret. Nothing as uninhibited had ever adorned so many speculative houses. Borrowed from Norman barns, the device was taken up by devotees of the Romanesque and the Queen Anne alike. It is difficult to imagine anything more cumbersome to position; in fact, this impracticality has greatly contributed to the rarity of the towers' survival.

Harlem's finest round towers are found on a pair of attached dwellings at 729–731 St. Nicholas Avenue (1886). Theodore Minot Clark, their architect, observed the source of his inspiration first-hand. French originals were characterized by rubblestone masonry reinforced with reddish brick to improve structural strength. Clark reproduced all elements of the original structures with great originality. The better part of the facing material is gray Manhattan mica schist, quarried on site. Molded brick voussoirs with delicate beading form an arcade at the basement. Engaged in a gabled roof, the towers have the expected conical roofs and aligned windows. But on the parlor level are yellow terra-cotta flat arches, introducing yet another color and texture. Additionally, the roofs are covered with cedar shingles, as is the tower's final story. Clark's talent for manipulating scale and materials is surely unmatched.

Failure of the Hamilton Grange subdivision struck a heavy blow to the notion of making each house in a row unique. Such individual attention now appeared disastrously extravagant, and it was never copied. More typical was a judicious differentiation of houses, apparent in the row

Theodore Minot Clark, 729–731 St. Nicholas Avenue, 1886

OPPOSITE
729–731 St. Nicholas Avenue

by architect Adolph Hoak at 311–339 Convent Avenue (1890; see pages 142 and 160–61), where an individual center house is flanked by five distinguished matching pairs. As New York began to weary of architectural pastiche, Montgomery Schuyler's criticisms were ever at the ready:

> The monotony which prevailed in the appearance of private dwellings for fifty years has been superseded by the utmost variety both of material and design . . . each [row] house claims the distinction of an individual . . . It is not too much to say that this claim is frequently made in the most deliberate and pretentious manner. Whatever such a [row] house may be, it must at any rate be different . . . It seems settled that New York shall symbolize in design of its private dwellings the incoherent multiplicity of its origins.

## The Golden Mean in Harlem: Strivers' Row

It is no surprise that the pendulum of taste swung back in the direction of subordinate houses in monumental rows. Yet picturesqueness and variation were not rejected outright. For instance, five houses designed in 1889 by James Brown Lord on the northeast corner of Seventh Avenue and West 130th Street followed the example of McKim, Mead & White's groundbreaking 1885 complex for the family of jeweler Charles L. Tiffany, which was designed in consultation with his son Louis C. Tiffany, at the northwest corner of Madison Avenue and East 72nd Street. Lord's designs were unique in their genuine gables: other houses merely pretended not to have the prevailing flat roof. Lord used the gable to marshal his houses into a cohesive unit. With a long slope to the side street, the roofline stressed the expressive integrity of the group. Uninterrupted by bays or other protrusions, with openings aligned below prominent gabled wall dormers, the brick-and-brownstone facades reinforced this impression. It is a shame that such a successful group was razed in 1993, just as its inspiration had been in 1935.

Today well known as the architect of several flamboyant Fifth Avenue mansions, C. P. H. Gilbert was a skillful designer of restricted row-house groups as well, in both Brooklyn and Harlem. Attesting to his ability are the houses at 456–460 West 152nd Street (1889), with Queen Anne facades between projecting towerlike bays.

Conceived as prototypes to house with dignity "genteel persons of moderate means," the 160 David H. King Jr. model houses, or Strivers' Row, remain Harlem's best-known addresses. A successful building contractor, King acquired two entire blocks of lots from the Watt-Pinckney estate, comprising nine acres along West 138th and 139th Streets between Seventh and Eighth Avenues. King commissioned three architectural teams—Bruce Price and Clarence Luce; James Brown Lord; and McKim, Mead & White—to design his development. White, a personal friend, was responsible for the concept of the overall layout. The group, a unified, restrained ensemble with three distinct treatments, went against the trickle-down architectural fashions typical of New York, offering trend-setting ideas to the middle class.

The 1811 gridiron plan for Manhattan was devoid of the back alleyways that were common on the East Coast for deliveries and trash collection. Believing that rear yards were little used by inhabitants, who conventionally spent the warmer months at resort towns, King lopped twenty feet from each backyard to provide this amenity. Architectural treatment gave his houses affordable, uniform, yet subtly differentiated designs that avoid monotony by adapting modified interpretations of Colonial Revival, Italian, and Northern Renaissance precedents. Along with apartment blocks on Eighth Avenue, this is the consummate local example of the integrated, mixed-use plans employed by enlightened designers during the period.

If Lord's sober brick and brownstone houses on the south side of West 138th Street are the embodiment of Victorian conformity, Price and Luce's collaborative efforts (on the north side of West 138th and the south side of West 139th Street) are pure representations of gaiety. High Renaissance, cream-colored, glazed terra cotta decorates these yellow-brick, otherwise Federal-style designs, deliberately conceived without concern for strict authenticity. Exploring anew the disciplined and coolly elegant Italian Renaissance neoclassicism, derived from Rome's Cancelleria, that the firm had so brilliantly used earlier for journalist and railway tycoon Henry Villard at 451–455 Madison Avenue (1884), McKim, Mead & White's houses, on the north side of West 139th Street, were the project's most original. As with the other rows, the centermost house was "precisely articulated by slight projections" on the tawny ocher-colored ironspot brick walls, detailed with matching terra cotta. Similar were the additional stories added to houses on and adjacent to Seventh Avenue. However, McKim, Mead & White's adaptation of the so-called American basement plan, which dispensed with high stoops and provided entry at a rusticated brownstone basement story, is a decided departure.

James Brown Lord, 202 West 138th Street (Strivers' Row), 1891

OPPOSITE
Bruce Price and Clarence S. Luce, 203–271 West 138th Street (Strivers' Row), 1891

Heralding a more highly unified urbanism, the King model houses were a reaction against the often confused intricacies of the Aesthetic Movement. Montgomery Schuyler, for one, praised King as "a public benefactor, and if he had seen his way to covering the whole [Harlem] flat from Morningside to the Harlem River with like houses, he would have been a public benefactor of the very first order." King ought to have reaped great rewards for offering so much to families of modest means. Instead, his lender, the Equitable Life Insurance Company, foreclosed in the wake of the crash of 1893. When African-Americans first moved to Harlem, the insurance firm refused to rent or sell them long-vacant houses. Opened to blacks only in 1919, Strivers' Row quickly attracted some of the most notable African-Americans in the nation, including architect Vertner Woodson Tandy (211 West 139th Street), composer W. C. Handy (232 West 139th Street), and eminent Harlem Hospital surgeon Dr. Louis T. Wright (218 West 138th Street).

McKim, Mead & White, 203–269
West 139th Street (Strivers' Row),
1891

OPPOSITE
Frederick P. Dinkelberg, 401–409
West 147th Street, 1895

Nowhere are tried and true materials used so engagingly or with such refined sensibility as at 401–409 West 147th Street (1895). The stoops of these houses are embellished with machine-made S-scrolls atop stepped parapets. The facades have a spartan simplicity; incised carving, Byzantine in inspiration, is the sole purely decorative emphasis. Architect Frederick P. Dinkelberg was a true American hybrid: the son of an Italian countess and a well-to-do Pennsylvania contractor. Training in Philadelphia architectural offices was followed by the opening of his own firm in New York in 1895. An unsuccessful participant in the New York Public Library competition, he also submitted plans for Brooklyn's Erasmus Hall High School. Disappointed by not receiving these major commissions, he left New York and went to work in the office of Daniel Burnham in Chicago.

Dinkelberg's largest undertaking in Harlem was an unusually long row on St. Nicholas Avenue between West 148th and 149th Streets (1896). Repeated bulging bow fronts that extend for four floors create an almost hypnotic rhythm, despite the alternating materials used. The two corner houses are entered from elegant semi-elliptical porches with polished granite columns and bronze capitals. Only these two make use of the American basement plan; the remainder employed the standard straight stoop.

Clarence F. True was somewhat at odds with his colleagues, who found speculative house building unprofessional. Not only an innovative architect but also a developer and contractor, he was largely responsible for the development of the area between West End Avenue and Riverside Drive

from West 79th to 84th Street. As a designer, he was a steadfast champion of the American basement plan for its provision of full-width reception rooms.

Placed above rusticated basements with arched openings, True's row houses at 469–475 West 143rd Street (1896) have slightly bowed or canted fronts. The infrequent ornamentation consists of carvings of quaint putti and fruited festoons. While the style is a pastiche of Renaissance balustrades, Gothic dormers, and Flemish gables, the ensemble is utterly harmonious. Clad in limestone and buff brick, the group includes an apartment building at number 477, on the northeast corner facing Amsterdam Avenue (see page 160).

Archival information concerning 471 West 143rd Street provides a glimpse into the area's residents at this time. The house was first owned by Dr. Ernest J. Lederle, described by his biographer as "a forceful blue-eyed man who stood six feet one inch and filled a Santa Claus suit without padding for Christmas hospital parties." The founder of Lederle Laboratories, today a division of the American Cyanamid Company, Dr. Lederle served two terms as New York's health commissioner under Mayors Seth Low and William J. Gaynor. In 1895 he married Margaret C. Taylor, and one year later they purchased number 471 for $15,000. The top-floor nursery was the domain of the Lederles' daughter Mary, as well as living quarters for the cook, parlor maid, and waitress. A member of the Century Association and the Waverly Club, and president of Harlem's Heights Club (see page 127), Dr. Lederle maintained a summer residence in Stamford, Connecticut.

Nearby in the neighborhood are the distinguished houses of Henri Fouchaux, an architect born in Coytesville, New York, to a French émigré family, who settled in Harlem at Audubon Park. While working as a carpenter, Fouchaux pursued his professional education at Cooper Union's night school. He was later employed by the firm of Schickel & Ditmars; in 1886 he established an independent practice and seems never to have lacked for work. In addition to churches and commercial buildings downtown, he designed dozens of uptown houses and apartments. Some are low-key, harmoniously contributing to streetscapes that include some of Harlem's last row houses. Such houses, however, are the exception; Fouchaux more often designed work distinguished by a Gallic verve. Occupying the west blockfront of Convent Avenue between West 141st and 142nd Streets, his heavily embellished Louis XV limestone group of 1902 provides an interesting comparison to a somewhat later, Louis XVI group on St. Nicholas Avenue between West 153rd and 154th Streets. Both are knowledgeable exercises, revisiting Paris in the eighteenth century.

Beginning their careers as specialists who planned speculative row houses, Thomas P. Neville and George A. Bagge also designed apartments. They rank as Harlem's most prolific planners of private dwellings. One of their most exceptional commissions was for six houses on the south side of West 144th Street between Convent Avenue and Hamilton Terrace (1897), a high and handsome row faced with limestone, brick, and terra cotta derived from Robert Mook's Marble Row of 1869. With mansard roofs and rusticated American basements, the row's similarity to a Parisian hotel lends to the group a monumentality that would have been impossible were the houses treated individually.

The largest and probably the final such project designed by the firm of Neville & Bagge—455–465 West 140th Street and 456–474 West 141st Street—was built in 1906 by Gustavus L. Lawren. The red brick and white limestone facades are complemented by cornices that were originally painted a stone color; today they are painted black or green. The eighteenth-century three-part keystone at the lintels reappears, along with strictly symmetrical fenestration. In the small

Henri Fouchaux and others,
south side of West 147th Street
between Broadway and Riverside
Drive, 1896–1900

Henri Fouchaux, 282–286 Convent
Avenue, 1902

John Hauser, 453–475 West 141st Street, 1905; Neville & Bagge, 456–474 West 141st Street, 1906

vestibules, however, it becomes apparent that facade and plan are not scrupulously matched. The inner door is not aligned with the outer one, because of the position of the service entrance to one side of the front door. In order to reestablish a balanced hall while providing a separate long and narrow passage for tradesmen, the off-center entrance was imperative. Ornate interior plasterwork was produced by the firm of Patrick McNulty of 473 West 141st Street, a first-generation Irish immigrant. The Neville & Bagge houses are closely imitative of a group completed the previous year at 453–475 West 141st Street by the Picken Realty Company, based on designs by John Hauser, who worked locally for over twenty years. Such homages to earlier houses occurred with some frequency in Harlem during this period, a means of ensuring architectural harmony.

The exterior of row houses built before 1900 typically had a white-painted rear wall, to reflect sunlight; nine-foot-high wooden-sided fences enclosing yards; and brightly striped canvas awnings above both windows and doors to shade and cool rooms inside. Since rooms at the back of a house seldom had interior shutters, exterior shutters were also routinely employed. The sturdy (if highly decorative) wrought-iron bars that protected and adorned the lower windows of most nineteenth-century New York houses indicate that crime prevention was a concern then as now. According to the *New York Herald* of December 10, 1910, three bandits burglarized the residence of Edgar Lockwood at 4 West 121st Street: "Examining a large quantity of silver plate and appropriating the servants' savings . . . [they] got away with gems [Mrs. Lockwood] valued at about $2,500.00."

## The End of the Row-House Era

In the face of an unsure future, people such as former mayor Thomas F. Gilroy held fast to Harlem. Like most Irish immigrants, most Tammany Hall politicians, and most Harlemites, he was a self-made man, appreciative of the city's boundless opportunities, with high hopes for the future. His six daughters and four sons were recalled as "the envy of the neighborhood . . . and it is a pretty sight to see them ranged in a line rising one above another like the steps of stairs."

Without a zoning ordinance to protect the value represented by their fine row houses, Harlem leaders, including responsible developers, resorted to restrictive deed covenants that set as conditions of sale prohibitions against using properties for factories, stables, "bawdy houses and other nuisances." Initially these covenants were the only means available to protect neighborhoods from incompatible development. Later, they were increasingly used to prevent the acquisition of Harlem property by Jews and African-Americans.

In this period of uncertainty, row houses were perceived by developers as a safe bet, with a modest reward if sold and a slightly better return if rented. Apartment buildings of all sorts—tenements, French flats, and "first-class" elevator buildings—were potentially far more lucrative propositions, since they were inhabited not by one but by dozens of families who would pay and keep on paying. The problem was how to bring these people into Harlem in sufficient numbers: even the combination of elevated trains, streetcars, the Amsterdam Avenue cable car, the viaduct, and the Hudson River and Harlem railroad lines was not sufficient to convey that many people uptown. The subway, projected as early as the 1860s and approved by 1888, was held up until 1904 by the private interests of streetcar owners. During the period of subway anticipation, developers and householders hedged their bets on Harlem's future with restrictions that applied for periods of ten to twenty years. Sure enough, as most of the clauses prohibiting multiple dwellings expired, Harlem's row-house era also came to an end.

CHAPTER THREE

# AT HOME IN HARLEM

St. Nicholas Avenue and Place looking north from West 148th Street, 1909: Frederick P. Dinkelberg, 757–775 St. Nicholas Avenue, 1896; Frank Wennemer, 810–814 St. Nicholas Avenue and 11–19 St. Nicholas Place, 1894; Henri Fouchaux, Arundel Court, 772–778 St. Nicholas Avenue, 1905; John P. Leo, Purling, 768–770 St. Nicholas Avenue, 1902; Paul Franklyn Higgs, 762–766 St. Nicholas Avenue, 1895

William E. Mowbray, 464 West
144th Street (now Alexa and Bethany
Donaphin house), 1890. Parlor

T he interiors of Harlem's houses never fail to surprise visitors. Just as the exterior of
the speculative row house had taken advantage of newly available ready-made
components, so the millwork, stained glass, and plasterwork required for interior
construction and decoration could be ordered as machined, standardized elements.
Far from encouraging repetitiveness or anonymity in domestic interiors, these
common and related features allowed for much greater creativity and innovation.
As preservation of Harlem's extraordinary architectural legacy becomes a firmer reality, a fuller
picture emerges of what a proper urban home environment meant to middle-class occupants
in the nineteenth and early twentieth centuries. The common interior areas—parlor, dining room,
and so on—of the diverse buildings of this period present a composite portrait of life at the time.

The rigid hierarchies that pervaded every aspect of Victorian life are even today betrayed by
details of interior decoration and layout, while other aspects of daily life, such as lighting and
hired help, require imagination to envision. In any Harlem town house, villa, or mansion, there
is a similar decorative stratification: greater attention to ornament, materials, and craftsmanship is
lavished on reception rooms open to guests and strangers, while private family spaces are less
elaborately appointed. The parlor's mahogany or cherry woodwork gives way to curly birch or
bird's-eye maple trim in the principal bedrooms. The quality of materials reaches its nadir in
the utilitarian domain. Meant to be invisible, servants' rooms, kitchens, and laundry rooms were
fitted out as economically as possible.

Only the most elaborate mansions in Harlem included an elevator. Gaslights prevailed well into
the first decade of the twentieth century, despite the availability of cheap reliable current by 1895.
Rich individuals such as James Bailey and Jacob Baiter did make use of electricity well before
then, but in a rather limited fashion. Electric light in their St. Nicholas Place reception rooms was
only a supplement for gas fixtures, much as prominent and decorative mantelpieces with gas logs
augmented coal-fired furnaces. Electricity was more often used to ring the front doorbell and the
servants' call bells.

The sets of double outside doors and the marble-tiled or mosaic-floored vestibules of Harlem residences today are the same as in the nineteenth century. Through an additional single inside door is inevitably a staircase constructed from a lustrous hardwood, most usually quartered oak, although gumwood, mahogany, cherry, or black walnut also appear. The staircases of Harlem's row houses are frequently elements of great charm: the most elaborate and expensive woodwork in the building, expressive of a particular period and reigning style. In houses surviving from Harlem's early days—the Italianate rows of wood, brick, and brownstone situated east of Fifth Avenue just north and south of East 125th Street—the staircase takes the form of uninterrupted flights. Midway, these stairs gently and gracefully curve onto a landing, which is emphasized by an arched niche. The mahogany handrail often has supporting balusters of white-painted pine; in other instances they are composed of solid sections of turned walnut with matching newel posts. In the 1870s, representations of female figures in diaphanous garments, or round-faced cherubs, began to be cast from bronze, iron, and pot metal to support fancy lamps atop the

Theodore Minot Clark, Nathan Hobart house (later the Heights Club), 727 St. Nicholas Avenue, 1886

OPPOSITE
464 West 144th Street (now Alexa and Bethany Donaphin house). Staircase

newel posts. Generally, the mid-1880s saw greater creativity in the design and ornamentation of more interesting and varied stairways in residential Harlem. Particularly notable are John E. Terhune's staircases from this period. In an improbably eclectic row at 240–248 Lenox Avenue (1883; see page 58), the halls have English encaustic-tiled floors with polychrome geometric patterns reminiscent of medieval decoration. The stairs are of oak planking embellished with an abstract Ruskin-inspired cut-out floral design.

The stairs at 464 West 144th Street, a house designed by William E. Mowbray and completed in 1890, are of cherry with a satiny grain; both the turned balusters and carved newel posts were standard ready-made elements. Mowbray, while not a great innovator, had a genius for making ordinary elements into extraordinary architecture. Here he turns the back of the stair toward the front door. In this way, the curved landing assumes a balcony-like aspect, which for most of the year, if only for a short time each day, was bathed in shafts of sunlight falling from the stained-glass skylight.

Both complex and subtle, the staircase design in a residence by architect Horace E. Hartwell at 420 West 143rd Street (1890) has the sleight-of-hand quality delighted in by Harlem's merchant class. A corner site allows the hall to be both generously proportioned and well lighted. The use of marble, oak paneling, and a beamed twelve-foot ceiling lends considerable dignity to the space. Opposite the entrance, the stairway, substantial and handsome, commands attention. Originally, gas-fueled logs below the oak mantel provided a warm gesture of welcome. (Fumes were vented through a chimney ingeniously running under the stairs and up the north wall.) The same warm atmosphere is created with considerably less drama in the entrances to James Brown Lord's Strivers' Row houses on West 138th Street (1891): here stairs ascend behind a colonnaded screen, beyond which after only two steps a landing is offered. After three more steps another landing occurs, and at this point the flight turns, continuing its progress along the back wall.

In contrast to such inventiveness is Neville & Bagge's 1894 approach to the hallways of 348–356 Convent Avenue, a row so decidedly conservative that it could have been formulated twenty years earlier. Yet once inside the decor is so satisfying that fashion is hardly a consideration. Mostly intact, the hall at number 352 exhibits particularly appealing qualities of the architects' work: spiraling baroque balusters complement the robust newel post with its bulbous finial. Daintily cusped, the Near East–inspired spindlework archway, positioned just in front of the staircase, is an effective means of delineating the more private areas of the house. Complete with a convenient stand for calling cards and a lidded seat for putting on and storing overshoes, the towering coat tree still has its original double hooks, which are long enough to hold high silk hats. Still more rare is the original pendant lantern reflected into infinity by mirrors in the hall and parlor.

The stairs designed by Stanford White for McKim, Mead & White's West 139th Street row for the King model houses (1891) are also in a sense conservative. They are scaled-down and simplified versions of grander flights created by the firm in Boston and New York residences. Leaving the ground floor's gracious but low-ceilinged reception hall, the visitor climbs to the parlor floor and is greeted by a flood of sunlight. It is here that the architectural accomplishment is seen to best advantage. Because of a back stair and butler's pantry, the stair halls here extend for only half the building's width. At the parlor level, White translated his sybaritic taste into a quartered-oak columnar screen. A high-backed seat suggests both momentary repose and welcome, while the railing's three distinctly turned balusters recall colonial examples.

Horace E. Hartwell, 420 West 143rd Street (now Robert Van Lierop office), 1890. Stair hall

OPPOSITE
Neville & Bagge, 352 Convent Avenue (now Patricia Jones house), 1894. Stair hall

These stairs on Strivers' Row were not only followed by similar versions by White but were copied by other Harlem architects at the turn of the century, content not to alter a winning arrangement. Clarence F. True, at 469–475 West 143rd Street (1896), retained the seat featured in McKim, Mead & White's King houses, but the grace of his arcaded screen gives his design originality. The stair at 465 West 140th Street, designed by Neville & Bagge and completed in 1906, also reveals the prevalence of White's influence. It is distinguished by fluted columns, a seat with a low, curving back, and identical balusters.

Neville & Bagge, 465 West 140th Street (now Peggy Shephard and Charles Lovejoy house), 1906. Staircase

OPPOSITE
McKim, Mead & White, 227 West 139th Street (Strivers' Row; now Mr. and Mrs. Randy Dupree house), 1891. Stair hall

Adolph Hoak, Richard Leeland
Sweezy house, 329 Convent Avenue,
1890. Double parlors

## The Parlor

The French root of parlor—*parler* ("to talk")—tells the story of this rarefied room. The stiff little suites of chairs and settees seen in old photographs are also clear indicators. The parlor was primarily the province of women, who sat and talked here. Endless rules of etiquette governed what to do or say in the parlor and when and how to say it. A small industry was devoted to supplying manuals that dictated just what was correct and what was not.

During the cooler months, when families stayed in town, women selected a day to be "at home." On this afternoon, the hostess's circle of friends was welcomed—indeed, almost compelled—to call and chat for fifteen minutes to half an hour. Generally, tea was served to the group of, typically, two to six. Some teas were larger than others. In *Harlem Life* of February 3, 1894, for instance, it is noted that "Mrs. William A. Martin of 4 West 122nd Street entertained about 250 guests at her second and last tea of the season on Saturday last. Mrs. Martin's sisters, the Misses Beck, assisted in receiving. Mrs. Martin's gown was opal shaded moire, with chiffon draperies in the same tints and opal set passementerie—worn with a full set of diamonds."

Andrew Spence, Thomas Jacke house
(now Valerie Jo Bradley house),
144 West 120th Street, 1887. Parlor

In addition to social calls and tea parties, the parlor was the setting for games of whist, bridge, or charades. Invariably the parlor was equipped with a piano, and musical evenings, at which refreshments were served, were quite popular. Sometimes such interludes preceded or followed a dinner; dinner parties constituted the most frequent use of the parlor. Both before and after sitting down to table, company was entertained in the parlor. On Saturday, or on Sunday following religious services, the family sometimes awaited dinner here as well, but most households reserved the room strictly for company. Parlors were also used for weddings, funerals, and other ritual gatherings, making it imperative that this "best room in the house" be ordinarily shut tight, in immaculate readiness.

Harlem row-house parlors reveal infinite clues to the lives once lived there. Number 144 West 120th Street is one of a row of brownstones designed by Andrew Spence and completed in 1887. The exterior of the house is fairly standard, although the entrance cornice features an oversized egg-and-dart molding. The house was originally owned by Thomas Jacke, a wholesale glass dealer, and inhabited by his family of four and their three servants. The parlor provided Jacke's neighbors with tangible evidence of his status. The deep plasterwork frieze, which looks like so

133

much icing on a cake, and the mass-produced mahogany millwork are indicative of genteel aspirations. However, along with the mirror between the windows, this type of decoration was by this date somewhat old-fashioned. Jacke's moderate fortunes are expressed more by what is missing from his parlor. The absence of stained-glass transoms and the architect's inability to provide a regular, rectangular space without a narrowing bend at one end (accommodating the entrance-hall staircase) are telling signs that limitations exist in this household.

Architects of high-stooped row houses were always faced with the problem of providing maximum dimensions for the parlor while still accommodating other reception areas. At 456–460 West 152nd Street (1889), C. P. H. Gilbert's solution to the tight fit was the regularization of rooms. However, the semi-octagonal treatment at one end dictates an odd triangular closet in a corner. For narrower rooms at 133–143 West 122nd Street (1887), Frances H. Kimball made similar concessions, employing corner fireplaces as well. H. L. Page and W. W. Kent's 1890 houses in the Hamilton Grange subdivision also used corner fireplaces to help solve the problem. These houses were seventeen and a half feet in width. The twenty-foot width of William Mowbray's nearby houses on West 144th Street allowed him more freedom in the interior arrangement, yet he still had to weigh space requirements against purely aesthetic considerations. At number 464, the contractor's son widened the parlor adjoining the entrance hall—a solution that, while practical, resulted in an irregularly shaped room. Nevertheless, stained-glass transoms with iridescent, Sandwich glass–like rosettes and an Adamesque festooned mantlepiece make it stylistically up-to-date.

Since all Harlem row houses built after the mid-1870s had central heating, the presence of so many fireplaces comes as a surprise. It is important to note that providing warmth was only a secondary function; visual interest was the primary motive. Fireplaces contributed to an ambience that was common in late-nineteenth-century domestic interiors, one accurately described by Victoriana scholar Denys Hinton as that of a "private museum." Interiors were intended not merely to be decorative in themselves but to provide an environment for the exhibition of various bibelots and artwork that announced the owners' taste. From as early as the beginning of the nineteenth century, particularly during the Federal and Greek Revival periods, over-mantel mirrors were popular; they were often related to the design of the chimneypiece. Under the sway of the Aesthetic Movement introduced by English architects such as William Eden Nesfield and Richard Norman Shaw, there arose a new taste for individual "artistic" ornaments shown as a collection against a unifying backdrop.

Exemplary in this respect are the parlor mantelpieces in Kimball's Harlem houses. Stylistically innovative, they adopt the eclectic vocabulary of the Queen Anne mode, combining Eastern and Western references alike. The swirling rosettes carved on the frieze between acanthus-leaf consoles appear to draw on European sources but are actually derived from Japanese porcelain. In outline, if not detailing, the three-staged, partly glazed cabinets flanking the over-mantel mirror recall the delicate, Anglo-Japanese cabinetry of designer Edward William Godwin. In all six of Kimball's Harlem houses, mantels were provided with distinctive character through the judicious use of fittings. Surrounded by a narrow brass band and terminating as an embossed hood, the fire box at number 137 is flanked by angled tiled jambs. A roughly textured, richly colored border of narrow tiles surrounds pictorial tile panels in pastel tones. The latter illustrate two of the four seasons, which are personified as young girls. Manufactured at the famous Dalton Works at Minton, England, they are believed to be designs of Walter Crane.

In the parlor at number 133 a different but equally felicitous arrangement of tiles forms the surround. The border again consists of deeply colored tiles, a harmony of rich rose-red and

Francis H. Kimball, Mrs. Charles D. Gambrill house (now Josephine Ebaugh Jones house), 137 West 122nd Street, 1887. Parlor mantelpiece

turquoise-blue. Reliefs of flying fish alternate with larger reliefs of robins, perched diagonally on the canes of a briar rose, a design clearly inspired by Japanese prints. The cast-iron fire box is set inside a Greek-key framework with squared stars emblazoned with four repeated motifs: a handsome youth rowing a shell-shaped boat through rough water; a seahorse; a winged lion holding a bunch of grapes; and a beribboned shield decorated with a lion's head and positioned in front of a drawn sword. It was precisely this sort of mood-creating but culturally non-specific mass-produced decorative element that designers like Kimball relied on to set one house in a related grouping apart from another.

Kimball doggedly enlisted everything at his disposal to reinforce his stylistic theme. His beautifully designed parlor-floor transom lights have vibrant, highly contrasting colors. Featuring husk garlands and other hybridized details, they were considered "colonial." The same interpretation was given to his built-in coat trees, by virtue of their scrolled pediments. The panels of the various sliding doors on the parlor level are of leaded bottle glass—medieval in derivation, but colonial by contemporary inference.

Kimball's satisfying stylistic admixture was not easily emulated. In the parlors of William B. Tuthill's nearby houses, the interior design was less accomplished and innovative. Even so, at 4 West 122nd Street (1889), the staircase was pushed into the center to wrap around itself in the new manner. The resulting reception hall has a stagelike landing behind an arched opening, which resembles a proscenium. This landing, just above a built-in bench, confronts the most imposing extant Victorian fireplace in Harlem. Curving jambs overlaid by Romanesque scrollwork of the

135

William B. Tuthill, William A. Martin house (now Martha Chandler Dolly house), 4 West 122nd Street, 1889. Reception hall

William A. Martin house (now Martha Chandler Dolly house). Parlor

William B. Tuthill, 10 West 122nd Street (now Rev. Eugene and Thelma Adair house), 1889. Double parlors

type found on church doors frame the fireback, which has been cast with a François I salamander emblem. Above the mahogany mantelpiece's corbeled shelf is a beveled mirror with flanking tabernacles intended to display statuary. Most magnificently, the gabled ends of these shelters, topped by pomegranate finials, engage a bracketed mahogany hood. Carefully, convincingly, it is carved with overlapping shingles. Two arched stained-glass windows flank the chimney and are set into the wall. A bold composition, the decoration of Tuthill's reception hall is meant to evoke Romanesque splendor. Tuthill's archaeological plasterwork frieze in the adjacent parlor is identical to Frank H. Smith's parlor frieze in the John Dwight house, built the following year at 1 West 123rd Street. Also of interest are the classically inspired sconces, with snaking gas jets. Sadly, the accompanying ceiling fixture no longer survives.

At Tuthill's 10 West 122nd Street (1889), an ornate polished-brass gasolier is found at the center of the elongated double parlors, suggesting the scale and prominence of the fixture missing at number 4. Partly obscuring the bay window is a fretted columnar screen evocative of the Levant, the ideal setting for the era's beloved "cozy" or "Turkish" corners. The parlor mantelpiece is the same as at number 4: paired, elaborately turned posts are reflected in separate arched mirror panels supporting a display shelf. However, here the flowered garland carved on a lozenge at the center of the fireplace is not reiterated in the plaster frieze. Instead, the frieze of number 10 was probably papered; period photographs of Harlem's most elaborate examples also suggest the possibility of stenciling, with touches of hand painting.

## *Hints on Household Taste* and *The Decoration of Houses:* The Color and Pattern of Harlem's Interior Walls

In most parlors of the late nineteenth century, walls, friezes, and even ceilings were originally covered with printed papers of contrasting color and design. Appearing in the United States in 1872, Charles Eastlake's guidebook to refined decor, *Hints on Household Taste in Furniture, Upholstery & Other Details,* arrived just in time to transform the parlors of Harlem's speculative rows during the area's second building boom. It was received with the same degree of enthusiasm, and had an equal influence upon interior decoration, that the works of Andrew Jackson Downing had enjoyed a generation earlier. As decorative-arts arbiter Harriet Spofford wrote, "Not a young marrying couple who read English were to be found without *Hints on Household Taste* in their hands, and its dicta were accepted as gospel truths."

Eastlake disliked the fashion of displaying strips of paper in isolated panels around a room in imitation of a French salon, calling it "attractive from its novelty . . . [but] false in principle." On the other hand, he also did not like papering walls in one pattern, deeming it a monotonous

227 West 139th Street (now Mr. and Mrs. Randy Dupree House). Parlor

OPPOSITE
465 West 140th Street (now Peggy Shephard and Charles Lovejoy house). Parlor with decor (designed by Patrick McNulty) inspired by Marie-Antoinette's boudoir at Fontainebleau

alternative. What he did praise were walls divided into three unequal horizontal sections or zones. At the bottom, he favored a wooden wainscot, or the effect of one, about three feet high. At the top was the frieze, one to two feet deep. The largest area was the remaining "field." Explaining why areas should be decorated in a varied manner, critic Henry Hudson Holly, in *Modern Dwellings in Town and Country,* explained that "furniture and costume show to a better advantage when walls of an apartment are dark, while pictures look well upon a light background." Only in a vague way appreciating such subtleties, many Harlem decorators ignored the balance of light and dark and altered the proportions, merely aware that their walls had at all costs to be tripartite.

By the following decade, a radical change in aesthetic sensibilities had taken place. Harlem developers, decorators, and homeowners were happily taking the advice offered by Edith Wharton and Ogden Codman Jr. in their *Decoration of Houses,* published in 1897. On the second floor of Stanford White's Roman-derived Strivers' Row houses on West 139th Street are, for the first time since the 1830s, white, or nearly white, parlor walls. But color and pattern were not banished entirely. White's gilded neoclassical frames were meant to contain panels of fabric or fabriclike stenciling. Stanford White was among America's foremost stylistic trendsetters, always well ahead of other designers in his novel approach. His pioneering appreciation of eighteenth-century decor caused his friend critic Mariana Van Rensselaer to playfully dub his firm "McKim, White & Gold." For Fifth Avenue millionaires, or the handful of similarly rich Harlemites, a white-painted parlor in the last decade of the nineteenth century did not seem to be so daring. But the solidly middle-class clientele expected to buy or rent the King model houses was less worldly. Outside of growing numbers of how-to books and journals devoted to the decorative arts, such rooms were completely unknown. The time was right, however, and many Harlemites were ready for something new and different, which they hoped would distinguish them from people who lived in more ordinary houses.

With regard to the decorative arts, it is interesting to note that in the late nineteenth century and the early years of the twentieth, wallpaperers, painters, plasterers, and furniture firms had a far greater role in conceiving decorative schemes than they do today. The parlor of Neville & Bagge's

house at 465 West 140th Street, inspired by Marie-Antoinette's boudoir at Fontainebleau, is a case in point. The complex ornamentation that today is painted white was formerly gilded composition. Patrick McNulty was not only the plastering contractor for the room; he actually designed it, as well as the remarkable parlors of other houses in the same row and of row houses on both sides of West 141st Street, between Convent and Amsterdam Avenues, by Neville & Bagge and John Hauser. Certainly Wharton and Codman, champions of the creation of a new and forward-looking aesthetic, would have approved. Under their tutelage, in what had once been the forests of Harlem, ordinary people were creating parlors that would help to definitively banish Victorian gloom.

## The Dining Room

If the parlor, with its ceremoniousness and stiff decorum, was only occasionally opened for family gatherings, the dining room was far more accessible. Here visitors were bidden not merely to break bread but also to glimpse a household's most sacrosanct daily ritual. In an era when well-ordered meals, well served, were anticipated by even the ordinary citizen as what King Edward VII referred to as "life's only dependable pleasures," the dining room was very important. Thus considerable care and thought went into both its placement in relation to other rooms and its distinguishing decor.

Because of practical service considerations before the general employment of electric call bells and dumbwaiters, most Harlem dining rooms were on the ground floor, slightly below grade and facing the street. Representative of the earliest row-house dining rooms is the one at 20 East 127th Street. Part of a brownstone group designed by Alexander Wilson and completed in 1869, the Italianate-style structure is today famous as the home of poet and writer Langston Hughes. Like the majority of Harlem's first wave of speculative town houses, it is of little interest architecturally. Indeed, its extremely conservative design treats the dining room in an identical fashion to the two first-floor parlors above it. Apart from a lower ceiling, it is interchangeable.

How rapidly and thoroughly this situation would change can be gauged by an inspection of the dining rooms of the houses at 133–143 West 122nd Street. Francis H. Kimball's striking row of 1887 retains basement siting, but nothing else about them is the least bit old-fashioned. They are, however, quite small, at least relative to the size of the reception rooms and parlors upstairs. While the scale may be less than expansive, the craftsmanship is superb. A panoply of built-in shelves, cupboards, closets, and cabinets makes these compact rooms veritable Chinese puzzles. They are also advanced in their use of the Queen Anne style's evocative vocabulary. Arcades with slender columns are the major feature of both the quaint corner fireplaces and the recessed, built-in sideboards.

Less original is the 1889 dining room designed by William B. Tuthill, in the house originally belonging to developer William A. Martin at 4 West 122nd Street. Here a more orthodox version of the Renaissance Revival mode was used. Representative of local late-nineteenth-century dining rooms, the Martins' was located on the first floor as the last among three reception spaces. This house, twenty-five feet wide, was five feet wider than its related neighbors. Not surprisingly, none needed an alcove to contain the sideboard. However, in the same block on West 121st Street, houses of eighteen feet in width designed by Cleverdon & Putzel in 1890 do include such alcoves, which were made necessary by the standard three-foot depth of the sideboard and the five-foot width of the butler's pantry. Identical architraves with composite pilasters, high wainscots, and

William A. Martin house (now Martha Chandler Dolly house). Dining room with Tiffany window

similar decorative ceiling and wall treatments are common to all of Tuthill's dining rooms. The Martin house was further enriched by parquetry floors.

Intricate parquet floors as a background for oriental carpets were the fashion in late-1880s Harlem houses. Crafted of as many as six different woods, the complexity of the designs belies the fact that they were often composed of prefabricated and mass-produced elements that could be selected from catalogs. Of the three parquetry floors in the Martin house—the others are in the entrance and stair halls—that in the dining room shows the greatest subtlety. This room's sophisticated appointments include an electrical outlet at the center of the dining room; it facilitated the installation of a call bell, which was mounted under the table to summon servants unobtrusively.

A highly polished, arabesque-adorned brass frame at the fireplace opening is a veritable second mantelpiece. It forms a border for both the tiled fire surround and the cast-iron fire box. Like the flooring, it and the carved oak mantelpiece were available from a catalog. Exhibiting well-executed craftsmanship, the mantel's pedestrian origins would never have been suspected: the stock materials that had increasingly become the norm were of high quality. Beyond choosing from a limited selection of available stock items, most architects involved in designing Harlem row houses relied on a lumberyard being able to fabricate whatever custom pieces were required, often working from preexisting plans. Inevitably, as long as ornamentation remained popular, there was pressure to utilize more and better machine-made cabinetry.

Eventually, increasing costs led builders to employ cast composition in place of hand carving. In exactly the same way as exterior terra cotta, such elements allowed architects to indulge in

Richard Leeland Sweezy house

exuberant interior decorations that would have been impossible to achieve in any other way. Less time-consuming to execute and install, these embellishments, glued on and stained or painted, were all but undetectable. After 1890, their use soared. At the Martin house a compromise was struck: the mantelpiece is carved, but the even more elaborate, arabesque frieze that crowns the high wainscoting (and matches the fire surround) is composition.

The pictorial stained-glass window in the southern wall of the dining room is a memorable focal point. Along with the house, the window was a wedding gift from Mrs. Martin's father; it fittingly features a theme of marital fidelity. Supplied by New York's foremost decorating firm, Tiffany Studios, it depicts Penelope, the wife of Odysseus, busy at the stealthy enterprise of unweaving her day's work as she waits patiently and faithfully for her husband's return. The Martins' window recalls an observation by Denys Hinton: "To Victorians, every picture told a story, and since in the main, there was a lack of understanding of classical symbolic language, the stories had to be simple ones with which the owners could identify themselves. And visual platitudes abounded."

Composed of the faceted jewels and the plated and textured drapery glass that so distinguishes Louis Comfort Tiffany's extensive output, this window is an almost unique survivor. (Although once numerous, there are almost none of this size and quality remaining in Harlem's private houses.) A more modest example is found quite close by at 7 West 122nd Street, completed in 1888 as part of a row designed by Cleverdon & Putzel. Highlighting the sideboard recess in the dining room is a small stained-glass panel. Less spectacularly but with equal luminosity, it portrays a garland of glowing fruit.

Richard Leeland Sweezy house.
Dining room

Far easier to find but by no means commonplace are dining rooms with built-in buffets. Like hall coat trees, inglenooks, and built-in seats and cabinets, they were an attempt on the part of the designer to exert more control over an interior's unity. Lawyer Richard Leeland Sweezy's dining room, in a house that is part of the 311–339 Convent Avenue group designed by Adolph Hoak and completed in 1890, was designed in the same Renaissance Revival style as that at the Martin house. It featured mahogany woodwork, including a built-in buffet. Both the deeply colored wood and the beveled mirror installed directly above the sideboard must have created an impressive tableau at a candlelight dinner, with delicate reflections of glittering silver and cut glass.

While the ceiling of a dining room in Horace E. Hartwell's 420 West 143rd Street was cast from plaster, originally its heavy beams were painted in a faux-grain pattern to match the oak paneling and buffet. The latter is surmounted by mirrored panels, which are embedded into the wainscoting between pilasters. The room's great proportions are such that the buffet appears overwhelmed in comparison to the imposing mantelpiece and the curving leaded-glass bay window.

This sort of massiveness seems to have appealed mightily to Victorian families. Throughout the 1880s and 1890s, the Romanesque Revival style was determined to be eminently suitable for the most scrutinized room in the house. The dining room at 411 West 148th Street, a house designed by Christian Steinmetz and completed in 1890, requires shoulder-high wainscoting to maintain its imposing scale. Carving on the mantelpiece frieze represents lion's heads and alternating rosettes within an interlacing guilloche. With contrasting expanses of alternately curved and rounded

143

420 West 143rd Street (now
Robert van Lierop office). Dining
room

Christian Steinmetz, Morris Tuska
house (now Robert Van Lierop
house), 411 West 148th Street,
1890. Dining room

unadorned quartered oak, accentuated by concentrations of bas-relief carving, the mantelpiece is a tour de force. In addition, it is superbly appointed with a broad fire surround of Mexican onyx, dazzlingly rich in effect. Yet the room is knowingly balanced. The coloration and texture specific to the various materials and their finishes are sensitively handled as an integral aspect of the design. With great attention to historical accuracy, Steinmetz decorated the double parlors in an interpretation of the High Italian Renaissance. The choice of materials—maple for the mantelpiece, architraves, and high dado, and scagliola for the Corinthian columns and pilasters marking the division of the two rooms—is still essentially Victorian, but the fidelity of proportion and crisp detailing forecast a new epoch.

The house was owned by Morris Tuska. In addition to supporting and directing some of New York's most important Jewish charities, Tuska was a retired upholsterer. This was an era when upholstery firms, cabinetmakers, and wallpapering establishments served in the capacity today reserved for professional interior decorators. It is therefore tempting to wonder whether Tuska played a role in planning the decorative format, since the materials, color schemes, and shapes are set against one another with great élan. Furthermore, they are uniformly representative of the best design obtainable at the time.

William E. Mowbray, Mr. and Mrs. William Kaupe house, 459 West 144th Street, 1888. Christmas dinner, c. 1908

Neville & Bagge, Mr. and Mrs. Joseph Guttenberg house, 118 West 120th Street, 1893. Golden anniversary dinner, 1902

## Remembrance of Things Past

The house at 459 West 144th Street, one of William Mowbray's row, belonged to Mr. and Mrs. William Kaupe, the sister and brother-in-law of the architectural photographer L. H. Dreyer. One of his views is a faithful portrait of his family's annual Christmas festivities, which transports the viewer back to about 1908. Unlike Dreyer's renowned depictions of Pennsylvania Station, which are filled with grandeur and frozen shafts of light, this semicandid shot is intimate, celebrating a family's joy. The dining-room table has been extended to make room for everyone. Newly electrified, the lighted gasolier provides a dramatic spotlight for the feast.

The walls are painted a solid color, not papered, and have no wainscoting. The cherry door and window surrounds are decorated with composition Colonial Revival garlands, echoed by the stenciled frieze. The fireplace is a reminder that these houses were not entirely finished before the developers, William De Forest and his son, ran into financial difficulties in the late 1880s:

147

a close look reveals plain sawn oak and coarse detailing. But most of the details of the scene are not very different from what might be found in the majority of middle-class Harlem dining rooms of the period. While the display of small racks of antlers may appear barbarous, they and other ornaments were precisely what gave this interior its Teutonic identity.

Another of Harlem's many German-American households was one headed by Joseph Guttenberg, who had arrived in New York from Hamburg at the age of nineteen, penniless. By the turn of the century, he had retired from the garment industry and was a prosperous Harlem developer. Since the mid-1890s, the family had resided at Neville & Bagge's 118 West 120th Street, completed in 1893. To celebrate their parents' golden wedding anniversary in 1902, their children planned a dinner. The dining room is papered in what for the period was a subdued pattern. On the round table is an arrangement of daffodils and maidenhair fern, with a trail of bridal tulle. Charming, though not unusual, pierced silver candle shades lined with pink silk have an inner lining of mica to protect against the flame. The refinement of the silver candlesticks is more unusual. Composed of brass scrollwork, a gasolier provides the main source of light; it combines a utilitarian, shaded lamp with more decorative candlelike gas jets. However, in this instance, the center light, all but hidden by the florists' worthy efforts, is fueled by old-fashioned kerosene instead of gas or electricity. Both period photographs, taken within a few years of each other, record not only memorable occasions but also typical households in homes characteristic of their times.

Paul Franklyn Higgs, William Haigh house (now Eleanor Eastman house), 412 West 147th Street, 1890. Dining-room sideboard

OPPOSITE
William Haigh house (now Eleanor Eastman house). Pantry with dumbwaiter and icebox

The dining room of William Haigh at 412 West 147th Street, designed by Paul Franklyn Higgs and completed in 1890, is neo–Italian Renaissance in style. The sideboard is flanked by tabernacle-like glass cabinets and appears to be a kind of altar laden with innumerable gleaming relics of business success and social attainment. (Haigh was an agent of the Equitable Life Insurance Company and the president of the Realty Construction Company; upon his death he was to leave a considerable estate.) The serving pantry and dumbwaiter in the house were typical of the period, an essential connection between kitchen and dining area. The dumbwaiter was a marvel of convenience. Some—such as those at 4 West 122nd Street and 352 Convent Avenue—rose all the way to the top floor; more frequently they only reached the first story, as at the Haigh house, where a glass-doored icebox is also preserved in the pantry.

Between 1895 and 1905, Harlem's last years of speculative row houses, the Classical Revival was the favorite mode for dining rooms. Yet although these spaces became far less masculine and overbearing, they were nevertheless a counterpoint to the feminine sphere of the parlor. Neville & Bagge's and John Hauser's related rows on West 140th and 141st Streets both have handsome, almost identical basement dining rooms, which are entered through a spacious hall. Designed as neo-Renaissance spaces with beamed ceilings and high wainscoting, these entirely American dining rooms also resound with Georgian overtones.

In Henri Fouchaux's high-stooped row on the west side of Convent Avenue between West 141st and 142nd Streets (1902), somewhat larger and higher dining rooms are upstairs rather than at ground level. Company was served here, while family meals were taken downstairs. The two dining rooms found in many houses of this period allowed for more flexibility. Some families adapted one of the rooms as a library or family sitting room.

William Ström, in his 21–49 Hamilton Terrace row of 1899, designed some houses with American and others with English basements. None, however, have ground-floor dining rooms. The houses were built on a gentle rise of glacial bedrock dropping off dramatically to the east, Alexander Hamilton's onetime terrace. The first five houses employed the American plan to compensate for lower building sites.

At 37 Hamilton Terrace the dining room is representative of others in the group. A sign of the times, it is neoclassical; with much restraint and sensitivity, it looks to early Stuart England. A finely carved strapwork panel framing one large faceted "jewel" and several cabochons decorates the fireplace that dominates the room. As in Ström's other rooms, selective ornamentation embellishes quietly; it does not draw attention to itself. The rhythmic volume of the parlor's bow window is not suggestive of any particular period, and not a single element of its spare decoration has a definite historical source. In the hall, the balustrade of narrow, repetitive oak slats evokes both Japan and Gustave Stickley's Arts and Crafts sensibility. Like other designers who were his contemporaries, Ström does not attempt to show off his knowledge. Instead, much decoration created during this period may be read as a powerful representation of self-assured inhabitants who were able to appreciate their great good fortune in inhabiting such fine houses.

Richard Leeland Sweezy house.
Son's bedroom

## Bedrooms, Billiards, and Baths

> Upstairs were the bedrooms; "mother-and-father's room" the largest; a smaller room for one or two
> sons, another for one or two daughters; each of these rooms containing a double bed, a washstand,
> a bureau, a wardrobe, a little table, a rocking-chair, and often a chair or two that had been
> slightly damaged downstairs, but not enough to justify either the expense of repair or decisive
> abandonment in the attic.
>
> —Booth Tarkington, *The Magnificent Ambersons*

The "chambers," or bedrooms, of row houses were more homogeneous, both generally and within
a given house, than were other rooms. For the most part, the upstairs area enjoyed a great deal of
informality and flexibility. In many Harlem row houses, the family sitting room was directly above
the parlor and otherwise would have been used as the front bedroom of the second floor. In high-
stooped houses, the family chose the room below the parlor; at 420 West 143rd Street, a corner
house, plans designate this space as "the billiard room." However, this room was situated so that
it was often used for other purposes, including, on occasion, the servants' brief moments of leisure.
Compared to the main entrance with its several steps up, the room below the parlor required only
a few treads down; it was thus an ideal location for the bedroom of an elderly family member.

Technology and the quaint Victorian equation of cleanliness with godliness had brought about
a widespread demand for bathrooms. Following the long-anticipated opening of the Croton
Aqueduct in 1842, New York's sanitation was transformed, and by 1880 nearly all houses built
in Harlem had bathrooms. A private bath adjoining the main bedroom was still considered
quite deluxe. James Bailey and his wife in the 1888 house at 10 St. Nicholas Place had one

that adjoined their bedroom and sitting room. A similar arrangement could have been found in almost any of the stately residences along the street.

Yet many New Yorkers still had misgivings about too frequent bathing. In 1854, while his seaside house was under construction, James Rhodes received a note from a friend, James Moran:

> Dear Jim: I'm much worried about you. I hear that in your house in Newport you are putting in two bathrooms. I never thought that you would be such a damn fool, and I expect to hear any day that you've been drowned.

James Moran might have taken solace in the fact that before rear L-shaped extensions became common in row houses in the mid-1890s, in Harlem it was virtually impossible to fit in even one private bathroom and still provide for the rest of the household. By way of compromise, the second-floor bath at 4 West 122nd Street opened into the stair hall as well as into the adjacent main bedroom. Additionally, two connecting dressing rooms were usually placed back to back between two bedrooms. The dressing rooms were separated by a sliding door and generally had porcelain washbasins set into marble counters. Above the basin would have been a medicine cabinet faced with a beveled mirror. The dressing rooms were also fitted with built-in wardrobe closets with paneled doors.

352 Convent Avenue (now Patricia Jones house). Bath

Lavish baths had stained glass and fireplaces. On the upper floors of the house, the bath generally occupied the space used for dressing rooms below and was entered from the middle of the hallway. Occasionally servants' rooms had washstands; a tub was placed in the hall bathroom and the toilet relegated to a closet—hence the term "water closet." Alternatively, there might be a bathroom in the basement for the servants' use. A basement room might also be utilized as a laundry, which was otherwise relegated to the cellar below. Advances in plumbing did not ease the drudgery of washing. A built-in copper wash boiler stood next to soapstone, porcelain, or galvanized-iron washtubs on cast-iron stands. A small stove nearby was used to heat "flat" irons of various weights. By 1890, laundry rooms and sometimes kitchens were clad in white-tiled wainscots, thought to be antiseptic. The reflective surfaces of such tiling also helped to brighten basement rooms.

In row houses built before 1900, the most popular means of heating water was the kitchen's cast-iron range, which was contained in a protective brick vault or fireplace and fueled by coal or wood. The range was used to heat water because in fall, winter, and spring it was kept burning day and night. The furnace, by contrast, was used only in the coldest weather. Water was piped through the range firebox and stored in copper tanks. With time these tanks were supplied with a gas-fueled burner, which heated water more efficiently.

The cellar furnace was also made from cast iron. It burned as much as one and a half tons of coal every year to heat the average row house, and twice that amount for a double-width mansion. Hot-water or steam radiators heated individual rooms. Those in the main rooms of the John W. Fink house at 8 St. Nicholas Place, designed by Richard Rosenstock and completed in 1889, took the form of squat pillars with round marble tops. Three houses designed by C. P. H. Gilbert at 456–460 West 152nd Street in 1884 had large floor registers with decorative grilles that emitted hot air, but generally such systems came to be considered less desirable than radiated heat. Dust rising up via the ductwork presented a problem, and hot air removed moisture from the air, to the detriment of woodwork and sinuses alike. This is one reason for the frequent appearance of corner steam pipes for radiators that replaced hot-air systems.

10 West 122nd Street (now Rev.
Eugene and Thelma Adair house).
Kitchen

# CHAPTER FOUR

# APARTMENTS

St. Nicholas Avenue looking south
from West 150th Street, 1909: Frank
Wennemer, 810–814 St. Nicholas
Avenue, 1894; Samuel Sass, Plaza,
795–797 St. Nicholas Avenue,
c. 1903; Neville & Bagge, 809–813
St. Nicholas Avenue, 1898

Schwartz & Gross, Riviera Apartments, 790 Riverside Drive, 1910; Schwartz & Gross, Rhinecliff Court, 788 Riverside Drive, 1911; George and Edward Blum, Vaux Hall, 780 Riverside Drive, 1914

I n the early twentieth century, the streets of Harlem were changing rapidly and single-family homes were quickly disappearing. In the 1890s, subway lines had invaded the neighborhood, although it was not until 1904 that the initial phase of construction was completed, with the Lenox Avenue line extended to West 135th Street. During this uncertain time Harlem was prey to tremendous upheaval as the possible changes in store were contemplated. While, as historian Gilbert Osofsky has noted, erratic development of land along new transportation routes had occurred before—as when charters were granted to horse-car companies in the early nineteenth century—at the turn of the twentieth fevered dreams of unprecedented wealth seemed to take hold. New York's big builders were able to raise large sums of industrially based capital. Furthermore, the population of New York grew tremendously during this same period, as multitudes of immigrants from Europe arrived and the first wave of black migration from the South occurred.

Steven Ruttenbaum's thoughtful study of Emery Roth's work, *Mansions in the Clouds*, carefully delineates the range of options available to turn-of-the-century tenants in Harlem's multiple dwellings:

> A tenement house was a building in which its many suites of rooms were provided with neither separate baths nor elevators; a [French] flat was a suite of rooms with a private bath in a "walk-up" building; and an apartment was a suite of rooms with a private bath in an elevator building.

Large numbers of each of these housing types were built north of Central Park between Lexington and Seventh Avenues in the 1890s. Joining more established German-Jewish families, some Eastern European Jews who had prospered celebrated their upward mobility by moving from the Lower East Side to Harlem.

Market collapses similar to the catastrophic Panic of 1904–7, which came about just as the subway turned from dream to reality, had occurred before. While at one time Harlem had been

157

an aristocratic summer resort, with just a few resident families, new means of transit brought more and more people with fewer and fewer resources. Elite Knickerbocker clans were mostly long gone by the time the subway debuted, but many remaining upper-middle-class residents had viewed the new trains not through the rose-colored glasses of real-estate investors but as the bearer of bad tidings: the disadvantaged. In areas with covenants limiting building to row houses, prohibitions against multiple dwellings were not renewed; new covenants restricted the religion and race of a tenant or buyer. Apartments had been built in anticipation of the subway, and several mansions and row houses less than twenty years old had been demolished to provide space to build more densely. Clearly, the neighborhood was changing, and this must have prompted lively conversations and even arguments in many Harlem households. Often fueling the debate were incendiary reports in newspapers. An editorial in the *Harlem Local Reporter* noted in 1893: "Foreigners are crowding up the whole length of the island"; an August 31, 1913, *New York Sun* headline announced by way of warning: "Took Negro Tenants, Now Sued; Harlem Woman Asked to Pay $10,000 for Breaking Agreement."

The speculative middle-class apartment house has received little scholarly attention, although it has been discussed in texts such as Elizabeth Collins Cromley's *Alone Together*; M. Christine Boyer's *Manhattan Manners*; and Robert A. M. Stern's *New York 1900* and *New York 1930*. As Stern has observed, above midtown it is a building type that is responsible for the appearance of the Manhattan residential streetscape as it appears today. Preoccupied with architecture with more upscale associations, many have failed to see the fine qualities of the typical Harlem apartment house. Montgomery Schuyler, for instance, derided these buildings as "over-ambitious" and "too pretentious." His special disdain was reserved for the grand facades of structures of six to twelve stories, with their boldly rusticated basements and hierarchical arrangement of ornamentation culminating in the upper stages, where exuberant decoration ran riot.

He was critical mostly of the hypocrisy of such grandeur, for inside these buildings suites typically contained from four to eight repetitive spaces; all rooms were comparatively small and "strung along seemingly endless corridors." There was no piano nobile with grander suites among these tightly packed units. Indeed, the fanlight culminating the grand two-story main entrance of many of these buildings was very likely to be a bedroom window. Yet the same criticism could have been leveled at Jefferson's similar compromise between noble facade and practical interior at Monticello, and the eighteenth-century Parisian *hôtel particulier* also very often expressed this same dichotomy. While for the purist the blind doors sometimes employed by Emery Roth must be anathema, they nevertheless seem a reasonable, indeed clever, means of providing a subordinate axis. Likewise, the towers of Harlem apartment houses, appealing though they are, have offended some critics who learn they mask water tanks within.

For their designers, these grandiloquent gestures related to the standard established by institutional buildings and private houses uptown, without compromising the interest of their clients. The names of Harlem's late-nineteenth- and early-twentieth-century apartment houses—Riviera, Beaumont, Graham Court, Jumel—with their references to historic figures and places, were intended to evoke a sense of stateliness and romance. Neighboring buildings on Seventh Avenue were named for French royal residences—Chantilly, Versailles, and Fontainebleau. Like much post–Civil War Harlem architecture, some apartments emulated far grander downtown structures. Even in approximation, however, lower Manhattan's palatial apartment blocks and towers were slow to appear here. Indeed, widespread middle-class misgivings persisted as to the propriety of living in an apartment house, as opposed to a private residence or even a boardinghouse. Accordingly, specialist apartment designers were careful to provide their earliest efforts with reassuringly homelike features.

158

## Row Houses in Miniature

Inspired by Dutch Renaissance houses, Clarence True's French flats, at 477 West 143rd Street at Amsterdam Avenue (1896), epitomized this approach, as did Louis Entzer's Marion Apartments at 100–108 St. Nicholas Avenue, at the intersection of Seventh Avenue and West 115th Street (1898). The latter building is deceptively simple: half a block long and six stories high, it must have seemed unworthy of any special attention when it was built. Yet the facade's six gabled ends are surmounted by scrolling finials, much like the decoration on the neck of a fiddle. They organize the building's bulk into six residentially scaled bays, creating a rhythmic emphasis at street level. Projecting above a mansard roof between intervening chimneys, the gables also assert a sense of domesticity, belying both the building's massiveness and its relative austerity. The varied but disciplined fenestration of rectangular and arched windows provides the only other notable ornament.

More typical apartment buildings were built in 1887 by Berg & Clark. Located at 187 and 188 West 135th Street and 2299 and 2301 Seventh Avenue, they imitate various features associated with Harlem houses and evince the rugged intractability of the Romanesque Revival style. In place of elaborate embellishments, the four brick structures are trimmed with brownstone and employ curving corners and deep bracketed cornices to provide interest.

At numerous other Harlem apartment houses, lobbies feature such domestic gestures as prominent fireplace mantels and stained-glass windows. Gilbert A. Schellenger's Haberman building at the southeast corner of St. Nicholas Avenue and West 116th Street was an imperious seven-story neo-Romanesque structure built by developer Simon Haberman in 1892, at a cost of $100,000 (it was later renamed the Wilhelmina). Designed to house nineteen families, the building featured a lobby richly paneled in ornately carved oak. In the Berg & Clark buildings on Seventh Avenue, however, the entrances were far more reticent. In the tradition of Parisian apartments for the middle class, plain and simple hallways were treated as a realm of transition and considered almost as public as the street.

By contrast, the apartment suites in the West 135th Street group were built just two to each floor; extending front to back, they were really row houses in miniature, rearranged on one level. Two connecting reception rooms, separated by sliding doors, faced the street. Mahogany woodwork included a parlor chimneypiece. A third adjoining front room could be used in a variety of ways: as a library, office, family sitting room, or bedroom, as requirements demanded. Along a lengthy passageway, beyond three bedrooms and a bath, lay the dining room, pantry, and kitchen. Even farther on was a maid's room and bath. Initially a characteristic of most multiple dwellings in Harlem, such spaciousness quickly became a luxury reserved only for the wealthy. Exemplary of the sometimes overexuberant suite decor found in such French flats are the parlor, dining room, and bedroom of Mrs. Leoni on Morningside Avenue in 1894.

As developers slowly reduced the size of apartments, they preferred to keep the same number of rooms and reduce the overall area. They also introduced compensatory features of style and convenience. Once electric light, steam heat, gas ranges, mechanical refrigeration, tiled bathrooms with porcelain fixtures, and elevators were considered unobtainable frills. But between 1900 and 1915 all of these amenities, reinforced by new building regulations, became standard for middle-class residents of Harlem. To maintain a competitive edge, some shrewd building owners even started providing features of architectural distinction, which were to become as vital as provisions for more efficient layouts.

West 143rd Street looking east from Amsterdam Avenue, 1909: Clarence True, 477 West 143rd Street, 1896; Adolph Hoak, 311–321 Convent Avenue, 1890; Neville & Bagge, 480 West 143rd Street, 1897

Louis Entzer, Marion Apartments, 100–108 St. Nicholas Avenue, 1898

Mrs. Leoni apartment, Morningside Avenue. Parlor, Christmas 1894

For many architects the task of imbuing an apartment house with glamour was often interpreted as a simple matter of piling on more and more ornament. Usually this meant use of terra-cotta decorations, which by now were quite inexpensive—at least when standardized elements requiring no new molds were ordered from catalogs. At first straightforwardly rendered in red clay, as on Edward L. Angell's brick apartment buildings on the east side of Seventh Avenue at West 118th Street (1889), increasingly these embellishments came to be regarded with scorn. In order to redeem this effective and pragmatic substitute for carved stonework, terra-cotta decorations, polychrome or glazed to imitate stone, were more frequently specially designed by an architect to enliven a specific spot on a particular building.

Other builders protected their investments with a guarded, less decorative strategy. Developer Franklin A. Thurston, cautious as an investor, had been reluctant to employ an experimental design for the walk-up tenements he erected on the south side of West 133rd Street between Seventh and Eighth Avenues in 1892. Designed by C. P. H. Gilbert, who was to be increasingly occupied planning handsome, highly integrated row-house groupings and lavish Fifth Avenue mansions, these apartments were well built with materials of high quality. Their form, however, was calculatingly related to that of high-stooped houses, assumed to be more familiar to prospective tenants of moderate means.

## Mansions for the Masses: The Legacy of Emery Roth

Arriving as an immigrant from Hungary in 1884, Emery Roth overcame extraordinary obstacles, including prevalent anti-Semitism, to become one of the city's most highly regarded architects. Despite his lack of formal training at a university or the Ecole des Beaux-Arts, which by the

Mrs. Leoni apartment. Dining room

turn of the century was considered a prerequisite for a flourishing and fashionable practice, Roth made a name for himself by endowing speculative apartments and commercial structures with dignity and distinction. The dramatic skyline framing Central Park, especially along its west side, may be traced more to his contributions than to those of any other architect. The growth of his career was directly linked to the frenetic development of upper Manhattan at the turn of the century. He was greatly aided in his rise by a mutually beneficial association with the prolific developers Alexander and Leo Bing. The subtlety with which Roth quoted past architectural successes by prominent designers, transforming them into something distinctively his own, was noteworthy in a field in which "borrowing," although widespread, was only occasionally inspired. This was particularly true for buildings with limited budgets—the sort that secured Roth's reputation. He went to great lengths to maintain at least a semblance of classical balance in his interior allocations, a task often challenged by nervous builders.

Apartments extending along the north side of West 136th Street between Broadway and Riverside Drive (1904, with More and Liesidal) date from so early during Roth's steady rise that the Bing brothers were unwilling to entrust him with planning the layouts. Unquestionably, they had been impressed by his combination of Viennese Secessionist and Beaux-Arts styles at the Hotel Belleclaire at Broadway and West 77th Street (1901). But otherwise, Roth was unknown to them. His ability to wrest the maximum amount of rentable space from a plan was a critical matter. They might have worried that this young man, who had worked for society architects Richard Morris Hunt and Ogden Codman Jr., would not be able to adhere to a strict bottom line. Perhaps they merely hoped that he could impart stylishness to more modest structures. Instead, with scores of subsequent collaborations during their long association, he was to satisfy them in every regard.

Emery Roth, Halidon Court, 3681 Broadway, 1910. Colored concrete and carved-stone ornament

Halidon Court. Lobby staircase

OPPOSITE
Julius A. Schweinfurth, Jumel, 405 and 407 West 142nd Street, 1901

Bing and Bing's apprehension had stemmed primarily from Roth's reputation for extravagance, which was unmerited: he was extremely conscientious. He had been a determined advocate of enhancing or even upgrading French flats into fireproof apartment houses. Whenever possible, he would provide elevators in place of stairs and secondary stairs in place of fire escapes. Roth also would come to be known for his propensity to screen unsightly water tanks with picturesque towers. Ultimately, his great contribution to the field of speculative multiple dwellings intended for the middle-class market was a gift for tactfully educating his clients. Again and again, Roth convinced his clients to spend money on "non-essentials" as a sure means of realizing greater profits.

In order to maintain architectural principles of balance, Roth employed the tripartite formula associated with McKim, Mead & White, which was based on the disposition of a classical column. Ornately embellished basements and top floors, corresponding to pedestals and capitals, complemented plainer floors in between, corresponding to the shaft. Typically, the ground floor was built from stone, even when the upper stories were not. On West 136th Street, Roth's basements had robustly banded rustication with highly modeled architraves, superbly crafted from limestone. On the upper four floors, however, terra cotta and brick masonry, both glazed to imitate limestone, were used. Symmetrically balanced, aligned window groupings concentrated all ornamentation upward. Projecting pavilion-like bays flanking the entrances also emphasized the verticality of these relatively low structures. At the same time, they framed the fire escapes (newly mandated in 1901) within an arched recess. No less decorative than the building's other elements were their deep cornices, stamped from sheet metal but painted the color of limestone.

Representative of Roth's early commissions are the Halidon Court and Trinity Studios, which stand across from each other on Broadway at West 153rd Street (1910). Roth's unusual embellishments, inspired by Art Nouveau and the Viennese Secession, transform these conventionally configured structures into something exceptional. All the while mindful of the bottom line, Roth employed an economy of means that transformed the sensuous mosaic designs of Otto Wagner into prefabricated colored concrete panels used both on the facade and as a courtyard frieze. The Art Nouveau balustrade of the lobby stair was likewise a stock item. What remains a mystery is how Roth managed to provide these buildings with such distinctive stone carving. Although motifs like the bundled laurel leaves and bejeweled heads of exotic sirens appear on other buildings by Roth, they are not found on structures designed by his competitors—which would suggest that they were specially commissioned. The end result was a level of sophistication that is today difficult to imagine being lavished on the dwellings of the middle class.

## The Age of the Opulent Apartment:
## The Jumel, Arundel Court, and El Nido

Brilliant application of custom-created terra-cotta ornaments was not by any means the exclusive province of Roth. At the Jumel at 405 and 407 West 142nd Street (1901)—cream-colored French flats—unique terra-cotta decorations complement Roman brick and limestone in an arresting manner. Quatrefoil windows, profusely embellished by arabesques, run in lines up and down the center of the facades to light the staircases. A banded, engaged colonnade—interspersed with roundels depicting Spanish worthies in profile—frames the windows of the top floor. Such details, in combination with the elegant yet simple iron fences and delicately detailed interiors with handsome gas fireplaces, must have almost made up for the owners' failure to provide elevators. The pair of flats was designed by Boston's Julius A. Schweinfurth, who had trained as a draftsman for thirteen years with Peabody & Stearns before studying at the Ecole des Beaux-Arts. Immensely

Henri Fouchaux, Arundel Court,
772–778 St. Nicholas Avenue, 1905

talented, he was one of four brothers who were to practice architecture in different regions of the country. An avid traveler, Schweinfurth compulsively documented visits to Europe and the Caribbean with skillful sketches and photographs. Pen-and-ink drawings made during his tour of Spain and North Africa in the 1890s clearly show the source of the Jumel's ornamentation.

Even when designers were less gifted and ornament was ordered from stock, exceptional architecture was occasionally the result. Completed in 1905, Henri Fouchaux's Arundel Court at 772–778 St. Nicholas Avenue is a case in point. It was not distinguished by decorations; its elements and organization were also, on the whole, unoriginal. What was striking was the way in which Fouchaux made a virtue of the 1901 Tenement House Law, which stipulated that each room of an apartment suite have an exterior or courtyard window and that buildings without a separate rear staircase be adequately equipped with fire escapes. Unornamented and faced in common brick, a narrow court divided the building in half, addressing requirements for adequate light and air. Set into central recesses on each section, exterior fire escapes fulfilled the rules for secondary egress: neighboring apartment houses built before 1900 employed clumsily retrofitted additions to comply with the law. Fouchaux's deep court was surmounted by an arch; considerable visual impact was provided by what amounted to three arches upholding a deep modillioned cornice. With its arcade, the building's facade shared the dignity associated with an ancient aqueduct or triumphal entryway. Arcaded entrance loggias were employed at Henry Andersen's Minerva at 357 and 363 West 118th Street (1901); it was here that choreographer Agnes de Mille was born in 1904. That features such as these add tremendous distinction is well illustrated by Benjamin Levitan's Temple Hall of 1907 at 207–215 Lenox Avenue, where the impressive cornice has been recently restored.

Seventh Avenue's El Nido (Spanish for "the nest") Apartments were designed by Neville & Bagge in 1901 at the northwest corner of St. Nicholas Avenue and West 116th Street. Once again the catalyst for great architectural accomplishment was derived from limitations. St. Nicholas Avenue was the longest of a small number of uptown roadways that predated the gridiron plan; it cut a diagonal swath through central Harlem. As a result, Kilpatrick Square, between West 115th and 116th Streets, west of Seventh Avenue and east of St. Nicholas Avenue, was among New York's many irregularly shaped plazas.

To accommodate this site, El Nido assumed an awkward trapezoidal shape. The problem was disguised by the repetition of the building's rounded corner in a series of sensuous bows along the exposed sides. Along with the lobby's colonnaded spaciousness and long-vanished potted palms and liveried attendants, this infusion of style imbued what would have been a commonplace building with dynamic presence.

El Nido is an excellent example of architects who designed apartments for wealthier inhabitants emphasizing an elite group identity within ever more grandiose, luxurious, and anonymous buildings. Modeled directly on the world's first apartments in European urban centers—suites of rooms in royal residences reserved for courtiers—these apartment houses were regally scaled and elegantly appointed.

Gilbert A. Schellenger's substantial Wilhelmina (formerly known as the Haberman) stood diagonally opposite El Nido. Nearby Thomas Olyphant Spier's massive Monterey, at 351 West

Young & Wagner, Deluxe,
900–910 Riverside Drive, 1915

114th Street at Morningside Avenue (1890), provided a distinguished backdrop for Frédéric-Auguste Bartholdi's bronze sculpture group of 1891 depicting Washington and Lafayette on yet another misshapen "square." (Buildings by Spier, while accomplished, are very rare; a onetime Princeton football star, he died in 1892 of an accidental, self-inflicted gunshot wound.)

## Harlem Apartments with Palatial Attitudes

Buildings such as El Nido were certainly Harlem's finest versions of the neo-Romanesque genre, but other apartment houses emulated palaces with far greater specificity. The meandering Boulevard Lafayette, long ranked as Audubon Park's premier address, was crowned by the temple-fronted wood-frame mansions of Mayor Ambrose Kingsland, at today's Fort Washington Avenue and West 161st Street (c. 1851), and Shepard Knapp's Melbourne, at West 162nd Street north of Riverside Drive, which after 1900 became the aptly named Grand View Inn (see pages 84–85). These buildings, both razed about 1914, survived from a lost era, when the Kingsland and Knapp families were two of a handful of neighbors of the Audubons.

When the subway arrived, it was accompanied by new names, and Boulevard Lafayette became Riverside Drive. Stately houses were quickly supplanted by a series of palatially inspired apartment houses. Most were designed either in partnership or independently by local architects Harold L. Young and William H. Wagner between 1915 and 1920; they forthrightly emulated European architecture that their middle-class tenants could be relied on to recognize as icons of elegance. The Deluxe, at 900–910 Riverside Drive (1915), was based on Henry VIII's Hampton Court, while the Loyal, at 884 Riverside Drive, mimicked the Doge's Palace in Venice. Both employed elaborate terra-cotta embellishments supplied by the New York Terra-Cotta Company. (Unfortunately, the Loyal's rooftop cresting of pinnacles was removed about 1979.) Comparable embellishments appeared at the Armidale, at 894 Riverside Drive; its entrance loggia and bowed facade were derived from Rome's celebrated Palazzo Massimi. Like its model, the Armidale had a convex contour that followed the street's curve. Adjacent concave or even S-curve apartment houses of six stories also reiterated the snaking roadway. Their shape was an embodiment of their owners' desire to maximize rentable space, but the unintentional result was the creation of an appealing contrapuntal rhythm. Inside the buildings, however, the irregular shapes posed more of a problem.

Achieving a palatial attitude without benefit of such definite foreign sources were several Harlem apartment buildings that echoed others downtown. The name of one notable example by Schwartz & Gross, the Grinnell at 800 Riverside Drive (1910), was arrived at logically enough. Over half the properties making up Audubon Park had been purchased by George Bird Grinnell by 1895. A park resident since the 1860s, Grinnell inhabited a substantial house designed by Vaux & Withers on the future site of the Riviera Apartments. One of his sons, William Milne Grinnell, was an architect active uptown, and another, George B. Grinnell Jr., achieved fame as a naturalist and writer. Following their father's death, his children sold the estate for development. Modeled after William L. Rouse's 1907 Hendrik Hudson Apartments in Morningside Heights (a faint echo of the Villa Medici), the Grinnell contained curved parapets pierced by decorative cutouts. The courtyard, with lofty arched gateways, was one of the most impressive in the city.

Nearby, Emery Roth's Sutherland, at 611 West 158th Street (1910), emulated the greater elegance of his earlier Hotel Belleclaire, which in turn had been at least partly derived from Graves & Duboy's Ansonia Hotel, on Verdi Square at 2101–2115 Broadway (1904), with all its Parisian verve. Schwartz & Gross's 1916 Colonial Parkway Apartments at 409 Edgecombe

George and Edward Blum, Beaumont,
730 Riverside Drive, 1912

Emery Roth, Sutherland, 611 West
158th Street, 1910

Avenue was fourteen stories high; it towered over the Harlem Valley as uptown's highest apartment house for almost forty years. In the same year the firm designed the Roger Morris Apartments at 555 Edgecombe Avenue. The latter evoked the ambience of Madam Jumel's life in France, with lobby decor inspired by the Napoleonic era. The neighboring Alberta at 461 West 159th Street was completed in 1910. No less handsome, it was slightly less fashionable, since there were fewer floors from which to enjoy the spectacular views.

The Grinnell, Sutherland, Roger Morris, and neighboring buildings designed by George and Edward Blum represented a new type of apartment house unseen above 110th Street prior to 1910. Nine stories or more, such buildings were required by the municipal fire code to be fireproof. The additional investment necessary to satisfy this provision had made most builders willing to spend more for alluring extras, which they hoped would attract a clientele who could afford the higher rents they now needed. The Blums' Beaumont at 730 Riverside Drive (1912),

Clinton & Russell, Graham Court, 1925 Seventh Avenue, 1901

OPPOSITE
Graham Court

delightfully decorated with vibrant terra-cotta parrots and owls supplied by the Federal Terra-Cotta Company, is a case in point. Other such apartment buildings included George Frederick Pelham's Sound View at 260 Convent Avenue (1911) and Frank H. Norton's 270 Convent Avenue, built in 1915 by plastering contractor Patrick McNulty. Italian Renaissance in style, both of these buildings had high, handsomely ornamented facades and spacious, graciously appointed lobbies, which belied well-appointed but modestly scaled apartment suites. This was also true of Schwartz & Gross's Colonial Parkway Apartments, though to a lesser extent.

## Graham Court

Still considered Harlem's finest luxury apartment house, Graham Court at 1925 Seventh Avenue (1901) was conceived by Clinton & Russell as a Renaissance palace, without any source more definite than McKim, Mead & White's 1891 Plaza Hotel. Each occupies an entire blockfront, is built from light-colored masonry, and is ornamented with wrought-iron balconies. Graham Court, however, was distinguished not only by its Venetian arched entrance but also by the commodious open courtyard beyond. Landscaped with walks and a driveway surrounding a fountain, the court was a superb means to introduce cross ventilation and additional light and air into the generously sized apartments. Four separate stately lobbies gave access to suites via two elevators and stairs at each corner. They were decorated in a low-key manner: delicate plasterwork adorned the walls and marble mosaics paved the floors. Entered via spacious anterooms, which also boasted marble mosaic floors, the typical apartment featured a parlor and dining room en suite with a pantry, kitchen, and maid's room and four or more bedrooms and up to three baths, thoughtfully segregated along separate passageways.

Unseen and, according to an advertisement, sweet smelling, Graham Court's underground stable was situated directly below the court. The facility was built by S. F. Lindstam of Minneapolis in collaboration with Fleming & Company of 123 Liberty Street. The stable was considered a major amenity for tenants, as was the roof's warren of extra servants' rooms. It is no surprise that this exceptional structure was built for one of the world's richest men, who was also one of the largest owners of Harlem real estate: William Waldorf Astor. Even today Graham Court is embellished with the WWA monogram. The firm of Clinton & Russell may be considered the house architect of the Astor estate; both men had started their careers in the employ of ecclesiastical architects Richard Upjohn and James Renwick Jr. Graham Court was held by the

Astor family until 1928. Although African-Americans had been living in the neighborhood for a number of years, Graham Court did not admit them as tenants until 1933. The new management's decision to "accept colored" was accompanied by a reduction in services and an increase in the reduced, Depression-era rents. New residents, including Dr. Cyril Harold Dolly, assistant visiting physician at Harlem Hospital and a native of Port-of-Spain in the West Indies, responded by forming the Consolidated Tenants League, which went on to assist countless Harlemites in search of decent housing.

## Combination Banking and Apartment Buildings

In several cases a very direct means of infusing Harlem's first apartment buildings with extra hauteur was utilized: the practice of including an ornate banking room on the ground floor. In fact, before 1920, bank buildings that did not include apartment suites, like Alfred C. Bossom's Columbia Trust Company at 153 West 125th Street (1922), graced by a festooned carving of a dime, were uncommon. The Mount Morris Bank/Morris Apartments building at 81–85 East 125th Street at Park Avenue was the result of a limited competition that included McKim, Mead & White. Designed by Lamb & Rich and completed in 1884, the structure housed apartments that were later transformed into offices. Splendidly devised and boldly massed, the cherry-red brick and terra-cotta structure exhibited a stylistic lineage deriving from Romanesque, Queen Anne, and Dutch sources; it was one of Lamb & Rich's great achievements. Born in Scotland, Hugh Lamb was largely self-taught, whereas Charles A. Rich had studied engineering at Dartmouth

Henry Andersen, Corn Exchange Bank, Hamilton Place branch, 500 West 143rd Street, 1899. View in 1909

College. Forming a partnership in 1882, the two architects were extremely active, their productivity well documented by the often humorous and frequently critical commentary of Montgomery Schuyler.

Largely favorable in his assessment of the Harlem building, Schuyler had been even more generous in his praise of its prototype, Carl Pfeiffer's Berkshire Apartments, built in 1883 on the northwest corner of Madison Avenue and East 52nd Street. The affinity of the two structures was unmistakable: both were quaintly gabled, with Dutch-inspired dormers, multifloor oriel windows, towering chimney stacks, and high, steep mansard roofs. Smaller and more compactly arranged, the uptown building had just six French flats and no elevator, as opposed to the two lifts and eighteen suites found downtown. As a consequence, in lieu of a secondary stair, Lamb & Rich's building employed exterior fire escapes. But instead of the expected diagonal skeletal stairs, these intricate cast-iron versions had less noticeable iron ladders along the building's wall. Sadly, the Mount Morris Bank/Morris Apartments was partially destroyed by arson in 1997.

One of about six small banks founded in late-nineteenth-century Harlem, the Mount Morris Bank was by 1913 absorbed by a mightier citywide financial institution, the Corn Exchange Bank. Beginning in the 1890s, the latter institution was the first bank in New York to establish neighborhood branch offices. Initially, most resulted from strategic mergers. The office at 500 West 143rd Street at Hamilton Place (1899) was a notable deviation from this pattern. Henry Andersen, the local architect in charge of the project, was best known for designing Harlem's most deluxe dining establishment, the Pabst Harlem restaurant, a few years earlier.

173

Henry Andersen, Hamilton Bank,
1707 Amsterdam Avenue at
478 West 145th Street/
477 West 144th Street, 1897

Having planned a large number of tenements, flats, and apartment houses, Andersen was
equal to the task at hand. In addition to the bank and the apartment lobby, the flatiron-shaped
building's rusticated base also contained several shops. Commercial tenants helped to subsidize
somewhat reduced rents for residential tenants. The bank office was located in the structure's
preeminent position, the squared-off corner. Every architectural detail and element of the
pavilioned building, inspired by Ernest Flagg's nearby St. Luke's Hospital (1896), on Morningside
Drive—pepperpot domes, crested mansard roof crowning the corner—proclaimed the prosperity
and prestige of the Corn Exchange Bank.

Across Amsterdam Avenue, only a few blocks north, Andersen was also responsible for an
earlier, less spectacular apartment/banking/commercial complex at 478 West 145th Street/
477 West 144th Street (1897). Occupying the entire block, the two palazzo-form buildings had
limestone ground floors; the upper floors were pale brown Roman brick decorated with cream-
colored terra cotta. Andersen's lively ornamentation—neoclassical wreaths, festooned husks,
and anthemions—was mostly made from terra cotta, like the first story's Greek-key banding
or the exceptionally elaborate architraves of the windows. The facade was also adorned with
three separate friezes, each more elaborately patterned than the next, although made from
successively humbler materials: limestone, terra cotta, and galvanized tin. On the ground level
along Amsterdam Avenue was a varied group of shops; the apartment entrances were on the side
streets. Andersen was again to accentuate the bank, this time positioning its entrance, a temple-
fronted, one-story structure, as a hyphen between the two apartment houses. The enamel face
of a clock set above the entryway had the letters HAMILTON BANK in place of the usual Roman or
Arabic numerals.

174

## Splendid Living: Lobbies and Interiors

Just as the facades of luxury apartment houses imitated the opulence of those downtown, so too did their lobbies. In some instances highly original design was the result of this imitation. One such building is Vaux Hall at 780 Riverside Drive (1914), designed by George and Edward Blum. The Blums' skill at utilizing common materials in an uncommon way is evidenced by the contrasts of color and texture in the rough tapestry brick and glazed tiles employed on the facades and repeated in the lobby, where a large brick fireplace is ornamented with jewel-like tiles made by the American Encaustic Tile Company. The specially designed molded plaster ceiling utilizes the stylized foliated patterns so characteristic of the Blums' work. Features like this were made possible by prefabrication from inexpensive materials; for example, a grille in the lobby decorated with representations of conventionalized pomegranate vines has been cast from pot metal.

The prolific firm of Schwartz & Gross was the designer of the Riviera Apartments at 790 Riverside Drive (1910). The limitations of the Riviera's lobby are typical of such spaces in speculative middle-class apartments of this period: the ceiling is low; the space is otherwise unsalable. Although somewhat stereotypical in its Italian Renaissance pretensions, it is nonetheless pleasing due to the designers' careful attention to detailing. The bronze entry screen with a pierced frieze of winged nymphs, the trabeated ceiling, leaded windows depicting Roman centurions, carved marble benches, and a double curving staircase with finely cast balustrades in the form of scrolling arabesques all combined to create a welcoming, even awesome atmosphere, now diminished by the loss of more ephemeral original details such as velvet curtains, oriental rugs, and potted palms.

George and Edward Blum, Vaux Hall, 780 Riverside Drive, 1914. Lobby fireplace

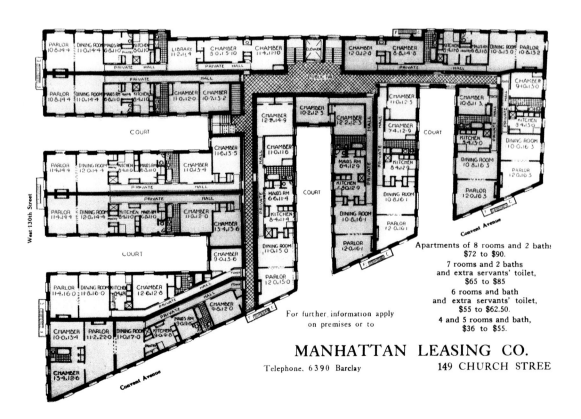

Henri Fouchaux, St. Agnes Apartments, 41 Convent Avenue, 1909. Standard floor plan

Among other families, the Riviera was once home to the Gustave Cerfs. In 1911 the Cerfs left the Douglas Apartments at 201 West 121st Street in central Harlem and came here with their thirteen-year-old son, Bennett. The future founder of Random House was to recall the Riviera not only for its hypnotic river views but also for its neighbors and friends. Here he met Howard Deitz, who became a composer, as well as Merryle Stanley Rukeyser, future financial analyst for the Hearst newspaper chain. Across the street lived Elliot Sanger, of the Dallas family, who would help to establish WQXR Radio.

African-American tenants found a somewhat less hospitable environment in the luxury apartments of Harlem, which in general did not begin to admit them until around the 1930s, nearly ten years after blacks had become a majority in Harlem. Even at this time, according to Harlem Renaissance writer Claude McKay, there were attempts to prevent white realtors from selling or renting to blacks, and some white residents of Harlem "sought to evoke city ordinances as quarantine measures." Henri Fouchaux's St. Agnes Apartments at 41 Convent Avenue (1909) did not admit black tenants until 1940, despite being part of a complex named for saints and built on land sold by the Sisters of Manhattanville College of the Sacred Heart. This otherwise typical middle-class apartment building has extraordinary ornamentation, inspired by the Gout Greque style associated with eighteenth-century French architect Claude-Nicolas Ledoux, among others, including a cyclopean modillioned cornice.

Beaumont (Anne and Dale Dobson apartment). Hall

OPPOSITE
Beaumont (Anne and Dale Dobson apartment). View from living room to dining room

Lit from above, the vaulted marble wainscoted lobby is also exceptional. According to historian Carolyn Kent, this was because the developer erected just one building on the Convent Avenue blockfront, pooling funds required for four small lobbies into a single splendid space. Less pleasant are the suites of numerous relatively small rooms running along lengthy narrow corridors. More problematic still are misshapen rooms, a result of the desire to build close to capacity on an irregular lot.

At the Blums' Beaumont, in contrast, great trouble was expended to avoid both excessively long passages and oddly shaped rooms. When absolutely unavoidable, slight irregularities were permitted in large bedrooms and entryways. However, reception rooms are always strictly symmetrical and are further distinguished by parquetry floors, high wainscots, and exquisitely decorative plaster borders. Foyers and baths are provided with extra natural light by means of stained-glass panels that depict simple motifs such as heraldic lions or jeweled garlands.

Graham Court. Parlor

Graham Court. Sitting room

OPPOSITE
Graham Court. Dining room

More than any other Harlem apartment house, Graham Court's expansive suites suggest the ideal of an entire row house set on a single level. Such éclat is accomplished in part by sheer spaciousness. Universal marble mosaic-paved reception halls connect the parlors and the dining rooms. A domestic touch is provided by as many as four Adamesque or Colonial Revival mantelpieces for coal and gas fireplaces. The illusion of being in a house is further reinforced by the separation of family bedrooms along a private hall beyond the public spaces and the similar isolation of the kitchen and servants' room.

## Harlem of the Bitter Dream

In some cases such surroundings were the homes of tenants whose rents were excessive in relation to their incomes, and the adaptability of the large spaces was appreciated as an advantage for those who needed to take in boarders. Certainly after the Great Depression the maids' rooms of such buildings became obsolete. Poet Langston Hughes, who rented a studio apartment in Harlem in 1938 and bought a house there about ten years later, wrote in his poem "Passing" that when

> . . . Harlem has its
> washed-and-ironed-and-cleaned-best out
> the ones who've crossed the line
> to live downtown
> miss you,
> Harlem of the bitter dream,
> since their dream has
> come true.

178

**CHAPTER FIVE**

# HOUSES OF WORSHIP

Riverside Drive looking west from
West 145th Street, 1909

Carrère & Hastings and
Theodore Blake, St. Mary's Church–
Manhattanville (Episcopal),
521 West 126th Street, 1909.
Rectory, Robert Oughton, c. 1840

H arlem is one of the few areas of the city where it is still possible to experience the
streetscape of New York as it was envisioned by the authors of the Commissioner's
Plan. On most corners, handsome houses of worship punctuate long, low, related
blocks of row houses and similarly uniform apartment buildings. Some churches
are small and intimate, distinguished by little more than an exclamatory steeple.
Others boast imposing porticos or are spatially elegant. But all express their
builders' highest aspirations, expressed in the finest workmanship and materials obtainable.

Even today these structures are compelling: gracious and enduring, they give every appearance
of calm stability. However, most of them represent at least the second incarnation of a single
congregation. Some have been outgrown; others were prey to fire. Quite often, when original
congregants dispersed or moved, abandoned churches were adapted for use by followers of
other faiths, ethnicities, or denominations.

Harlem's oldest Christian Dutch Reform congregation was organized in 1660, two years after
a permanent settlement was established. Two years more were necessary before a barnlike church
was erected. The placement was oblique in relation to what is now First Avenue between East
126th and 127th Streets. Square and shingled, this church was, not surprisingly, consumed by fire.
Replacing it in 1685 was a larger square stone edifice at First Avenue and East 125th Street.
Both buildings were extremely austere, possessing only one ornament. Even this was functional as
well as fanciful—a copper weathercock atop a belfry. Destroyed during the Revolution, the stone
church was rebuilt in 1789 and vanished at an undetermined date.

As the surrounding community became larger and more sophisticated, the church's congregation
grew. Its fourth home, completed in 1824 by celebrated architect Martin E. Thompson, was
located at today's Third Avenue and East 121st Street. Built of wood and painted white, it was
rectangular rather than square and was graced with elongated arched windows and a dentiled
pediment atop the facade of flush boards. It was an icon of early America; an essential part

Martin E. Thompson, Harlem Dutch Reformed Church, Third Avenue and East 121st Street, 1824, altered 1852

of this image was the belfry, emphatically neoclassical. Engaged Tuscan columns articulated the octagonal lantern, which was crowned by a copper dome and surmounted by the traditional spinning rooster.

Thompson's design was very successful. He had begun his career as a carpenter, but his talent was such that just a few years following completion of this church, he entered into partnership with the prominent architect Ithiel Town, although the association was to last only two years. Early views of the church, which show Thompson's extensive alterations of 1852 (lengthening the building to form a chancel, provision of two cast-iron stoves), are impressive. Particularly notable was his addition of an Ionic portico at the entrance and a columnar screen in the sanctuary. Church members of the next generation were largely unappreciative of Harlem's first significant example of sacred architecture. Welcoming the idea of perpetual progress, they began building a new church in 1885, well outside the community's traditional center. As rapid transit developed, the most desirable residential section had moved farther and farther west: the newly renamed Lenox (Sixth) Avenue was among the best addresses. The church, now known as the Reformed Collegiate Low Dutch Church, therefore moved to 267 Lenox Avenue and West 123rd Street; it was completed in 1887. The architect was John R. Thomas, a competent and prolific designer. The building was asymmetrically Gothic and built of Ohio sandstone. Where the wooden belfry of Harlem's earlier Dutch churches had acted as a device of distinction, Thomas's slender, dizzyingly high stone spire was a landmark for blocks around. One Harlem resident described it as "an index finger, pointed heavenward, which reminds us that God is always watching."

Thomas's imposing work, ornamented by gargoyles and cherubs, was largely funded by a bold transaction. The fourth home of the congregation had been built on one of Harlem's original town lots. Cleared of timber as early as 1666, it extended almost half a block into East 121st Street. Long anticipated, the arrival of the elevated train in 1879 had seen adjacent property skyrocket in value. In order to realize some of these profits, the church fathers decided to move Thompson's old building. In 1884 they turned it to face the side street, enabling them to sell their newly valuable corner lot. Next, immediately west of the old church they erected a modern parish house (c. 1890). The idea was to maintain both buildings as a mission and settlement house, addressing

184

the needs of East Harlem's rapidly increasing population of poor immigrants. Named the Elemendorf Dutch Reform Church (in honor of the Reverend Joachim Elemendorf, church and mission leader) long after its Lenox Avenue companion had been transformed into the Ephesus Seventh-Day Adventist Church, this successor to Harlem's oldest congregation survived. Unfortunately, when the church fathers again decided to sell off a portion of their East 121st Street holdings in 1908, it was Martin Thompson's noteworthy church that was sacrificed.

## Congregations Multiply:
## Churches in Harlem at Midcentury

Thompson's second Harlem church was erected about 1852 on the southwest corner of West 126th Street and Morningside Avenue (originally Ninth Avenue). The Manhattanville Presbyterian Church bore certain similarities to the earlier building as well as to Isaac Lucas's 1844 Mariners' Temple in lower Manhattan. A dignified if unflamboyant structure, the Harlem building served after 1875 as a municipal courthouse. Later still, prior to its demolition in 1920, it was a convent.

Nearby St. Mary's Church–Manhattanville (Episcopal) was built in 1824 on land donated by the town's principal founder, shipper, merchant, and druggist Jacob Schieffelin. Without any sort of portico, the white, short-steepled structure and its adjoining rectory (c. 1840) were not planned by a professional architect but by a respected carpenter and framer, Robert Oughton, a circumstance not unusual at that time. A glimpse of a June Sunday morning at this church in 1867 was provided by Laura Dayton Fessenden in the pages of *Valentine's Manual of Old New York* of 1923. She reported that as a child she often joined the group at about a quarter to nine in the morning, when the bell in the tower on Mount Morris Hill in Harlem rang out:

> All the way to church, from mild springtime to Indian summer days, we passed along a winding road, holding on either side homes with gardens about them, and white wooden fence palings were wide

Martin E. Thompson, St. Joseph's Convent (formerly Manhattanville Presbyterian Church), Morningside Avenue and West 126th Street, c. 1852

enough apart to afford opportunity for the reaching through and touching with gentle hands the petals of the great fragrant roses, the honeysuckle cups and innumerable other fragrant flowers . . . We took a cross cut through our own and our neighbors' orchards and fields and so came upon . . . the village of Manhattanville . . . Our church [St. Mary's] stood in the middle of a square, the rectory on one side, the graveyard on the other. Just beyond was the new Sheltering Arms [Charles C. Haight, 1869]. The Sheltering Arms was a home very recently built and now occupied by little boys and girls who had become fatherless and destitute through and by the Civil War.

Mrs. Fessenden remembered admiring gray, lichen-covered tombstones among the tall grasses, particularly one inscribed "Afflictions sore, long time she bore and physicians were in vain." She then continued with a description of St. Mary's:

St. Mary's was white and severely plain on the outside and square and bare within. The altar was unlike those one sees today, in fact, it looked more like an old-fashioned parlor with its table, horsehair sofa and chairs. The communion table was near the altar rail and, of course, there was a reading desk, and our pulpit had a winding stair that led up to it, and there was a top over the pulpit [a sounding board] that looked like an opened motherly umbrella, but this pulpit was not used in 1867. Our rector, who had served the parish for many years, had rheumatism and did not like the climb.

St. Mary's burned at the turn of the century. Still supported by the Schieffelins (newly enriched through an alliance with the Vanderbilts), it was quickly replaced and even enlarged in 1909. The rather unlikely architect was the team of Carrère & Hastings, authors of the opulent New York Public Library, and their associate Theodore Blake. Blake was soon to launch a career on the strength of the new church, an engaging if unassuming brick structure trimmed with concrete and equipped with pointed windows and thick aggregate mortar joints. Set sympathetically alongside the old clapboard rectory in a green garden from the Manhattanville of yesteryear, St. Mary's had all the ambience of an old English village church. With a long history of serving the poor and the working class, it would survive in a changing Harlem where other churches were to fail.

The original St. Andrew's Church (Episcopal) was established in 1829 on property provided by Harlem alderman Charles Henry Hall. The midblock site stretched from East 127th to 128th Street, between Fourth and Lexington Avenues. Shortly after it was built, the wooden church burned, and in 1873 a new St. Andrew's was designed by Henry M. Congdon at the same location. Congdon had served in the Civil War, enlisting as a private and leaving as a sergeant. A graduate of Columbia College and ultimately a fellow of the American Institute of Architects, he was to become a leading church specialist, active across the nation. The new building outdid nearly every other church built in Harlem up to that date, irrespective of style. Gothic and muscular, the building exhibits a sure handling of superb materials, including rose-colored granite and cast iron (for the columns of the nave). Cruciform, with four prominent gable ends and a deliberately defined polygonal sanctuary, St. Andrew's is the very embodiment of increasingly fashionable High Church tendencies. Its narrow Norman tower, in a dramatically calculated contrast, soars skyward. Originally painted a terra-cotta color, the vaulted interior includes a rich array of imported memorial windows, including one designed by Joseph Laubar. Congdon planned the church when he was twenty-nine years old, and his ambitious accomplishments in relation to St. Andrew's were to continue. In 1887 he was asked to dismantle, move, reconstruct, and expand the church at its present location—Fifth Avenue and 127th Street. He did so, completing the job in 1890.

St. Mary's Church–Manhattanville

Thanks largely to the efforts of St. Andrew's patron and member Charles Henry Hall, the neighborhood between Mount Morris Park and Hall's Fifth Avenue house at 131st Street was one of Harlem's most fashionable enclaves. Between 1860 and 1900, the neighborhood was at the height of its exclusivity. A spate of handsomely attired congregations with buildings clustered in close proximity around this hub attested to the area's cachet.

One such congregation worshipped in Hubert, Pirsson & Company's Church of the Puritans (1878), opposite Charles Buek's Astor Row, at 15 West 130th Street; it is now St. Ambrose Church (Episcopal). A new congregation, it had formed as the Second Presbyterian Church of Harlem. Then its members were offered a substantial gift by the Reverend George B. Cheever— with the proviso that the name be changed. In response to growing commercialization, the old Church of the Puritans on Union Square in lower Manhattan had just disbanded. The building had been acquired by Tiffany and Company for a new store, both prompting and enabling Dr. Cheever's generosity. Most unusually, much of the interior decoration in the new Church of

187

the Puritans—both carving and ornate plasterwork—was the design and handiwork of the founding pastor of the Church of the Puritans, the Reverend Edward L. Clark.

With exterior walls of rough-textured limestone, the Church of the Puritans had also been provided with a cross-shaped layout and pointed lancets. However, its design was not the equal of St. Andrew's: it was neither as clear in planning nor as liturgically exacting. Contained between asymmetrically placed turrets of unequal size, the nave and sanctuary were oriented toward the north. Although a more ample than usual plot included a garden, an east-facing altar was not important to Presbyterians. The east tower, intended to be as tall as that of St. Andrew's, was left unfinished after rising just two stories.

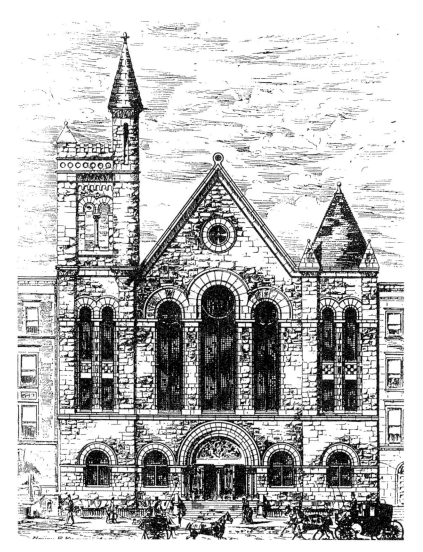

Henry F. Kilburn, Mount Morris Baptist Church (now Mount Moriah Baptist Church), 2050 Fifth Avenue, 1888. Rendering

OPPOSITE
Mount Morris Baptist Church. View from Sunday School hall into auditorium

## Alternatives to the Gothic

During the nineteenth century, there were continuous debates among churchmen and architects regarding the proper style and form of a Christian church. Adherents of the Church of England, as well as many influential American Episcopalians, asserted that Gothic buildings provided the only environments suitable for Christian worship, whereas members of other denominations showed a more flexible disposition toward styles as divergent as the Greek Revival and the neo-Egyptian. Increasingly, as the nineteenth century drew to a close, this dispute evolved into a contest between the conservative neo-Gothic and the more progressive neo-Romanesque.

Such debate had occurred before: at the beginning of the nineteenth century, Calvinist and Evangelical Protestants had caused Anglicans, Lutherans, and Episcopalians to eschew "papist" influences and ceremony. Dismissing ritual as meaningless and placing emphasis solely on scriptural readings and preaching, they devised open auditorium spaces for worship. That all could see and hear the sermon became paramount. Influenced by this imperative, in time most churches came to resemble more the barnlike meeting houses of Harlem's early Dutch settlers than the ancient cathedrals of European capitals. In the 1860s in Akron, Ohio, Evangelicals introduced to American church architecture the Akron Sunday School plan. Originated by Jacob Snyder, this plan emphasized a more open and flexible church space that could accommodate overflowing crowds in halls adjacent to the church proper with sliding, folding, or French doors. While Snyder never practiced in Harlem, a number of church architects had occasion to utilize his innovation.

One of them was Henry F. Kilburn, whose Mount Morris Baptist Church at 2050 Fifth Avenue (1888; originally First Baptist Church of Harlem and today the Mount Moriah Baptist Church) was the third home of the church on this site. In 1873 the congregation's polychrome Carpenter Gothic church building (c. 1854), attributed to Samuel A. Warner, had been destroyed by fire, and its

188

second brick church building was soon outgrown. Kilburn's gabled, Romanesque Revival facade, with repeated round arches, is described by historian Thomas Mellins as "severe." Built primarily from mustard-brown sandstone, it was meant to be framed by two unequal towers. Unfortunately, once again the larger, more picturesque and expensive tower remained incomplete, creating the sense of a fairly pedestrian exterior, almost resembling an ordinary brownstone row house.

Yet the utterly unflamboyant facade acts as a foil to the drama of the less predictable interior. Most churches in Harlem that utilized the Akron plan had only one hall, due to lot restrictions, and such was the case with the Mount Morris Baptist Church. The large auditorium is square and handsomely appointed, with curving oak pews, stained-glass windows, and a stained-glass skylight. By contrast, almost revolutionary is the fact that the stained-glass arch at the back of the balcony passes through to a large light-filled hall flanked by double-decker classrooms, rather than opening onto Fifth Avenue: it is a complete surprise. Certainly, it was far more elaborate than the rooms in the wooden structure housing the church's Bethel Chapel. Built in the mid-1840s, this mission on East 121st Street near First Avenue served African-American servants.

## Romanesque Revival: Church of the Holy Trinity, St. Luke's, and Harlem–New York Presbyterian Church

The Church of the Holy Trinity (1869) was the first in Harlem to employ the Romanesque idiom. It was favorably placed on the northwest corner of Fifth Avenue and 125th Street on a lot large

John W. Welch, Temple Israel
(formerly Church of the Holy Trinity),
2022–2030 Fifth Avenue, 1880

William A. Potter, Holy Trinity Episcopal Church (now St. Martin's Episcopal Church and Rectory), 18 West 122nd Street, 1888

enough to provide a pleasant lawn. Yet another Brooklyn-based church specialist, Scotland native John W. Welch, produced its uncomplicated design. Each element and every part of the brick and stone rectangular structure was forthrightly stated. Five pinnacles, reminiscent of rockets, divided the gabled front. Dominated by a St. Catherine's wheel window, the facade rose well above the sloping roofs of the aisles. The *New York Times* of May 6, 1870, reported:

> The new church . . . cost $65,000 in building . . . The interior is embellished with an open timberwork ceiling of very elaborate description, and polychrome decorations . . . The church is not altogether finished, but fit for use and will, when completed, be one of the handsomest in the city. The campanile tower is one-third built.

It was never three-thirds built. Burned and rebuilt in 1880, the church was sold to congregation Temple Israel in 1888 and demolished about 1903.

William A. Potter was selected as the architect for the new Holy Trinity Episcopal Church, built at 18 West 122nd Street, at Lenox Avenue, in 1888 (now St. Martin's Episcopal Church and Rectory). Potter was extremely well connected: his uncle, Horatio Potter, and his half-brother, Henry Codman Potter, were successive Episcopal Church's bishops of New York. Yet his extensive family ties to wealth and power should not obscure the fact that Holy Trinity could not possibly have selected a more able architect; his skills as a designer more than equaled the ambitious building program. The cruciform church, facing west, was neatly sandwiched between a parish house as extensive as a community center and a diminutive rectory (seventeen and a half feet in width). Holy Trinity's three buildings were coherent as a group, even if the components were also highly individual. On the avenue, the parish house maintained the scale and spirit of neighboring dwellings without diminishing the monumentality of the whole. For all its bravado—multiple gables and arched leaded windows—the facade was formally organized and symmetrically disciplined. A particularly masterful touch is exhibited in the cluster of homelike chimneys that balances the institutional center lantern. Prominently displayed, a second handsome chimney and pointed gable help to make the rectory a picture of domesticity. The dollhouse proportions, while undoubtedly an inconvenience for the inhabitants, were useful as a means of exaggerating the imposing massiveness of the adjoining church. Close to the corner and seven stories tall, the great bell tower formed a memorable counterpart to the overall horizontality of the complex. If the cross-crowned church was perhaps too obscured by the conspicuous parish house, Potter's tower more than made up for any crisis of identity.

Holy Trinity Episcopal Church

OPPOSITE
R. H. Robertson, St. Luke's Church (Episcopal), 285 Convent Avenue, 1889

Even from afar, in terms as unmistakable as they were compelling, it announced a sacred presence.

Inspired by Henry Hobson Richardson's Trinity Church in Boston (1872–77), Harlem's Holy Trinity was granite with bands of reddish brown Longmeadow sandstone. The church was fifty feet square at the crossing, with shallow transepts and a raised chancel embellished with carving, stained glass, and mosaics from Tiffany Studios. Lauded by Montgomery Schuyler in the *Real Estate Record and Builders' Guide* of October 12, 1889, as comparable to Richardson's Senate Chamber in the New York State Capitol, the church was considered worthy of imitation by other architects:

The introduction of galleries connecting the piers of the vaults becomes unobtrusive, as it can never do in a many-bayed Gothic church, while the whole interior has an aspect of seriousness and solemnity, which one must be very far gone in devotion to pointed windows to stigmatize as "unchurchly."

St. Luke's Church (Episcopal) at 285 Convent Avenue at West 141st Street was designed by Potter's early partner, R. H. Robertson, in 1889. "The austere St. Luke's, with its two shades of rough textured stone and its bold round arches, is one of New York City's finest essays in the Romanesque Revival Style," states architectural historian Andrew Dolkart. St. Luke's is indeed handsome, and it is still another among the ranks of Harlem churches with missing towers. Its incomplete state extends to uncarved stonework on the facade and in the nave. However, Bertram G. Goodhue's ornately inlaid marble and brass altar and ambulatory screen, introduced in about 1912, were magnificently realized—complete in every way.

If deficient in technical terms of materials and stylistic authenticity, Thomas H. Poole's Harlem–New York Presbyterian Church at 2 West 122nd Street (today the Mount Morris Presbyterian Church), Harlem's last Romanesque Revival church, was far more daring than either St. Luke's or Holy Trinity. Not built until 1905, it provided the west side of Mount Morris Park with a landmark of power comparable to that of Lawrence B. Valk's Church of the Pilgrims (1872) on the northeast corner of East 121st Street and Madison Avenue. (Embedded into the pulpit of the latter was a piece of Plymouth Rock; it was transformed into the Russian Orthodox Church-in-Exile—the Church of Christ the Saviour—in about 1920 and razed in 1970.)

A specialist in the design of Roman Catholic buildings, New Yorker Poole was extremely productive. However, he seldom designed Protestant churches, and his receipt of the commission for merging two of the area's oldest congregations remains a mystery. The church faced Harlem's long-favored residential square, Mount Morris Park. In poorer neighborhoods, Poole enjoyed renown as a designer skilled at producing impressively elaborate structures at comparatively low cost. This reputation as a resourceful and ingenious architect may have been sufficient recommendation for two congregations whose churches had been so expensive that both remained unfinished for decades. The Harlem Presbyterian Church on the north side of East 125th Street between Fifth and Madison Avenues, one of the congregations, was designed by D. & J. Jardine and built at a cost of $100,000 in 1874. It was razed about 1925. John R. Thomas (the architect of the Reformed Collegiate Low Dutch Church on Lenox Avenue) and Richard R. Davis, working from 1884 to 1885 and 1889 to 1890, respectively, failed to see the New York Presbyterian Church at 151 West 128th Street completed. It survives as the Metropolitan Baptist Church.

John R. Thomas, New York Presbyterian Church (now Metropolitan Baptist Church), 151 West 128th Street, 1885

OPPOSITE
Thomas H. Poole, Harlem–New York Presbyterian Church (now Mount Morris Presbyterian Church), 2 West 122nd Street, 1905

However it came about, Poole's new, almost Byzantine edifice was everything that the old churches were not, and like no other in the city. In place of the brownstone used before, Poole designed a striking combination of yellow-orange ironspot Roman brick, smooth bluestone, and rock-faced granite. Rather than projecting overly ambitious towers with tall stone steeples, he employed a more affordable copper-clad dome (the first of only three in Harlem). Often entrusted with translating an undervalued immigrant community's hope and pride into a tangible symbol of group identity, worth, and accomplishment, Poole took an unconventional approach toward church architecture, at odds with that of more academic practitioners. Whereas some architects disdained the use of materials other than stone or its faithful approximations in their attempts to recapture the atmosphere and antiquity of European churches, style for Poole was only a point of departure, used as a vehicle to dignify his buildings. Ordinarily given much less generous budgets than those enjoyed by other architects, he routinely used ribbed vaulting, as well as columns and domes made of plaster or terra cotta. Plaster was the chief medium of the splendid interior of the Harlem–New York Presbyterian Church. Without making any reference to marble, the high walls, painted to contrast with white ornamentation, sparkled in the sunlight. Arched, vaulted, domed, and demidomed, the soaring space was no less "churchly" than neighboring Holy Trinity.

194

## The Triumph of the Neo-Gothic

Thomas H. Poole's St. Thomas the Apostle Church (1907), on the south side of 118th Street near St. Nicholas Avenue—one of twelve contemporary Roman Catholic parish churches in Harlem—was one among many examples of the progress of the Gothic style uptown. The facade's architectural fanfare was a contrast to the tenements that surrounded it, as noted by *Architect and Builders' Magazine* in August 1907: "St. Thomas' Church does not possess the advantage of a fine location which would itself give majesty. Approaching . . . we are hardly aware of the edifice which fairly bursts upon us, truly a dazzling gem among the surrounding commonplaceness."

The animated, though towerless, roofline is alive with pinnacles. Below the Guastavino-vaulted porch is a diaper pattern of terra-cotta tiles; the source is England's York Minster Cathedral. The church's plan, with its stairway porticos and flamboyant silhouette, derived from Rhenish and Belgian town and guild halls. Described at the time of construction as "Gothic design with perpendicular lines well emphasized," the front features brick supplied by Harbison-Waller Refactories Company paired with "limestone"-glazed terra cotta, as well as gray eight-sided marble columns.

Thomas H. Poole, St. Thomas the Apostle Church (Roman Catholic), 260 West 118th Street, 1907

Recalling aspects of St. George's Chapel at Windsor Castle and the Henry VII memorial at Westminster Abbey, Poole's richly embellished painted plaster nave and aisles copied neither directly. Piers with clustered columns employed shields with emblems of the church's patron saint. Plaster-cast stations of the cross were specially commissioned from sculptor Joseph Sibbel, which lent another touch of refinement to the decorations. Of greater significance in terms of a unifying harmony are the stained-glass windows. Usually such windows were individually created, since they were typically given by church members to commemorate the death of a loved one. But at St. Thomas memorial requests were gathered for the fifteen years it took to build the church, enabling Mayer and Company, with studios in Munich and New York, to install a series of related windows.

The polychrome and parcel-gilt tapered pipes of the W. W. Kimball Organ Company's colossal instrument flank the great window above the entrance, although the sanctuary and high altar of translucent marble are St. Thomas's primary focus. Artificial lighting, concealed within the canopies of the altarpiece, reflects on inlays of gold and green Venetian mosaic. At the time of the church's construction, these effects must have dazzled parishioners, who still lived by gaslight. Dulled gold windows behind the altar form an effective backdrop while emphasizing the brilliant windows above and their depictions of angels.

Designed in 1875 by James W. Renwick Jr., who was also responsible for St. Patrick's Cathedral, All Saints Roman Catholic Church, at the northeast corner of Madison Avenue and East 129th Street, was completed in stages: the rectory in 1889 by Renwick, Aspinwall & Owen; the church in 1894 and the school in 1904 by Renwick, Aspinwall & Russell. The church was acclaimed by critic Montgomery Schuyler, who wrote in *Architectural Record* of July 1909:

> One can readily understand an architect's saying that he would rather have been the designer of the Church of All Saints than St. Patrick's Cathedral . . . There seems to be distinctly more freedom and individuality in the application of the Gothic of All Saints than of the . . . Gothic of the Cathedral.

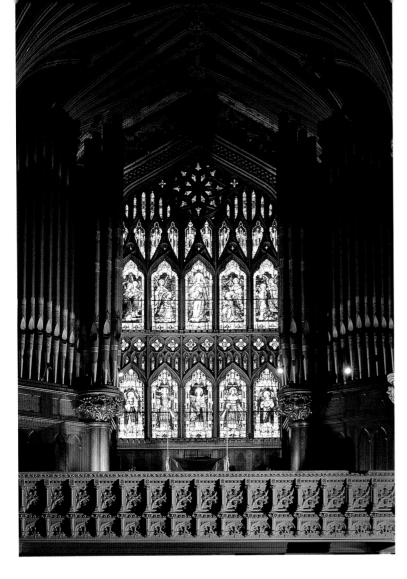

OPPOSITE
St. Thomas the Apostle Church

St. Thomas the Apostle Church. Organ
pipes and stained-glass window over
entrance

St. Thomas the Apostle Church. Porch

In large part this assessment must be viewed in the context of Schuyler's generation of critics. Harlem had seen a playfully interpreted, English-derived Gothic (exemplified by the first Mount Morris Baptist Church) evolve into something more substantial, academic, and finally more oppressive, leaving commentators ripe for the tenets of Ruskin, all of which are artfully expressed in All Saints. Renwick's earlier Italian Gothic essay in Brooklyn was St. Ann's Church (Episcopal) of 1869, today the auditorium of the Packer Collegiate Institute. Boldly massed, subtly colored, and economically built of brick and terra cotta, it shares most of the salient elements of All Saints. Schuyler, however, disapproved of the Harlem church's "unconsequential campanile." Unfortunately, today this tower is devoid of its original roof, and sadly, in 1999 the facade's canopied pinnacles, structurally deteriorated, were replaced with unattractive aluminum boxes. However, inside and out, many details of note survive. The rose windows, the gold stenciling on the high nave's vaulting, the bronze angel-form candelabras on the altar's reredos, and the quartered-oak pews with exquisitely pierced tracery all contribute to the interior's unrivaled magnificence.

William W. Renwick (with Renwick, Aspinwall & Russell) designed St. Aloysius's Roman Catholic Church at 209 West 132nd Street (1904). St. Aloysius's bears similarities to St. Thomas the Apostle, a parish with which it shared a usually friendly rivalry. Like that church, it bursts upon the viewer from the corner, but in place of Poole's spectacularly eccentric facade is a more subdued and intellectual presence, almost as if a fifteenth-century Italian church had been transported to the neighborhood. Commenting on the fine, seventy-five-foot facade (see page 17) and lengthy nave, Schuyler observed:

The coloring is very effective . . . a ground of excellent rough red brick, banded with gray terra-cotta, set off between courses of green glazed brick, the terra-cotta everywhere so elaborately molded as to show that the architect knew his material, and a sparing introduction of gold on fields of blue enamel. The interior has its interest also, though here the [transitional Italian Gothic] style seems to demand the mural painting which has not yet come to decorate the large spaces of the wall, the actual decorating in color being almost confined to the solid gilding of the deeply moulded recessions of the chancel arch, and in form to the Byzantine capitals of the wall arches.

James W. Renwick Jr. (with Renwick, Aspinwall & Russell), All Saints Roman Catholic Church, Madison Avenue and East 129th Street, 1894. Watercolor drawing

Made of pink-streaked scagliola, the columns of those arches provided some additional color. The deeply coffered ceiling was also gilded; it was lighted by electrified gasoliers with branches turned downward. A gold-framed window of yellow leaded glass produced a warm glowing focal point in this space of quiet repose. Yet Schuyler was correct that without further enrichment from strongly colored two-dimensional decoration, the nave of St. Aloysius's could scarcely be expected to live up to its exterior.

The window's glow abruptly vanished when a tall apartment building was built on the next block, finally prompting an intervention in 1911. William W. Renwick was an artist as well as a talented architect, and he had devised and patented a decorative technique called "fresco relief." This was employed in a magnificent depiction of Christ heroically towering in triumph while trampling Satan underfoot. The angel Gabriel sounds a fanfare, and the archangel Michael raises his sword. Higher up in the archway, amid a heavenly host, a bearded God extends his hand. Above all floats the dove of the Holy Spirit.

William W. Renwick (with Renwick, Aspinwall & Russell), St. Aloysius's Roman Catholic Church, 209 West 132nd Street, 1904. View with leaded-glass windows, before 1911

St. Aloysius's Roman Catholic Church. View with fresco relief by William W. Renwick

## An Enduring Sacred Tradition

As Harlem increasingly became home to less affluent residents, houses of worship were initially not made smaller or even simpler but rather from less costly materials. At Our Lady of Lourdes Church (Roman Catholic) at 467 West 142nd Street, designed by the O'Reilly Brothers and finished in 1904, an extreme measure was undertaken to cut costs: materials were salvaged from three famous, freshly demolished landmarks. Much of the facade incorporated elements from Peter B. Wight's National Academy of Design facade (1865), which was derived from the Doge's Palace in Venice. Consoles flanking the staircase came from the stair hall in the "Marble Palace" mansion of department store magnate A. T. Stewart (1869), designed by John Kellum. Three bays of the Madison Avenue end of James Renwick's St. Patrick's Cathedral, dismantled in preparation for a new Lady Chapel, were also reused here.

Less drastically, George H. Streeton used an economical combination of brick and terra cotta for his St. Charles Borromeo. Built on the site of an earlier church on the north side of West 141st Street between Seventh and Eighth Avenues, the structure featured Gothic ornamentation inspired by that of St. Gudule's in Brussels and supplied by the Excelsior Terra-Cotta Company.

The same company provided the similar flamboyant tracery and arches employed by Henry Andersen in 1898 at the Lutheran Church of the Atonement. Organized the year before by Harlem members of St. John's on Christopher Street in Greenwich Village, Andersen's church stood commandingly at the southeast corner of Edgecombe Avenue and West 140th Street. Economical terra cotta on the exterior, along with stamped copper embellishments at the top of the tower, made possible a costly altar of Numidian marble, which supports a larger-than-life-size statue of Christ.

## Synagogues in Harlem

Cost concerns also figured in the construction of Harlem's three largest synagogues. Terra cotta was a key component of two, but not of Temple Israel, established in 1870, the oldest and most prosperous synagogue in Harlem. Its members included Louis Blumstein, the owner of 125th Street's most successful department store (which bore his name), and Myron Sulzberger, an

Edward I. Shire, Temple Ansche Chesed (now Mount Neboh Baptist Church), 1883 Seventh Avenue, 1909. Skylight

OPPOSITE
Temple Ansche Chesed

attorney whose Harlem-born son would one day head the *New York Times.* They had formerly worshipped on Fifth Avenue at 125th Street in Temple Israel's first home, John Welch's converted Church of the Holy Trinity. The congregation sold this property for a handsome profit—underscoring just how much and rapidly Harlem was changing—and relocated to 201 Lenox Avenue, on the northwest corner of West 120th Street, within a few blocks of the new Church of the Holy Trinity.

Imperiously polished, the synagogue (now the Mount Olivet Baptist Church) was the work of the young Arnold W. Brunner. New York's first German-Jewish, second-generation architect had studied in Paris at the Ecole des Beaux-Arts. Begun in 1906 and completed the following year, the limestone synagogue appeared from a distance to be a bank or perhaps a courthouse. It featured fluted Ionic columns and was lighted by arched stained-glass windows. One cost-cutting measure appeared in the upper reaches of the synagogue: while the pedimented tabernacle that housed the Torah scrolls was made of finely veined marble, the paired shafts of Ionic columns above it were scagliola executed by the Artificial Marble Company, headquartered at 413 East 91st Street.

Hedman and Schoen's synagogue for the First Hungarian congregation, Ohab Zedek (1907), was an instance where budgetary considerations had a more serious architectural impact. Located on the southwest corner of Fifth Avenue and 116th Street in the heart of Harlem's largely Jewish, Eastern European and Russian neighborhood, the synagogue was of deep red brick trimmed with cream-colored terra cotta. It had a gabled facade, detailed to suggest a pediment, between two tapered, pylon-like pavilions. Curiously, the building, while primarily in the Beaux-Arts mode, included Tudor arches. The mystery of the arches is explained in the September 28, 1907, issue of *American Architect and Building News.* It explains that the members of Ohab Zedek's congregation, respectful of their traditions, had reproduced the Gothic interior of their former synagogue on the Lower East Side, which had originally been a church.

If apart from remodeled churches Harlem's Jews had avoided Christianity's definitive Gothic mode, they were not altogether reticent about presenting a "churchly" appearance. Resembling a two-towered porticoed church in early-eighteenth-century London, Edward Shire's Temple Ansche Chesed was completed in 1909. Now the Mount Neboh Baptist Church, it occupies a fine site on the northeast corner of Seventh Avenue and West 114th Street. Brick, limestone, and terra cotta, the synagogue was naturally lighted by means of an enormous skylight, the stained glass of which depicted traditional Jewish symbols. Unlike Ohab Zedek, Congregation Ansche Chesed had mixed seating for men and women and prayers conducted in English; it also boasted a fine organ.

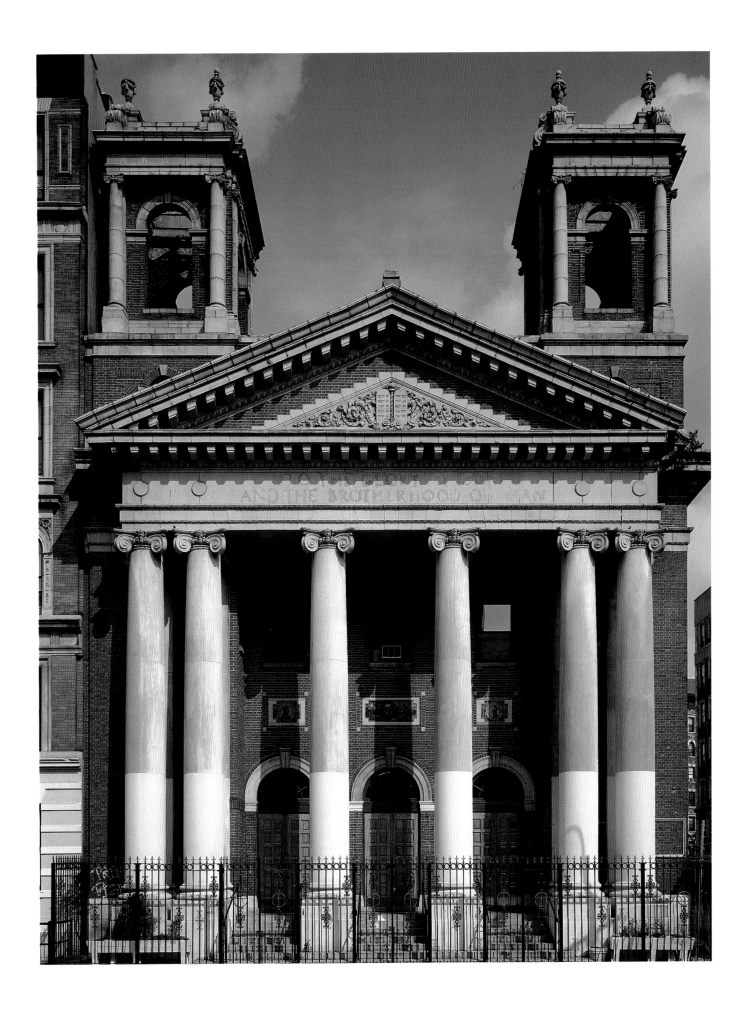

## Houses of Worship in an Age of Change

In East Harlem on elite East 118th Street, millionaire James Wood proudly funded Trinity Methodist Episcopal Church (1881), designed by Norris G. Starkweather. But not long after Wood's 1886 death, so few Methodists remained in this area that the building became the James Wood memorial "People's House," which performed settlement work among the poor. The nearby Presbyterian Church of the Ascension, at 422 East 116th Street, tried a similar strategy: the congregation included a settlement house when the firm of Ludlow & Peabody was engaged to produce a new church (1912). Brick and stucco outside, the Lombard Gothic edifice was vaulted and domed within, exhibiting a virtuoso tile-and-brick wainscot. Church officials hired the Reverend Francisco Pirozzini, an Italian-American pastor. But by the end of the 1920s, the church had been replaced by tenements.

Norris G. Starkweather, Trinity Methodist Episcopal Church, East 118th Street near Second Avenue, 1881

OPPOSITE
Vaux & Withers, Trinity Cemetery suspension bridge, Broadway and West 155th Street, 1872

After the subway-inspired apartment-house boom, many of the old Audubon Park families departed. At that time it must have appeared that the Church of the Intercession (Episcopal) at the northwest corner of Broadway at West 158th Street, designed by Rembrandt Lockwood and completed in 1872, might not survive. Its longevity is due to the vision of its rector, the Reverend Dr. Milo Hudson Gates. Considering the church an enlightening and edifying force, he set his sights on the anticipated tremendous population growth, convincing his small, insular parish to relinquish autonomy and become a chapel of Trinity Church, as was true when the church was founded in 1846. He pledged to the congregation that a church double the size of the old one would be built. Even more remarkable, in 1911 Dr. Gates convinced the vestry of Trinity to undertake a noble structure capable of holding nearly one thousand communicants.

In Bertram Grosvenor Goodhue, an original but scholarly designer, Gates found an able and equal partner. Together they created a house of worship so fine and grand that the loss of Vaux & Withers's elegant suspension bridge linking the two sectors of Trinity Cemetery—which had been divided in half when the Grand Boulevard (Broadway) was cut through in the late 1860s—may be forgiven. Completed in 1914, Goodhue's masterwork was positioned west to east at the southeast corner of West 155th Street and Broadway. By combining the church, parish house, and rectory into a unified composition linked by an arched cloister, he created a picturesque complex enhanced by an unspoiled setting. The site remains one of the few spots in Washington Heights where visitors may sense an approximation of the area's early-nineteenth-century atmosphere.

The interior of the nave was adorned by the most accomplished artisans and workshops of the era, creating an incomparable setting. The altar was embedded with hundreds of stones collected from holy places throughout the world by Dr. Gates; they were arranged in a conventionalized tree-of-life design. The neo-Gothic altarpiece in the vaulted Lady Chapel was painted by Boston's Taber Sears. The great east window is the work of Charles Connick, and Goodhue's effigy, set in an arch and decorated with illustrations of his most famous works, was sculpted by Lee Lawrie, who had a studio in East Harlem. All of these creative talents had collaborated on earlier projects; the group brought to the Church of the Intercession a common sympathy and understanding that were to produce unsurpassed beauty at the comparatively modest cost of $500,000.

ABOVE

Bertram G. Goodhue (with Cram, Goodhue & Ferguson), Church of the Intercession (Episcopal), Broadway and West 155th Street, 1914. Sanctuary showing altar inlaid with stones from holy places

Church of the Intercession. Doorway carved by Lee Lawrie

LEFT

Church of the Intercession

## "The Richest Negro Church in America":
## St. Philip's (Episcopal)

Along with the tale of determination fulfilled at the Church of the Intercession, it is inspiring to consider the story of an equally determined priest, Peter Williams Jr., the first rector of St. Philip's Church (Episcopal) and a passionate political activist and abolitionist. In the early years of the twentieth century, African-Americans were beginning to establish in Harlem the world's largest black city. Although they were as desirous as whites of worshipping within profoundly moving places, no black church had amassed wealth sufficient to approach the grandeur of the Church of the Intercession. The richest, St. Philip's Church, was one of New York's oldest black congregations, established by New York's first black Episcopal clergyman. It was organized in 1818, with the aid of Williams, who would serve as rector until his death in 1840. Initially, the church was located on Centre Street in lower Manhattan, not far from New York's first black church, Mother African Methodist Episcopal Zion, which had been founded by Williams's father in 1796. Following black Manhattan's northward journey, St. Philip's had moved from Centre to Mulberry Street and by 1886 reached the notorious Tenderloin.

Many of St. Philip's parishioners were members of what was then New York's extremely small "Negro elite." Through sacrifices and with contributions from compassionate whites, the congregation made a point of occupying only elegant, if simple, buildings. Some New Yorkers took exception to this assertion of African-American dignity: St. Philip's was vandalized or destroyed at least twice within a sixty-year period. One such instance, in 1900, was initiated by an off-duty policeman in plain clothes, and a three-day melee ensued. Patrolmen in uniform (mostly Irish) were observed assisting gangs of rioters (also mostly Irish, and living in the same slum area as the blacks) as they pursued and beat black men and women. At a subsequent investigation, the victims' lawyers were prohibited from cross-examining policemen and all officers involved were exonerated. This incident left people of color uneasy, and moving to Harlem appeared to be one possible counter to such insecurity.

The Reverend Huchens Chew Bishop was the rector of St. Philip's from 1886 to 1933. Born in Maryland during the era of slavery, he was the first black graduate of the General Theological Seminary. The cleric was an enterprising man and, beginning in 1906, began quietly investing in Harlem real estate, using proceeds from the sale of the church's Tenderloin property. That Bishop was aiming to purchase a church was left unstated; many of his transactions would probably not have taken place had the truth been suspected. Alarm in Harlem intensified with each new black arrival, and several unsuspecting owners had declared firmly to Bishop that they would never sell to African-Americans. By the time Bishop attempted to buy the Church of the Redeemer on West 136th Street, his intent was clear, and St. Philip's was foiled by a restrictive covenant. Feeling honor-bound to abide by an agreement with other property owners on the street, which barred sales to blacks, the vestry turned down Bishop's offer of $50,000. Sold to a white woman in 1914 for just $19,000, the church was immediately resold to Mother A.M.E. Zion Church.

In 1909 St. Philip's successfully acquired a new church site on the south side of West 134th Street near Seventh Avenue. (St. Philip's also purchased ten apartment houses on West 135th Street that had previously been restricted to whites. When the congregation began its move to Harlem, the white tenants living in the buildings were evicted and their places made available to blacks. For half a century the rents from these flats subsidized the St. Philip's endowment.) One of the architects was Vertner Woodson Tandy, the designer of Madam C. J. Walker's later West 136th Street town house/hair parlor and the first black architect to be registered in New York.

Just twenty-five years old in 1910, Tandy was younger, less experienced, and a much less gifted renderer than his partner, George W. Foster Jr. Foster had attended night classes at Cooper Union before briefly apprenticing with Daniel Burnham and Henry J. Hardenbergh, while Tandy was the product of a far more prestigious program at Cornell. Moreover, while studying at Ithaca, Tandy had helped to found America's first black college fraternity, Alpha Phi Alpha. Both advantages were enough to secure him top billing in his five-year association with Foster.

Tandy and Foster began designing St. Philip's Church in 1910 and completed it the following year. For $130,000, they created a conventional Gothic church with a Roman brick facade enlivened by cast-concrete gargoyles and two buttressed, arched entryways. The Reverend Bishop, familiar with the new St. Mary's Church–Manhattanville, insisted on a similar building with a brick interior and an open timber roof. Eager to celebrate the reputation of St. Philip's as black America's richest church, Tandy provided it with a more lofty scale and decorative flourishes; in the nave, he included corbels cast from artificial stone to represent the head of Christ, as well as a new marble altar finely carved with figures of the four evangelists and the Lamb of God.

An ornate limestone reredos and a credence were saved from the church's former home and reinstalled. These superb examples of 1880s excess are gabled, pinnacled, and embellished by cusps and crockets. The manner in which the St. Philip's altar was set off against bare bricks, rather than being placed in an ornate setting, today seems quite modern. Certainly the church impressed the publishers of *Architecture and Building*. With not a single reference to race, the June 1911 presentation of Harlem's newest house of worship constitutes the first publication of work by an African-American architect in a major professional journal.

St. Philip's led the way as New York's first African-American congregation to relocate in Harlem; others came soon after. As Harlem's real-estate bubble burst, many congregations found bargains in fine buildings abandoned by panic-stricken owners. Other black parishes proclaimed the arrival of the "New Negro" in the Promised Land with the construction of new churches. Yet in the two decades that followed *Architecture and Building*'s report on Tandy and Foster, the architects were able to attract comparatively few additional clients. Throughout this period Harlemites, black and white, most often relied on the services of white designers for the plans of all buildings, including churches.

A fresh start for the African-American congregation of St. James's Presbyterian Church had come with strings attached. Financed by the church's white national governing body, the parishioners were required to hire white designers Ludlow & Peabody when they moved to 59–61 West 137th Street from their former home on West 32nd Street, where they had been located since their founding in 1895. More prosperous than most black churches, St. James's had much in common with St. Philip's. Both congregations were Harlem pioneers, and both would erect new edifices. But the buildings differed dramatically. Faced in Harvard brick with limestone trim, St. James's, completed in 1914, followed the lead of Joseph Freedlander's nearby Harlem Hospital complex (c. 1910–27). It was an adaptation of the Georgian style's move toward the Federal idiom. This mode, just one step away from the Greek Revival, recalls the aristocratic Harlem of John McComb Jr.'s Hamilton Grange and Martin E. Thompson's Dutch Reform church. Faithful to the period, the design exhibited great delicacy and well-balanced refinement. However, both the complexity of the church's plan and its slightly asymmetrical facade betray its designers' Beaux-Arts training. Projected toward the street, the gabled main block was embellished by garlands, fanned lunettes, and a balconied Venetian window. Flanked by narrow recessed entry bays, this window was an expression of the nave. Yet as lower, arched openings suggested, an assortment of offices, classrooms, and clubrooms intervened between the street and the nave, an arrangement that would never have occurred in the early nineteenth century. Nor would any differentiation have been made between the two entrances, while here such divergence is essential: one leads to the sanctuary and the other is for tradesmen.

Lightly held aloft by a Corinthian colonnade, the barrel-vaulted nave broke open on the north wall into an inventive polygonal vaulted chancel. At the opposite end stood an elevated gallery. In an earlier Harlem this had been where African slaves were segregated during services. At the new St. James's, the balcony was a benign place, where latecomers and overflow crowds were relegated.

St. James's elegant interior must have been the perfect setting for the 1919 marriage of A'Lelia Walker, the daughter of the late Madam Walker. The country's greatest African-American heiress drew a crowd of guests that overwhelmed even the balcony and managed to make St. James's seem too small. And with African-Americans making their way to Harlem, America's new black capital, in record numbers, it really was not large enough for the new era. The congregation left the building in only a few years time, moving to St. Nicholas Avenue.

Ludlow & Peabody, St. James's Presbyterian Church, 59–61 West 137th Street, 1914

Designed in 1920 and completed in 1923 at 132 West 138th Street, the Abyssinian Baptist Church was another example of a black congregation engaging white designers. Charles W. Bolton & Son's Gothic edifice still features stained-glass images of blue-eyed blond angels, saints, and biblical figures— poignant reminders of the extent to which many blacks during this period internalized notions of white supremacy.

Transformation of Harlem's houses of worship represent perhaps the lowest ebb of local history. Whites initially—sometimes fiercely—resisted the integration efforts of blacks, and most ultimately fled. Catholic parishes, which even today retain white priests, gradually accepted black members. But St. Luke's, the Harlem–New York Presbyterian Church, and the Westminster Presbyterian Church (designed by Ludlow & Valentine and completed in 1908 at St. Nicholas Avenue and West 115th Street) were all handsome buildings in good condition that late in the 1930s were abandoned by their white congregations and locked tight.

By contrast, Temple Ansche Chesed was adapted to become Our Lady of the Miraculous Medal, a Spanish Roman Catholic church, and then the Mount Neboh Baptist Church, while Holy Trinity's vestry sold the building in 1927 for use by blacks. Sad to leave, the congregation gave one third of the $250,000 purchase price to the Episcopal Church Mission Society, stating: "In this way, we are leaving behind a part of our estate in the old neighborhood, looking forward to the day when church work might be more favorable among white people there."

211

# CHAPTER SIX

# CULTURE, COMMERCE, AND INDUSTRY IN HARLEM

F. Stuart Williamson, Riverside Park,
c. 1904. View looking north from
West 140th Street, 1908

George B. Post, City College of
the City University of New York,
West 135th to West 140st Streets,
St. Nicholas Terrace to Amsterdam
Avenue, 1903–7; Samuel Parsons Jr.,
St. Nicholas Park, 1909

**W**hen the members of Harlem's venerable Dutch Reform congregation moved their old Third Avenue church building in 1884 to make way for new commercial enterprise, they were only providing an example of an enduring truism. Then, as now, a building's artistic or historic significance did not always count for very much. Instead, immediate economic considerations often took precedence over all others. Sometimes, such an attitude was manifest in a speculative binge of indiscriminate building. At other times, it was evident in protracted neglect. Either way, too often this shortsightedness was to prove damaging to Harlem's architectural heritage. In its wake both commercial and civic architecture in the area has been particularly vulnerable.

During Harlem's gilded age, however, emphasis on the bottom line often had architecturally favorable results. As a rule, Harlem's hard-nosed capitalists of the era understood the economic sense of constructing well-planned designs, finely crafted from lasting materials. If developer David H. King Jr.'s model town houses of 1891 represent Harlem's best intact residential realization of this practice, Joseph Loth & Company's "Fair and Square" Silk Ribbon Factory, on Amsterdam Avenue between West 150th and 151st Streets, must be recognized as an exemplary industrial survivor—despite the considerable loss of the original clock tower. Apart from a smokestack, the tower was the sole vertical note in architect Victor Hugo Kafka's block-long building, which dates to 1886. Additional contrast is provided by projecting piers that divide the facade's aligned openings. The crowning parapets of subtly defined corner pavilions are emblazoned with "Joseph Loth & Company" in cut-brick letters. Nevertheless, the red Philadelphia brick structure, low in profile with light-colored granite lintels and sills, has been calculated to coexist well with nearby residential blocks. The tower exhibited much of the same dignity of expression as the neighborhood's institutional architecture, notably charities in the vicinity, such as John Duncan's orphanage for the Hebrew Sheltering Guardian Society on Broadway at West 150th Street (1892; incorporating the Hickson Field Mansion of about 1842) or William H. Hume's Hebrew Orphan Asylum on Amsterdam Avenue between West 136th and 138th Streets (1883).

215

Victor Hugo Kafka, "Fair and Square"
Silk Ribbon Factory for Joseph Loth &
Company, 1828 Amsterdam Avenue,
1886

John Duncan, Hebrew Sheltering
Guardian Society, Broadway between
West 150th and 151st Streets, 1892

William H. Hume, Hebrew Orphan
Asylum, Amsterdam Avenue between
West 136th and 138th Streets, 1883

In accordance with prevailing custom in American cities, Harlem's factories were generally situated in voluntarily designated industrial areas. The Loth building housed, in contrast, the only manufacturer in the neighborhood, so it was imperative that the structure look, as King's *Handbook of New York* boasted, "in appearance more like a public building than a factory." Over and over again in the Harlem of this era, model magnates pursued the goal of creating a positive impression with handsome headquarters. This was even true in commercial havens such as Manhattanville, the site of a rival ribbon factory, an extensive brewery complex, the glistening white-glazed terra-cotta "Sheffield Pure Milk" bottling plant on West 125th Street (designed by Frank A. Rooke and finished in 1903), an Armor meatpacking factory, and a massive gasworks, among other enterprises. All attested to their owners' good taste and public spirit.

Prior to the enactment of zoning laws, such displays of good will, along with restrictive deed covenants, were a property owner's only defense against unsightly or incompatible neighbors. Harlem's Standard Gas Works generating house (1888) at East 115th Street at the Harlem River was exceedingly elegant: at its base a square structure, it rose upward as a buttressed cylinder with a conical slate roof. However, no matter how well-intentioned, appearance could only go so far. The gas works' malodorous round storage tanks, marvels of cast-iron engineering, loomed as a neighborhood nuisance.

More successfully mitigated by design were area livery stables. Four stories tall and faced in pressed brick, F. W. Esper's Speedway Livery & Boarding Stables, designed by Henri Fouchaux and completed in 1891 at 459 West 150th Street, for instance, more closely resembled an office building than a stable. Patronized primarily by occupants of the surrounding row houses, its deceptive facade—round arched openings at the first floor and paired sashes above—was no accident. The stables were scrupulously arranged and planned to avoid odors; terra-cotta busts of lively steeds flanked the entrance, announcing its presence.

Devoid of horse heads, Carey Brothers Livery Stable (c. 1895) at 124–126 East 124th Street was even more carefully detailed. Its stylistic subtlety, particularly its fine brickwork, was particularly necessary because the stable was built in what had been one of Harlem's most exclusive residential districts and occupied the site of two razed brownstone houses.

Run by Harry L. Powers, one of the entrepreneurial sons of the well-known uptown politician and builder Jesse Wood Powers, the Excelsior Stables (1891), designed by French, Dixon & DeSaldern at 166–172 East 124th Street, was Harlem's most elaborate establishment for the leasing, boarding, and selling of horses. An exceptional building in the neo-Romanesque style, it had three floors of aligned windows grouped in four bays of paired arches between shallow piers. In the basement, each bay corresponded to a large Syrian arch; the exaggerated limestone keystones curved inward. Had it not been for a ubiquitous pair of horse heads, the Excelsior Stables might have passed for a post office or courthouse even more easily than the Loth factory.

Ironically, it was not until the 1920s that Harlem would finally have a federal post office building nearly as grand. As for panache, the Harlem Courthouse, located across from Sylvan Court at 170 East 121st Street, possessed all that the locals might have wished for. Designed by Thom & Wilson in the neo-Romanesque mode and completed in 1893, it cleverly combined courtrooms, offices, and jail cells in a single unified, picturesque building. Newly arrested offenders could be driven directly inside the building via three gated entrances. Like the judge's chambers, cells are immediately adjacent to the courtrooms. The most impressive courtroom—with a molded-plaster, barrel-vaulted ceiling and windows of stained glass—is expressed externally by a projecting bay

Thom & Wilson, Harlem Courthouse,
170 East 121st Street, 1893

Harlem Courthouse. Courtroom showing
mural by David Karfunkle, 1936

Harlem Courthouse. Staircase

OPPOSITE
Harlem Courthouse

surmounted by a pinnacled gable. In 1936 it was enhanced by a W.P.A.-sponsored mural by David Karfunkle. Unexpectedly, the principal public entrance, distinguished by a stone and terra-cotta porch, is off to the right. Expertly carved, the porch is decorated with a bas relief of mannerist cherubs and balancing scales of justice.

The courthouse corner clock tower, cylindrically engaged into the building to the height of the fourth floor, is the most pronounced feature of the building. Narrow, stepped windows light the exuberant and multicolored winding cast-iron staircase within. The tower culminates in an inventive octagonal lantern with eight gables and a tiled spire. Seeming to float magically above the trees of its brownstone universe, Harlem's courthouse must have presented to passersby an otherworldly vision of architectural fantasy.

A. B. Jennings, Mrs. Helen M. Scoville's School for Girls (formerly Lucien Calvin Warner house), 2042 Fifth Avenue, 1886

## The Schools and Colleges of Harlem

Just as with Harlem's early charitable organizations, the community's private schools initially adapted former private houses. By 1910, the Lucien Calvin Warner house designed by A. B. Jennings at 2042 Fifth Avenue (1886) had become Mrs. Helen M. Scoville's School for Girls and then the Mary E. Johnson Boarding School for Colored Children; the building was demolished in 1933. Around 1900, 721 St. Nicholas Avenue at West 146th Street (1891), designed by Thayer & Robinson, became the highly regarded Barnard School for Boys, while A. B. Ogden & Son's 423 West 148th Street at Convent Avenue (1895) became the Barnard School for Girls. The most notable conversion of this kind, occurring about 1903, was the Roman Catholic Academy of the Holy Child, at the southwest corner of Broadway and West 141st Street. Beginning as a country retreat, the yellow-banded, red brick Gothic "cottage" (1869) had originally stood on the east side of "the Boulevard" at West 140th Street. Inspired by Ruskin, it was among the earliest efforts of J. C. Cady, whose brilliant career was capped with the design of various wings for the American Museum of Natural History in the 1890s. The house was built for David Maitland Armstrong, an art authority and diplomat with an international reputation; he would later manufacture stained glass in partnership with his daughters. A Tile Club founder and intimate of Stanford White, Armstrong built his Harlem home assuming that he would never inherit the family ancestral seat, Danskammer at Newburgh. In fact, no sooner had the Harlem house been completed than this came to pass, and the new dwelling was offered for rental in the *New York Times*. It came to be the summer residence of Dr. and Mrs. William Rodgers, parents of the composer Richard Rodgers. Leasing Armstrong's aerie all through the 1870s, they called it "Cozy Nook."

222

Thayer & Robinson, Barnard School for Boys, 721 St. Nicholas Avenue, 1891

A. B. Ogden & Son, Barnard School for Girls, 423 West 148th Street, 1895

J. C. Cady, David Maitland Armstrong cottage, Broadway and West 140th Street, 1869

Joseph Wolf, F. W. Seagrist house (incorporating David Maitland Armstrong cottage), Broadway and West 140th Street, 1892

F. W. Seagrist moved and greatly enlarged the cottage in 1892. It incorporated a half-dozen fan-lit doorways from the Federal period, salvaged from Greenwich Village row houses and employed as windows; architect Joseph Wolf also utilized other historic architectural relics in a large new wing. Preserved while the building served as the Academy of the Holy Child, they were lost when it was traded in 1910 for a site at 630 Riverside Drive.

There, between West 140th and 141st Streets, a new facility was built by 1911. Renamed St. Walburgas Academy, it was designed by John W. Kearny. Collegiate Gothic in style, with crenellations and pointed arches, the school had walls of mica schist (excavated on site) animated by terra cotta. The imposing building stood near the center of the upwardly mobile apartment-house district that had been brought about by the subway. Typical of the area's residents were young George and Ira Gershwin at 520 West 144th Street. There were many Catholic households in the neighborhood as well, and the academy directed its efforts toward recruiting as its students the children of the most successful.

F. W. Seagrist house

## Manhattanville College of the Sacred Heart, the Magdalene Home, and Manhattan College

Dedicated to developing the intellects of women, the Sisters of the Sacred Heart was originally a French order. Daughters from some of America's most illustrious families were to be among the alumnae of the academy and college founded by the order in Harlem. The school's first multipurpose building (1841) contained classrooms and dormitories, as well as an elaborate chapel. Prominently placed atop the steep northern rise of Manhattan Valley (Convent Hill), it occupied the well-developed grounds of the former estate of tobacconist Pierre Lorillard. Octagonal in plan, the building's two-stage central lantern set high above dense foliage was visible for miles.

In 1888 disaster struck when the Gothic Revival building was consumed by fire. Undeterred, the sisters moved their classes to a nearby estate overlooking the Hudson, west of Broadway, between West 135th and 136th Streets. Here the nuns temporarily took up residence in a large, square, stuccoed Italianate house (c. 1850), which had been one of several in the neighborhood designed by Alexander Jackson Davis. By no means an exciting work of architecture, it nevertheless stood in close proximity to what was surely one of Harlem's most dazzling structures. A fantastic pavilion (1879) had been added to the garden by the house's current owner, Oswald Ottendorfer, who published New York's leading German-language newspaper, the *Staadt-Zeitung*.

This pavilion undoubtedly represented an attempt to impose a personal imprint on the newly acquired property. Ottendorfer was guided by the same romantic impulses behind other famous Orientalist confections of the day, such as the artist Edwin Church's Olana (1870–79) and Frederick Lord Leighton's Arab Hall (c. 1877). Ottendorfer's pavilion had a stained-glass-roofed square dome decorated with Stars of David and was stylistically similar to several contemporary synagogues. The nuns chose to utilize the pavilion as a chapel and, beguiled by their new environment, decided to engage the pavilion's architect to design their new building.

William Schickel, Oswald Ottendorfer pavilion, Broadway at West 135th Street, 1879. Rendering

William Schickel, a German native, had trained as a draftsman with Richard Morris Hunt. His partner was Isaac E. Ditmars. Predictably Gothic, Schickel's design for the nuns, completed in 1890 on the same site as their earlier building, was asymmetrically picturesque, with myriad dormers and conical roofed towers. It also housed an unexpected Italian Renaissance–style chapel. The beautifully landscaped campus would slowly grow to include additional, more specialized buildings; the first of these, predating the fire, were the spartan brick and brownstone convents (1880), in the form of semidetached paired row houses, on the north side of West 130th Street between St. Nicholas Terrace and what would aptly be known as Convent Avenue. The contractor in charge of most of these buildings was Harlem's native son Isaac Hooper, who was justly famous as the builder of the Montifiore Home (1889), designed by Brunner & Tryon with Buchman & Deisler for the east side of Broadway between West 138th and 139th Streets, and the H. C. F. Koch & Company department store (1891), designed by William H. Hume & Son at 132–140 West 125th Street (now the 125th Street Medical Building), in Harlem and William B. Tuthill's Carnegie Hall in midtown Manhattan (1891). Notwithstanding a reputation for academic rigor, Manhattanville College became popular nationwide as an elite "finishing school." However, its students were not always enthusiastic about the value of their experience there. For future actress Tallulah Bankhead, a congressman's daughter from the Deep South, it was "favorite among the different schools I was thrown out of. The subway went right down Broadway to the theaters." Another politician's daughter was promised that she might attend whatever school she wished; the young Rose Fitzgerald Kennedy chose Wellesley College, a Protestant school. In accordance with her family's faith and father's ambition, she was sent to Manhattanville instead; years afterward, she insisted, "I don't believe I have ever forgiven my father."

Meant to minister to spiritual needs and development, the Magdalene Home (1901) was located on Riverside Drive just south of St. Walburgas Academy between West 139th and 140th Streets.

Ottendorfer pavilion

226

William Schickel, Manhattanville College
of the Sacred Heart, West 134th Street
at Convent Avenue, 1890

Manhattanville College of the Sacred
Heart. Dormitory

Operated by the Sisters of St. Regis, the home was also known as "the cenacle," a reference to the Last Supper. At first, prior to the opening of Riverside Drive, the Magdalene Home had operated out of the nuns' convent, which was closer to Broadway. As the *New York Herald* wrote in 1901, "Many women of New York's most fashionable society come here for a few weeks retirement and prayer during the Lenten season and to receive religious teaching in the midst of the sylvan quiet that reigns in the shadows of the pines." One of these was Broadway's leading lady, Maude Adams, who so cherished her annual stays that she endowed a "cenacle branch" on her Long Island estate. W. E. Bosworth and W. C. Chase Associate Architects designed the Magdalene Home's Riverside Drive building in the guise of a Loire Valley chateau—yet on an intimate scale—in accordance with the wealth and taste of the people it served. It was analogous to Fifth Avenue mansions designed by Richard Morris Hunt.

The radically different nature of Manhattan College, to the south, was stressed with equal clarity by the appearance of its buildings. The school's founders, the Christian Brothers, had been attracted to West Harlem in part by the presence of Manhattanville College of the Sacred Heart. "You see, brother, the height crowned with a cross . . . Now we gentlemen have been thinking how gratifying it would be to Catholics of New York to see another cross crowning the summit opposite the Convent," one faculty member wrote to another after inspecting the proposed site. Purchased in 1853, the plot, eventually bound by Broadway and West 131st and 133rd Streets, had originally been part of the Findlay estate; its proximity to the working-class village of Manhattanville was also considered advantageous, since it was the brothers' goal to make scholars of orphaned and poor young Catholic men. Classes were initially conducted in the Findlays' former house. Empty barns and a stable were modified to serve as dormitories and a dining hall. Manhattan College's eventual buildings were of brick, with bracketed eaves and mansard roofs. Built in the late 1850s and the 1860s, they were almost as stylistically modest as those they replaced.

## City College

In marked contrast, the City College of the City University of New York, another beacon of opportunity for the poor, was an architectural masterpiece. Begun as a free academy for male New York high school graduates, the college moved uptown just before the subway did. Planned to dominate a hilltop site above St. Nicholas Park, designed by Samuel Parsons Jr. and completed in 1909, the campus was built between 1903 and 1907 and encompassed ten blocks between West 135th and 140th Streets west of St. Nicholas Terrace and east of Amsterdam Avenue. Convent Avenue, leading south past Manhattanville College, divided the grounds in half. Ornamental gateways spanning the roadway express the designers' determination to treat the city streets as assets that would integrate the college with its urban surroundings.

Far more than either of the prestigious private schools that were its neighbors, City College was highly restricted by budgetary constraints. George Brown Post, the principal partner of George B. Post & Sons, won the limited competition held for the institution's design, meeting the challenge with much originality and even humor. Educated at New York University, he had also trained in the New York atelier formed by America's first Ecole des Beaux-Arts graduate, Richard Morris Hunt. Fellow student Charles D. Gambrill would briefly become his partner in 1860. In the aftermath of the Civil War, in which he served as an officer, Post, practicing independently, steadily rose from success to success, with banks and office buildings predominating among his profitable commissions. He also occasionally designed stately houses, such as Cornelius Vanderbilt's palatial chateau (1882, 1894) at Fifth Avenue and 57th Street. A key participant in the design of the buildings for the World's Columbian Exposition held in Chicago in 1893, Post was highly and widely regarded for skillful planning. Designing much of the Statler Hotel chain, his firm was to assist in perfecting and popularizing the American Hotel plan, in which a private bath is provided for every room.

His design of City College benefited from familiarity with the district. Post's grandfather's country house, where he had spent several childhood summers, was the famous Claremont, a Federal-style landmark only a dozen blocks away. City College's many-gabled, towering Main Building (renamed Shepard Hall in 1950) was curved to follow St. Nicholas Terrace and caused some controversy in regard to its funding. For economic reasons, some trustees had preferred, of Post's original two designs, the simpler neoclassical scheme. Other trustees preferred Post's Collegiate Gothic designs, which made the most of a dramatic site and would contrast with the Beaux-Arts buildings then being constructed at Columbia—which poet Langston Hughes was later to deride as resembling a factory. While for a time the college faced the prospect of having Main Building stand as its sole institutional structure, sufficient private donations were raised to enable the construction of four more buildings. Overall, Post's methods were so inventive that it is hard to believe that cost-cutting played any role here.

Yet in fact both the style and the thoughtful selection of materials were gauged for suitability and practicality. Post's neo–English Gothic perpendicular style was associated with Oxford and Cambridge; yet, wishing to graphically identify City College as the workingman's academy, he employed not ivory or marble but Manhattan schist, excavated on site from deep foundations. To the disconcertment of the Italian-American stonemasons engaged in building City College, Post further insisted that rust-streaked and iron-spotted stones should be positioned prominently. His demand that the craftsmen desist in carefully and uniformly dressing the rock ran counter to all their training; only gradually would they come to appreciate that the very inexactness he sought required another kind of care, resulting in an appearance that suggested great antiquity.

Rusty, random stones and ivy were only a part of the Post alchemy, which distilled ambience from modern materials and new technologies. Modeled with precision and in intricate, seemingly infinite variety, the terra cotta employed at City College formed an almost startling juxtaposition with the mica schist walls. Crockets, bosses, and gargoyles were all in evidence. Whether depicting befuddled professors or scenes from Aesop's fables, inside and out Post's most inspired decorative elements were numerous corbels. Plaster versions in Main Building's lengthy entrance were especially adept, depicting the various ages of humankind from infancy to advanced age. On the outside of the building, the shining white glaze of the terra-cotta embellishments was sandblasted to better harmonize with the rough masonry. This experimental matte finish looked like marble when completed, testimony to Post's extensive knowledge in regard to manipulating materials to achieve an appropriate effect. Unfortunately, Post misunderstood the nature of the high-carbon steel used to support the college building; compromised by a microscopic network of cracks, the sandblasted terra cotta absorbed rather than repelled moisture, eventually leading to extensive corrosion of the building's framework.

Shepard Hall is easily identified: anchor-shaped, with embracing wings, it is lighted by long buttressed and mullioned windows, and the navelike interior "great hall" rising three stories is City College's most impressive space. Functioning as a chapel and exhibition and assembly room, the timber-roofed hall was meant to accommodate the entire student body and faculty. It is equipped with an enormous organ in a steep loft at one end and a deep stage at the other. Edwin Blashfield's allegorical mural serves as the hall's focal point. For all the allure of contrived distress or storybook charm of romantic massing, Post's buildings were strictly modern in their functionality. The lighting, heating, and ventilation of laboratories and classrooms were all state-of-the-art for the time, while woodwork, wainscoting, and plumbing fixtures are durable and easily cleaned.

South of West 138th Street, City College's athletic arena presented a severe, block-long masonry wall to Amsterdam Avenue. Behind that wall Arnold W. Brunner's neoclassical Lewisohn Stadium (1915), of reinforced concrete, was almost magical in its ability to complement Post's more aggressive designs; its curving colonnade echoed the wings of Shepard Hall. (Brunner was a former George B. Post & Sons draftsman.) A gift of philanthropist Adolph Lewisohn, it served as a summer venue for inexpensive performances from 1918 until the mid-1960s. Here Harlem's own George Gershwin played *Rhapsody in Blue*, child prodigy Phillipa Schuyler of 270 Convent Avenue performed her own compositions, and Marian Anderson, the New York Philharmonic, and the Denishawn dancers all entertained enormous crowds under the stars. The stadium was razed in 1973.

Arnold W. Brunner, Lewisohn Stadium, between Amsterdam and Convent Avenues, West 137th and 138th Streets, 1915

OPPOSITE
Crow, Lewis & Wicks, City College library, 1929. Rendering

More consistent with Post's design was Crow, Lewis & Wicks's extravagant library (1929). Planned to adjoin Shepard Hall to the north, the building was less than a third completed when it was demolished in 1955. Not as short-lived has been the school's history of offering a free education to all who qualified: tuition fees were imposed only in 1971. Purchased in the 1940s, the buildings of Manhattanville College were over the course of several decades demolished by City College, and about 1990 a new athletic arena was built in their place.

Highly esteemed academically, the finely conceived and wonderfully appointed institution must have been an inspiration for the immigrants, migrants, and local New Yorkers who would study there. Henry Roth, a Harlemite transplanted from the Lower East Side, provides in his novel *A Star Shines over Mt. Morris Park* a poignant and realistic account of the life of Eastern European and Russian immigrants living in Harlem during the first decades of the twentieth century. From tenements occupying the fringes of the city's most prominent middle-class Jewish neighborhood in southeast Harlem, poor children like Roth (who lived east of Madison Avenue near East 116th Street) were able to look out upon myriad manifestations of the American dream. Roth described the buildings of City College as being "like churches . . . seen in pictures in fairy tales, or formidable castles, gray and white." Adam Clayton Powell Jr., Lewis Mumford, Jonas Salk, Edward G. Robinson, and Bayard Rustin were all City College alumni. Women were first admitted as degree candidates in 1951.

## Public Secondary and High Schools in Harlem

By the close of the nineteenth century it was widely agreed that investing in public education represented good value for the money. With New York's population larger, more ethnically and culturally diverse, and often poorer, public grammar and high schools were increasingly seen as the best forum through which to provide opportunity. As much as salutes to the flag or demanding curriculums, architecture was enlisted in the effort to provide a free education that would create an assimilated, self-sufficient, and productive citizenry.

Decorated with star-spangled, stripe-emblazoned shields, C. B. J. Snyder's Lydia F. Wadleigh High School at 215 West 114th Street (1905) reflects the school board's decision to differentiate between its academic and technical training facilities by naming the former for individuals of importance to the academic community. Honoring an early advocate of increased educational opportunities for girls and women, Lydia F. Wadleigh, who died in 1888, the Wadleigh School cost $900,000 to construct, furnish, and equip. In 1896 the *New York Herald* was enthusiastic about prospects for the building, announcing that it was to be modeled on the Gothic Hôtel Cluny in Paris. The newspaper further reported that the architect declared that "light, space, quiet, health and cheapness will be assured." Specifications called for some eighty classrooms, more than a dozen laboratories, two elevators, three gymnasiums, a library, two study halls, and a 1,500-seat auditorium.

But before construction could begin, the unimpressed Manhattan borough president insisted that Snyder's estimates included $100,000 worth of "extra ornament which could be eliminated and not in any way injure the appearance of the building." Taking decisive action, the borough president put his own architect to work scaling back the plan. Anticipating trouble, Snyder, himself a talented politician, drafted a comparative study. It demonstrated how his design accommodated students for about half the cost of schools in Boston and Philadelphia. Members of the New York school board concurred and approved the original scheme with no changes, declaring that they did not desire "to erect a high school building which would be the subject of the scorn and ridicule of the entire country."

The new building was indeed worthy of the dignity of the city. Rather than resembling Hôtel Cluny, it evoked Louis XII's Chateau de Blois right down to its soaring, square corner stair-tower and steeply pitched, tiled roof (the tiles have since been lost). A beautiful and regal building, the Wadleigh School was a profound reminder to students of individual and collective dignity.

Years spent at study here were transforming ones for many students. Nineteen-year-old Elinor Sachs, after passing the state's Regents examinations, won a scholarship that augmented an award she had already received from Barnard College. Sachs was hailed in the pages of the 1913 *Harlem Home News*, which reported that instead of pursuing a conventional teaching career, Miss Sachs was "going to study law and be a suffragette." The reporter was pleased to discover that despite the scholar's "attainments, she is still a girl, vivacious, modest and has a pleasant smile for everyone." He further noted that "to hear Miss Sachs speak, one would hardly believe that nine years ago she did not know a word of English." When he asked her if she remembered anything about her old home in Russia, she replied, "No, I don't . . . I have long since relegated it to a forgotten corner of my brain. I am too much occupied to think of that dark period. I am now endeavoring to make the most of my opportunities in this wonderful land."

C. B. J. Snyder, Lydia F. Wadleigh High School (now Junior High School 88), 215 West 114th Street, 1905

All over Harlem, Snyder reinforced the notion of the specialness of young citizens with splendid new buildings. Most were by-products of New York's 1898 consolidation and probably deserved the claim of being "the best schools in the world." Snyder's H-shaped plan was particularly innovative. In combination with skeletal steel frames, it offered considerable savings by taking advantage of the properties of steel, which allowed expansive aligned windows. Thus adequate lighting and air could be provided without recourse to the costly corner lots that were once considered essential for schools.

One of Snyder's first efforts in Harlem, P.S. 103 (c. 1895), did occupy a prominent corner location at East 119th Street and Madison Avenue. An accomplished exercise in the Queen Anne manner of Richard Norman Shaw, the design employed baroque doorcases, fractabled gables, a tiled roof, and a domed cupola. The design was reemployed in 1899 for P.S. 157, on the west side of

St. Nicholas Avenue between West 127th and 128th Streets; despite the distinction of Snyder's buildings, duplication of various schemes was an economy he often adopted, although this one was somewhat simplified. In Harlem, none of his buildings was ever replicated exactly, but several were enough alike that their bricks and terra-cotta detailing could be commissioned as a single order, providing volume discounts. If P.S. 159 at 241 East 119th Street was, like the Wadleigh School, inspired by the style of a French royal chateau, P.S. 186 at 521–527 West 145th Street and P.S. 184 at 31 West 116th Street were both derived from an Italian Renaissance palazzo. Snyder applied the savings realized through such strategies directly to the schools, in the form of oak woodwork, marble and mosaic panels, mural paintings, wrought iron, stained glass, and decorative plaster. Snyder's choices of patriotic and symbolic art were determined attempts at instruction; good examples of the ennobling "extras" he pursued are the monumental busts of Minerva, the goddess of wisdom (supplied by the New York Terra-Cotta Company), which adorned niches above the main entrances of both P.S. 186 and 184. One of these schools is now a ruin, the other destroyed.

"These were peoples' palaces," wrote architectural historian Robert A. M. Stern in the New York Times in 1999, "not factories for learning, [but] . . . the everyday masterpieces of a talented, historically overlooked architect who devoted himself to the public. Here is architecture in the service of democracy."

## The Libraries and Museums of Harlem

Just as educational buildings of quality helped make Harlem more a part of an evolving New York City, new well-designed branch libraries would create a more cosmopolitan atmosphere. Harlem's seven libraries were among sixty-seven donated to the nation's great metropolis by the philanthropic industrialist Andrew Carnegie. Before 1901, there had been no municipally funded citywide library system. In Harlem just two privately maintained libraries had served the entire area. By 1892, the older Harlem Library, which had been built in the 1820s, occupied a domestically scaled, gabled-brick building, which combined chateauesque massing and neo-Romanesque elements. Adjacent to the Harlem Club at 32 West 123rd Street, it had been designed by one of the library's board members, architect Edgar K. Bourne. The library was closed in 1909 when a new library by McKim, Mead & White was built at 9 West 124th Street.

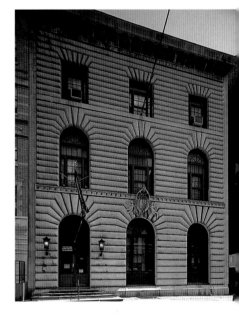

McKim, Mead & White, public branch library, 203 West 115th Street, 1908

LEFT
Charles Pratt Huntington, Hispanic Society of America, West 155th Street and Broadway, 1908. View in 1910

McKim, Mead & White designed most of the new libraries, and the buildings, while inspired by aristocratic European dwellings, were not at all suggestive of the domestic. The handsome branch at 103 West 135th Street (1905), modeled after a palazzo in Verona from the High Renaissance, is a fine example of the firm's work. However, the branch at 203 West 115th Street (1908), a miniature version of a sixteenth-century Florentine palace, must be singled out. Robustly carved from Indiana limestone, the building faithfully reproduces the mannerist rustication of the original as well as the facade's distinctive cherub-supported escutcheon. In the place of the ancient noble family's arms is displayed the great seal of the city of New York.

235

The central role that Harlem's public libraries played in helping poor residents discover a wider world and greater selves is perhaps best summed up by Henry Roth. Despite the proximity of exclusive shops and places of amusement, many New Yorkers had few opportunities to actually taste much of this bounty. Before 1910, freely circulating collections of books represented the best means to gain access to a wondrous world just outside a harsh reality. Books, Roth noted, were a godsend

> that [Ira] had kept under his bed . . . that he woke up to on Saturday and Sunday as a precious gift waiting for him to reclaim it . . . He tarried and reread, dreamed . . . Hundreds of new words . . . within the pages, unfamiliar words . . . and yet they offered no obstacle to understanding.

William M. Kendall of McKim, Mead & White, administration building, National Institute of Arts and Letters/ American Academy of Arts and Letters, Audubon Terrace, 633 West 155th Street, 1923

Hispanic Society of America

OPPOSITE
Charles Pratt Huntington, Audubon Terrace Historic District, Broadway between West 155th and 156th Streets, 1908. Statue in foreground: Anna Hyatt Vaughn Huntington, *El Cid,* 1927

Like libraries, Harlem's unique museums at Audubon Terrace, which occupied the easternmost portion of Audubon Park along Broadway, were meant to transport their visitors. This was especially true of the interiors, where a baroque Spanish courtyard, an Iroquois longhouse, and a Renaissance library each had been carefully replicated. The American Numismatic Society (1907), the Hispanic Society of America (1908), the American Geographical Society (1911; now Boricua College), the Museum of the American Indian (1916; now moved to lower Manhattan and to Washington, D.C.), and the National Institute of Arts and Letters (1923) were all institutions that reflected the interests of patron Archer Milton Huntington.

Enormously rich by the time he was eleven, Archer Huntington was a sensitive and intelligent boy somewhat traumatized by family scandals. His adoptive father was in fact his birth father, and his mother married, as her second husband, her nephew, Archer's first cousin (the builder of the famed Huntington Library). Educated privately, Archer Huntington focused on Spain and Portugal, leading to his founding of the Hispanic Society in 1904. Abandoned by his socially prominent first wife, who ran away with a younger man, he was despondent until meeting sculptress Anna Hyatt

236

J. B. McElfatrick & Sons, Harlem
Opera House, 207 West 125th Street,
1889

J. B. McElfatrick & Sons, Columbus
Theatre (later Proctor's Theatre),
114 East 125th Street, c. 1891.
Reception, c. 1905

Vaughn, a middle-aged New Englander. The felicitous match brought Vaughn's programmatic, academic, and beautiful sculptures to Harlem; they were displayed in an incomparable formally landscaped court. Vaughn's pieces celebrate Iberian heritage and prepare the visitor for the Hispanic Society's art collection, which includes the work of both academically trained and folk artists of Hispanic origin. Humanly scaled despite the grandeur of their Beaux-Arts classical style, most of the complex's buildings were the work of Huntington's Paris-trained architect cousin, Charles Pratt Huntington. The administration building of the National Institute of Arts and Letters, however, was designed by William M. Kendall of McKim, Mead & White and finished in 1923; the auditorium and gallery, completed in 1930, were designed by Cass Gilbert.

The complex also includes one of the city's first Roman Catholic churches with a Spanish-American congregation. Our Lady of Esperanza at 624 West 156th Street was designed by Charles Huntington and completed in 1912; it was refaced by Lawrence G. White of McKim, Mead & White in 1925 in order to enclose the exterior staircase, thus eliminating the original high portico. Not only was the church notable for its harmonious gold and green decor, it was equally unusual in its distinguished donors. These included not only Roman Catholics—including King Alfonso XIII and millionaire Thomas Fortune Ryan—but distinguished Protestants as well, such as J. P. Morgan. Audubon Terrace represents a remarkable and generous effort at providing amenities for Harlemites while preserving a tiny portion of Audubon Park's open space; the building group was reoriented from its original northern outlook along an east-west axis when neighboring apartments blocked the view of the distant horizon. *Architectural Record* of January 30, 1913, praised the complex when it opened, stating that "outside of a university, this is educational centralization unique in America."

## Theaters, Opera Houses, and Ballrooms of Harlem

Another exponent by which Harlemites were encouraged to expand their horizons was local theaters. One of the earliest venues for the dramatic arts uptown was Harlem Hall, built in the 1870s; its distinctive dormers and end pavilions rose on East 125th Street just east of Fourth Avenue.

Impresario Oscar Hammerstein's 1,800-seat Harlem Opera House (1889), located at 207 West 125th Street and designed by one of the city's most productive nineteenth-century theater specialists, J. B. McElfatrick & Sons, was ornately embellished with arabesque panels and a hierarchy of pilasters; allegorical statuary surmounted its crowning parapet. Its interpretation of European architecture was as free as any Disney castle. About a year later, Hammerstein, not content with providing Harlem with one of the city's most pretentious facades, built another theater with the same architect, the Columbus at 114 East 125th Street. Far less assertive, the brick and brownstone structure is of uncertain stylistic derivation, aside from being somewhat Victorian. Both theaters were intended to launch the national tours of shows that had opened downtown; theatergoers could attend performances for a fraction of the downtown cost. Alas, this hardly justified Hammerstein's lavish expenditures, and by 1900 both theaters had been acquired by his rival F. F. Proctor.

McElfatrick's massive 1905 Manhattan Casino, at 2114 Seventh Avenue, was of contrasting brick and terra cotta; it was firmly grounded in neoclassical conventions and confidently planned. Shortly after completion the building reemerged as the Alhambra, where Ella Fitzgerald would one day sing. George Zucker's Harlem Casino (1889), a short distance away at 2081 Seventh Avenue, had a ballroom and private dining rooms available for rent. It was a whimsical rendition of a Venetian Gothic palace, with terra-cotta reliefs of putti-supported escutcheons and repeated pointed arches. Like the Alhambra, the Harlem Casino provided vaudeville entertainment; it also boasted the first uptown sidewalk café ever seen by the young Henry Roth:

How sumptuous, how decorous, the tubs and tubs, a whole row of wooden tubs with short evergreen trees in them . . . On the other side stood neat round tables covered with blue-and-white checkered cloth, and in the midst of each round table stood a trim, creamy vase with flowers in it. The blond bow-tied waiter, in his plum-striped jacket, lifted his head . . . He gave no sign of having caught sight of the trio of Jewish gamins . . . [We] dashed past him as he came out running.

Soon enough such frills would be eliminated in Harlem. The casino was remodeled by S. S. Sugar as a movie theater and renamed Loew's Seventh Avenue Theatre.

Billed as "Harlem's Exclusive $600,000 PhotoPlay House," Thomas W. Lamb's Regent Theatre (1913) at 1910 Seventh Avenue was inspired by the Doge's Palace in Venice. Clad in a copper-studded covering of terra cotta without and elaborately decorated within, the Regent was among the first specially constructed picture palaces in America. The Regent's proscenium was adorned with Romanian painter Jean Poleologne's *Surrender of Granada*, which may have been read as an instructive racial allegory: Ferdinand and Isabella receive the keys to the city, from which the black Moors and the Jews have just been driven. As at other theaters, African-Americans were routinely relegated to the balcony. A few years after construction, manager Samuel "Roxy" Rothafel, who would go on to the Roxy Theatre and Radio City Music Hall, radically transformed the interior with a new dome and other embellishments.

One of the world's most prolific and talented theater architects, Lamb went on to design for B. S. Moss the Hamilton Theatre (1913) at Broadway on the northeast corner of West 146th Street. This building of glistening white terra-cotta arches playfully utilizes a classical vocabulary, replete with Ziegfeld-girl-like caryatids. Lamb's Washington Theatre (1914) at 1801–1807 Amsterdam Avenue was more modestly made of tapestry brick and used comic and tragic masks as keystones. Here, the proscenium painting was an eighteenth-century pastoral scene; the fireproof asbestos stage curtain displayed Washington crossing the Delaware. Today the building is a church. The Adamesque Loew's Victoria Theatre (1918) at 235–237 West 125th Street was another of Lamb's notable achievements.

S. S. Sugar, Loew's Seventh Avenue Theatre (formerly Harlem Casino), 2081 Seventh Avenue, 1889

Thomas W. Lamb, Regent Theatre (now First Corinthian Baptist Church), 1910 Seventh Avenue, 1913

Most resplendent of all was Lamb's Audubon Theatre and Ballroom (1912) on the east side of Broadway between West 165th and 168th Streets. Yet another arcaded pleasure pavilion, it is graced with segmented arches made of polychrome glazed terra cotta. The entrance's relief of a Viking ship guided through rough seas by a naked Titan goddess is not as droll as the fox-

Thomas W. Lamb, Hamilton Theatre,
Broadway and West 146th Street,
1913

Thomas W. Lamb, Washington
Theatre (now a church), 1801–1807
Amsterdam Avenue, 1914

Thomas W. Lamb, Audubon Theatre
and Ballroom (now Mary Woodard
Lasker Biomedical Research Building),
Broadway between West 165th and
168th Streets, 1912. Alterations,
Perkins & Will and Bond Ryder James,
1990

OPPOSITE
Audubon Theatre and Ballroom.
Entrance with sculptural relief

head trophies positioned at the springing of each arch. The latter are a sly allusion to the builder of the Audubon, William "20th Century" Fox. A venue for Fanny Brice as well as for the Marx Brothers, who lived nearby, the Audubon is now best remembered as the place where Malcolm X was slain in 1965.

## The Business of Harlem

In 1896 the *New York Herald* announced, "It is the set ambition of New Yorkers above the Park to have a railroad station which will have every possible convenience, and they will not be satisfied until every fast train which goes by, including the Empire State Express, will halt to take aboard the man from Harlem." Accompanying the article was a drawing prepared by the New York Central's architect, Morgan O'Brien. When completed at Park Avenue and East 125th Street in 1897, the station was a fairly modest structure, which now appears quaint. The new facility did encourage increased commercial development in Harlem's primary shopping area, giving rise to several fine business buildings. (As usual in Harlem, no sooner had rumors surfaced of plans for the station than structures of unprecedented elaboration began to appear all around its eventual site.) George S. Drew Jr.'s Twelfth Ward Bank, built in 1893 at the northeast corner of Lexington Avenue and East 125th Street, was among the earliest. A brick and sandstone essay in the Richardsonian Romanesque mode, it was accompanied by a conspicuous wooden flagstaff mounted to a corner of the building with iron scrollwork, and cost a princely $80,000.

At twelve stories high, C. P. H. Gilbert's mixed-use structure for Charles Ward Hall (1901), at the northeast corner of East 125th Street and Park Avenue, was Harlem's highest office "tower" for over fifty years (see page 172). Opened just in time to take advantage of the new train station, it was placed directly opposite the former Mount Morris Bank/Morris Apartments, which had been bought by the Corn Exchange Bank. After it was completed, Gilbert's office tower was put on the market; combining retail at the street level with offices and a warehouse above, it sold for the elevated price of $311,000 to the Lee Brothers storage firm. Profusely ornamented with a sophisticated, arched entry, an iron balcony, and a series of festooned aegricanes at the first story, the building provided local concerns with especially elegant headquarters.

Equally chic but of only three stories, Charles B. Meyers's red brick and terra-cotta Marion Building (1904) still manages to dominate its West 125th Street site, on the southeast corner of Lenox Avenue. The building is self-assured, devised as a double-height arcade of elliptical arches atop a rusticated base. Meyers was later to design several important courthouses and public buildings; his main building of Yeshiva University (1928) at 2540 Amsterdam Avenue ranks as a masterpiece.

The Marion Building and others from this period present an extraordinary paradox. The turn of the century was a moment amid a building boom inspired by the long-hoped-for subway. Movers and shakers such as the Harlem Board of Commerce (with offices in the Marion Building), confidently optimistic about the area, were also aware of the very beginning of an influx of black residents. Hoping this pattern was an unfortunate anomaly, they came to view the erection of ever newer and more deluxe commercial buildings as an effective means of stemming the "invasion."

Journalistic reports provide tragic testimony of extreme attitudes. Newspapers routinely announced both growing cause for alarm in the face of the "Negro menace" and proposals to "stabilize" local real estate. "I advocate the organization of a property owners' realty company to take over

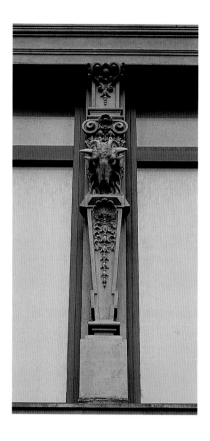

C. P. H. Gilbert, Lee Brothers building, 103 East 125th Street, 1901

OPPOSITE
Charles B. Meyers, Marion Building, 290 Lenox Avenue, 1904

244

JUNE—1912

15c. A COPY

# HARLEM MAGAZINE

OFFICIAL ORGAN OF THE  HARLEM BOARD OF COMMERCE

the property now occupied by Negroes, or in danger of being taken over by them, to renovate it and put white tenants in. I am sure . . . that if the tenants are white and not colored, it will immediately raise the value of the property," insisted one local businessman at a 1912 meeting covered by *Harlem Home News.* Another concerned citizen at the same meeting, Henry Holding of 111 West 130th Street, was reported to have "bitterly assailed the Negroes and denounced their immorality and shiftlessness . . . The Negroes are Negroes and that's all there is to it . . . Their mode of living is not the same as ours, and the two races cannot live together in peace." Holding is reported to have shouted "Drive them out!" while the audience applauded: "Drive them out and send them to the slums where they belong, and don't let them turn our beautiful Harlem into a cheap settlement district."

B. Hustace Simonson's buff brick and terra-cotta Park & Tilford store and office complex (1907) at 314–316 Lenox Avenue figures prominently in the movement to keep Harlem white and middle class through better buildings. Park & Tilford was one of New York's most prestigious purveyors of fine spirits, choice groceries, and tobacco. Simonson had emerged at the forefront of designers who specialized in planning duplex apartments, such as the Central Park Studios (1906) on West 67th Street, and he was quite capable of appealing to elite taste. His fashionable reserve is well represented by the Park & Tilford building, a chaste neoclassical work. Ionic pilasters on the upper floors correspond to the ground story's Ionic piers and engaged columns. Only the entrance to the offices was permitted any decorative flourish—a flowery garland.

This was the subdued, marble-countered and polished-brass environment where the rich of Harlem shopped and teenage Henry Roth worked. Delivering groceries throughout the neighborhood, Roth observed that Harlem was a divided community: white gentiles primarily shopped on 125th Street;

Jews on 116th Street; and African-Americans on 135th Street. Roth appreciated all too well that there were many places where he, a Jew, was no more welcome than were blacks. Faced with an increasingly poor and black presence and hard hit by the enactment of Prohibition, Park & Tilford closed its doors in 1919.

Perhaps no other edifice from this period of transition better exemplifies the threatened exclusivity of Harlem than the tall and shining white-glazed-brick and terra-cotta Hotel Theresa (1913) at 2090 Seventh Avenue, built by Gustavus Sidenberg, a lace dealer who named the hotel for his late wife before marrying another Theresa. Heralded as a triumphant testament to Harlem's arrival, it is a singular work by the firm of George and Edward Blum. It has all the quiet assurance of Park & Tilford and even employs the same combination of materials. But it also has something extra: it was the tallest Harlem structure of its day, retaining that distinction until 1973, when the Adam Clayton Powell Jr. State Office Building was erected. More fundamental to its considerable visual impact than mere height, however, was the Blums' forward-looking system of geometric ornament. Repeated motifs, including formalized flowers and vines, crisscross the facade in a diapered network. Such personalized decorations, which included a recurrent HT monogram, were influenced by cutting-edge French architecture and were applied to every element, from the wrought-iron balconies at the first and top floors to the windows. The designers' stylized sunrise symbolized the builder's hope for all the good things modernity was still to bring to Harlem.

## The Sun Goes Down on Harlem

For the poor and the African-American in Harlem, however, this embellishment of the Hotel Theresa was rather to represent the sunset of their hopes and aspirations as Harlemites. Sidenberg was to maintain a strict policy that excluded blacks, except as servants. Not until 1937, nearly twenty years after blacks came to dominate the population of Harlem, was this discriminatory policy rescinded. By then, the home away from home of Joe Louis, Lena Horne, Josephine Baker, and

Neville & Bagge, Hotel Olga (formerly North End Hotel), 695 Lenox Avenue, 1902

Georgi's River View Hotel, between West 149th and 150th Streets above the Harlem River, c. 1845

Fidel Castro was black-owned. Malcolm X would found the Organization of Afro-American Unity in the top floor's double-height dining room; with the Theresa as his backdrop, presidential aspirant Senator John F. Kennedy would ask Harlem blacks for their support.

Before 1937, according to an article in the January 1925 issue of *The Messenger*, a left-wing journal cofounded in 1920 by A. Philip Randolph, leader of the nation's first black labor union, the Brotherhood of Sleeping Car Porters, the best Harlem hostelry open to African-Americans was Edward H. Wilson's Hotel Olga (1902). It stood at the southwest corner of Lenox Avenue and West 145th Street and occupied the old North End Hotel, which had been built by brewer Jacob Rupert in anticipation of the subway to a design by Neville & Bagge. The Olga had limited accommodations on just two levels: in this regard it resembled a far earlier Harlem home for travelers, Georgi's River View Hotel of the 1840s, perched high above the Harlem River between West 149th and 150th Streets. A shuttered clapboard structure with a cupola, roof balustrade, and two porches, the River View Hotel was prepared to receive trotting-horse racers as well as Harlem railroad and steamboat passengers. Despite the fact that the Olga was so constricted, it was the habitual destination of Nancy Cunard, who in 1935 published the monumental anthology *Negro*, as well as of Howard University department head Alain Locke, godfather of the Harlem Renaissance.

It was not only theaters and hotels that discriminated against blacks. Harlem's finer stores, like Blumstein's Department Store (1923) at 230 West 125th Street, looked askance at African-

American customers. Blumstein's was designed by Robert D. Kohn, and its elegance, complete with Spanish baroque columned bronze window enframements, was intended to attract equally elegant patrons. Blacks, no matter how accomplished, cultivated, or well-to-do, could not, in the eyes of many white store owners, restaurateurs, and landlords, be so regarded; they could not even be considered as employees. Many "better" shops, such as J. M. Horton's ice cream parlor at 142 West 125th Street, designed by Edward Rodler and newly remodeled and improved with Austrian crystal chandeliers and stained-glass lamps as recently as 1913, went out of business rather than cater to black residents.

Not surprisingly, even African-Americans who were skeptical about Marcus Garvey's pan-African movement appreciated his efforts exhorting them to "buy black." Despite Harlem's evolution as the cultural capital of black America, comparatively little property has ever actually been owned by blacks. Nevertheless, exceptional black institutions and businesses arose. Most occupied existing structures adapted to new uses. Jardine, Kent & Jardine's enchanting Equitable Life Insurance Company office of 1893 at 252 West 138th Street, featuring Byzantine plate tracery and limestone Romanesque arches, was in 1923 adapted by Vertner Woodson Tandy for the hall of the Coachmen's Union League, a combination labor union and fraternal organization established in 1864. It is now Victory Tabernacle Church.

Harlem's pioneer black settlers were a positive and forward-looking group, as evidenced by the astonishingly ambitious million-dollar New Negro Social Center announced in the *Real Estate Record and Builders' Guide* in 1918. This plan called for a new facility on the site of the former Watt-Pinckney pasture, the southeast corner of Seventh Avenue and West 138th Street. Designed by architect Arne Delhi, a native of Norway, the project accommodated a roof garden, 160-by-50-foot swimming pool, restaurant, banquet hall, bank, dance hall, barber shop, Turkish baths, bowling alley, and billiard room. The center looked very much like three theaters of the size and style of J. B. McElfatrick & Sons' Alhambra strung together. The identity of the builders, listed as the Van-Astor Company, Inc., and presided over by William H. Butler, remains a mystery.

Delhi's plans did not take shape, but the concept, on a much smaller scale, was realized in 1921 by Harry Creighton Ingalls in his design for the Renaissance Casino at 2359 Seventh Avenue, between West 137th and 138th Streets. With its shops, stores, restaurants, theater, and ballroom (added in 1923), the casino may have lacked some of the amenities envisioned in the earlier project, but until 1930 it was owned by Afro-Caribbean immigrants, members of the Universal Negro Improvement Association founded by Marcus Garvey. Decorated with a frieze of brilliant tiles, the casino was an accomplished work that replaced Mamie Smith's open-air dance hall, designed in 1919 by Vertner Tandy. With a canvas canopy, the building at night resembled not the Alhambra but a sort of gigantic lampshade.

Such buildings, built by black owners or planned by black architects, were exceedingly rare. Moreover, for the most part the requirements of African-Americans flocking to turn-of-the-century Harlem were at odds with those of many existing deluxe shops, such as Park & Tilford or Horton's ice cream parlor. An influx of residents, generally much poorer than those preceding them, triggered the widespread conversion of single-family row houses into apartments and rooming houses. It also accelerated the subway-inspired proliferation of commercial enterprises on what had once been exclusively residential streets. One existing facility where African-Americans were welcomed, at least as patrons and on segregated Negro League teams, was the Polo Grounds sports stadium at West 157th Street and the Harlem River. Designed by Henry B.

Jardine, Kent & Jardine, Equitable Life Insurance Company (now the Victory Tabernacle Church), 252 West 138th Street, 1893

Herts, it opened in 1911. Highly embellished, with ornate neoclassical stamped sheet metal, the New York Giants, Yankees, and Mets all played here. So did the Howard and Lincoln University football teams—and in time, Hank Thompson and Willie Mays. Like so many other Harlem landmarks, it was removed in 1964 without leaving even a fragment.

From 1910 to 1920, a new economic imperative was at work in Harlem, one in which a less affluent population of necessity occupied both living quarters and workplaces divided and even subdivided into smaller and smaller units. Typically the high stoops of old-fashioned former town houses were removed in favor of new street-level entrances, while windows on the ground and first floors were reconfigured into larger plate-glass openings meant for retail display. Commercial conversions such as these—groceries, shops, funeral parlors, offices, small "storefront" churches—helped to keep small black architectural practices like Vertner Tandy's afloat. But normal wear and tear was greatly exacerbated by Harlem's overcrowding and relative poverty. Due to bias-generated economic inequality, the worst fears of Harlem's white defenders came to pass. Their prophecy of decline into a "settlement district" was as swift as it was self-fulfilling.

The visitor or resident of Harlem today will witness the appalling state of old buildings on 125th Street, many of which have upper floors that have been deliberately kept vacant for years. Absentee owners find a tax loss more profitable and trouble-free than routine maintenance. Moreover, the advent of wraparound nylon signs provides owners with unexpected revenue. Stretching across as many as three levels of blocked windows, the signs transform these often largely empty structures into ungainly and unattractive billboards.

Walking past such streetscapes, it is possible to feel that nothing has changed since 1962, when James Baldwin published his novel *Another Country*. Describing a walk made by his lead characters, he wrote:

> They had come out on Lenox Avenue, though their destination was on Seventh; and nothing they passed was unfamiliar because everything they passed was wretched. It was not hard to imagine that horse carriages had once paraded proudly up this wide avenue and ladies and gentlemen, beribboned, beflowered, brocaded, plumed, had stepped down from their carriages to enter these houses which time and folly had so blasted and darkened. The cornices had once been new, had once gleamed as brightly as now they sulked in shame, all tarnished and despised. The windows had not always been blind. The doors had not always brought to mind the distrust and secrecy of a city long besieged. At one time people had cared about these houses—that was the difference; they had been proud to walk on the Avenue; it had once been home, whereas now it was prison.

# THE EVOLUTION OF A COMMUNITY

Top left to bottom right: Alfred and Katherine Williams; Barry Bergdoll and William Ryall; Josephine Ebaugh Jones; Bethany and Alexa Donaphin; Valerie Jo Bradley; Margaret Anderson; Marvin P. Smith; Martha Dolly; Grace Williams; Beth Venn and Thomas Draplin with Ella and Owen Draplin; Lana Turner; Robert Van Lierop; Peggy Shephard and Charles Lovejoy; J.-L. Osei Mevs, Dr. Jeanne Adair, and Dr. Thelma Adair

How compelling, enduring, and vigorous is the legend of Harlem. Well before the hopelessness James Baldwin wrote of, another Harlem existed. Before the protracted decline of the area, witnessed by inhabitants who saw no means of arresting the transformation of their cherished homes into places unfamiliar and unlovely, a brighter community thrived. It was filled with optimistic newcomers from downtown New York, the rural South of the United States, and the islands of the Caribbean. They rejoiced at the new opportunities for better housing as economic depression drove down Harlem real-estate prices.

At first, about 1906, Negro Harlem was confined to a few blocks north and south of West 135th Street between Fifth and Eighth Avenues. It was here that speculative developers had enjoyed a spree of building, buying, and selling in the previous decade, expecting to become millionaires overnight by erecting apartment houses near the subway. After the Panic of 1904–7, no eager renters materialized. Owners slashed rents heavily, but to no avail.

Philip Payton, a black New Englander, saw possibilities for the formation of a black district in Harlem. He noted that New York's blacks, confined to streets in the west thirties through the west sixties in the Tenderloin, Hell's Kitchen, and San Juan Hill areas, were slowly being displaced by development that included the theater district, Macy's, Gimbel's, the U.S. Post Office, Pennsylvania Station, and the Hotel Pennsylvania. A custodian for white real-estate brokers, Payton envisioned a new black community with fine housing, majestic churches, and good schools. His employers were skeptical—at first. But soon enough it was shown that blacks, who had an average income of only $800 yearly, versus the $2,500 earned by whites, would pay a premium to occupy such an attractive and previously unimaginable environment.

Between 1906 and the beginning of the 1920s, Harlem became the largest settlement of black people in the world. They occupied more well-maintained buildings of greater architectural distinction, comfort, and convenience than at any previous time in the history of the United States.

255

Within this "city within a city," a new African-American leadership emerged, outstanding black professionals dubbed the "talented tenth" by W. E. B. Du Bois. Many insisted that a new epoch was at hand—an era receptive to and encouraging of the artistic and academic attainment of the "New Negro."

The extent to which Harlem between the wars became the nation's—perhaps the world's—capital of diversion is well documented in books by Ted Fox, Jervis Anderson, Steven Watson, and many other historians of its celebrated entertainment venues and cultural lore. Black Harlem's economic well-being was undergirded by its nightlife. In such clubs as Small's Paradise, the Savoy Ballroom, the gangster-controlled Cotton Club, and Connie's Inn, visitors set about "giving their morality a vacation," as local clergymen bitterly complained.

The phenomenon referred to as the Harlem Renaissance, which occurred during this same period, was a cultural manifestation far less exploitative or frivolous. Backdrop to the careers of such Harlem legends as Duke Ellington, Langston Hughes, and Zora Neale Hurston, this artistic movement helped to set in motion the current acknowledgment of African-American culture as a basis of American culture as significant as any European or classical antecedents.

## Take the A Train: Life on Sugar Hill

Toward the end of the nineteenth century, European—primarily Irish—immigrants had gazed longingly from the Harlem Valley toward what was known by first Dutch and later English settlers as Harlem Heights. In about 1870 it was dubbed Washington Heights, both to commemorate Revolutionary War battles and to set it apart from the neighborhoods where these impoverished and working-class people lived. When blacks began to move into the area after about 1920, the area became known as "Sugar Hill," the place where life is sweetened by piles of "sugar"—money.

African-Americans, told that Charles Buek's Astor Row or David H. King Jr.'s model-house neighborhoods were "too good for the likes of them," only desired these exclusive sections all the more. With the Panic of 1893, King was foreclosed by his backer, the Equitable Life Insurance Company, which kept houses vacant rather than let them to blacks. The diligent striving of black homeowners toward an elite address in the King houses section brought the appellation "Strivers' Row" into being. The neighborhood that came to be known as Sugar Hill was thought choicest of all. Small at first, it sat opposite the rocky promontory of St. Nicholas Park, crowned by City College's Shepard Hall. The buildings at 80 and 90 Edgecombe Avenue, designed by Gronenberg & Leuchtag and completed in 1915, are the neighbors of handsome late-nineteenth-century row houses and, in terms of the people who have lived there, have an unequaled historic resonance. When A'Lelia Walker moved out of her mother's West 136th Street mansion in the early 1920s, seeking a more private life, it was in the "unremarkable" 80 Edgecombe Avenue that she established her new, luxurious, but quite small residence. The fact that blacks had previously been barred from the building only made it more irresistible. Relatively new, it boasted steam heat and private baths, electric lights, a doorman, and porters. Walker's one-bedroom suite, decorated by Paul Frankel, was the setting for what must have been some memorable exchanges between blacks and whites in the Roaring Twenties. Princess Violette Murat, Lord and Lady Louis Mountbatten, the crown prince of Sweden, Tallulah Bankhead, Countée Cullen, and many other luminaries met here over glasses of vintage champagne and bootleg cocktails and plates of spaghetti, pigs' feet, and caviar.

As for number 90, at the time when Harlem was the center of the universe, this unlikely building was the heart of that center. It was here that Jules Bledsoe—a Columbia medical student who went on to become a singer, starring as Joe in the premiere of *Showboat*—lived as a boarder. Stardom arrived just as a much grander Edgecombe address opened to African-Americans: in 1927 Bledsoe was one of the first blacks to inhabit Schwartz & Gross's towering Colonial Parkway Apartments (1916) at 409 Edgecombe Avenue. Civil-rights activist Walter White also moved from 90 Edgecombe Avenue; he was joined by W. E. B. Du Bois, Thurgood Marshall, and a host of other famous Harlemites. With spectacular views over the Polo Grounds, Long Island Sound, and Yankee Stadium, it quickly became Sugar Hill's most desired address. By 1940, the former servants' cubicles on the top floor were converted to penthouse apartments, as was the case at the firm's Roger Morris Apartments (1916), at 555 Edgecombe Avenue. In 1939 the latter building—"the home of the Triple Nickel"—became an equally sought-after accommodation, boasting residents such as Paul Robeson, actor Canada Lee, and other leaders of New York's African-American community. In the 1930s, 409 Edgecombe Avenue was purchased by an African-American. Augustine Austin, from the West Indies, acquired number 409 just before he bought 270 Convent Avenue in 1939. Considering that Austin had arrived in New York penniless, this was an extraordinary feat. Shortly afterward, the Roger Morris also became black-owned, when it was purchased by the colorful evangelist "Daddy Grace."

Harlem's first black cooperative building was a 1917 conversion by Philip Payton on West 141st Street. But it was the Garrison Apartments at 435 Convent Avenue that came to be known as the first black cooperative; designed by Neville & Bagge and built in 1910 as Elmsworth Hall, the building opened to blacks as a cooperative in 1929, the same year another black cooperative was opened at Gronenberg & Leuchtag's 1890 Seventh Avenue (1914).

The decline of Harlem—and the reasons for that decline—has been written about extensively, but perhaps no account is as well crafted as the final chapter of David Levering Lewis's *When Harlem Was in Vogue*, unflinchingly titled "It's Dead Now." By the end of World War II, following the example of Jews who throughout the Great Depression had successfully challenged discriminatory covenants, affluent blacks began to abandon Harlem and move to "suburban Sugar Hills."

From the 1930s onward, the combined impact of the Depression and racist attitudes saw property values plummet, particularly for row houses. By the 1940s, it was possible for a house as capacious as developer William A. Martin's 4 West 122nd Street, designed by William Tuthill, to be acquired for as little as $7,500—half of its original 1889 projected price (and just a tiny fraction of its current estimated value, which is in excess of $800,000). Because the incomes of most blacks during this period still lagged far behind those of whites, only a few Harlem residents could afford to take advantage of such "bargains." As of 1940, fewer than a thousand black New Yorkers owned their own house or apartment. Paradoxically, African-American ownership in Harlem is still the exception rather than the rule.

Yet if today Harlem's cultural life leaves much to be desired and developed, there is a decided impetus for revival in the ironic form of an influx of foreign tourists. Along with bargain-hunting prospective residents, they seek the legend of Harlem, visiting churches that have become world-famous for their choirs and hunting for space and stylish surroundings on an impossibly congested island. Encouraged in their uptown treks by the establishment of multinational chain stores, such as Disney, Starbucks Coffee, and Old Navy, some observers are convinced that a total transformation—of the sort that made fashionable enclaves of West Hollywood, Georgetown, South Boston, and Park Slope—cannot be far off.

This is the neo-Renaissance vision of Harlem. Extolled by real-estate brokers, it was foreseen long ago by James Weldon Johnson, who in his unsurpassed 1930 history, *Black Manhattan*, wrote that "it is probable that land through the heart of Harlem will someday so increase in value that Negroes may not be able to hold it." For many long-term, old-time Harlemites, the pressures to sell out and move on are great: at the Grinnell, at 800 Riverside Drive, a handsomely restored five-bedroom apartment—with two and a half baths, a large living room, dining room, entry, and kitchen—that rented for less than $1,000 monthly as late as 1985 sold in 2000 for $850,000, setting a record for real-estate sales in Harlem.

## Preservationists at Home in Harlem

Today numerous residents, both old-timers and newcomers, maintain, restore, and sometimes even improve the district's irreplaceable legacy of superlative buildings. Whether they realize it or not, these owners are preservationists, determined to safeguard Harlem's extraordinary architectural heritage, one that lacks landmark protection commensurate with either its inherent value or the comparative worth of buildings that have been landmarked elsewhere in Manhattan. A unique perspective that speaks of Harlem life in the present arises from the examination of a number of these historic homes from the inside out with those who now own, love, and care for them. They know best the history of a community's sacrifice and commitment, a history to which their homes bear vibrant testament.

### MARTHA DOLLY: 4 WEST 122ND STREET

Haitian-born Martha Chandler Dolly, the current owner of 4 West 122nd Street (see pages 136, 141), is such a figure. The family of her late husband, Harold Dolly, purchased the row house, designed by William Tuthill for William A. Martin and completed in 1889, in 1943. Harold Dolly's father, Dr. Cyril Harold Dolly, arrived in New York from Port-of-Spain in 1922; prior to leaving Trinidad he had worked as the manager of a furniture company, a position that instilled in him an appreciation for fine craftsmanship. Earning a bachelor of science degree from Columbia University in 1927, he went on to receive a medical degree from Bellevue Hospital Medical College. He maintained a private practice, was a physician at Harlem Hospital, and acted as physician to famed evangelist Father Devine's "peace mission" in the former Harlem Club building.

Wedding of Harold and Martha Dolly, 1957

Martha Dolly recalls that her mother-in-law, Ida Roslyn Eligon Dolly, was at first unappreciative of the quality of the splendidly outfitted residence, and two mahogany mantelpieces were discarded before her husband intervened. The preservation activities of Harold, the Dollys' older son, culminated in his leading the effort to landmark the Mount Morris Park Historic District in 1971. While Martha Dolly's work as a preservationist has been somewhat overshadowed by her late husband's, she is widely recognized throughout the surrounding community as "the star that shines over Mount Morris Park." Her low-profile work is carried out as a member of numerous local organizations. She was first inspired to act when, in the 1950s, as a graduate nursing student at Columbia, she went on a tour of what was described as having been an "obsolete, ill-equipped public school" (now condominiums). This was P.S. 157, on the west side of St. Nicholas Avenue between West 127th and 128th Streets, designed by C. B. J. Snyder and finished in 1899. "It is such a handsome building . . . The stairs were marble with wrought-iron balustrades and polished brass railings," Dolly recalled. She felt keenly its devaluation and remembers thinking, "In Haiti, what a fine national school of nursing this would make."

**THE REVEREND EUGENE AND THELMA ADAIR: 10 WEST 122ND STREET**

Determined to reopen the abandoned 1905 Harlem–New York Presbyterian Church designed by Thomas H. Poole, which faces Mount Morris Park, the late Reverend Eugene Adair related some of the hardships that he and his family endured in the February 25, 1967, issue of the *New Yorker:*

> My son, who is now in medical school, slept in a Rinso carton . . . We went out on the street on Thanksgiving Day and got people to help. Some gave bricks, some gave labor, and we got the job done on a shoestring. We nursed this building through thick and thin, and somehow in the meantime I got my Master's degree . . . I forgot about going back to Chester [South Carolina].

Dr. Adair's wife, Thelma, is a retired professor of education and a National Presbyterian Church presiding elder. The couple raised a family and in 1966 acquired William Tuthill's 10 West 122nd Street (see pages 137, 153) for $26,000. The former home of a retired judge, a white resident who had remained on the block until the sale, the row house retained original furnishings and decor but lacked electric lighting. Dr. Adair meticulously restored rare features such as elaborate gasoliers and the kitchen's working woodstove. Today his daughter Jeanne and her sons share the house and, along with Thelma Adair, carry on the "Rev's" work, the restoration of both the church and their heirloom home.

**JOSEPHINE EBAUGH JONES: 137 WEST 122ND STREET**

Hailing from a small Southern town replete with cotton mills and a feudal dynasty (the Shell family of Gray Court, South Carolina), "Jo" has been a resident of Harlem since 1941. She has embarked on an ambitious project that people half her age would find daunting—restoration of Francis H. Kimball's 1887 Mrs. Charles D. Gambrill house, at 137 West 122nd Street (see pages 108, 135), to its original splendor. A single parent, she worked at two jobs in order to raise and educate her daughter, Wendy Diana Jones, an award-winning author and English professor. "If anyone can rescue this incomparable landmark," Wendy says, "Mama can." Jo Jones loves her home in Harlem:

> When I arrived here there was the Hotel Theresa; it was a lovely place . . . You should have seen my Harlem. Clean, it was as clean as a pin. You could have eaten off of the streets. Men going to work in the morning on the subway, they might have only been elevator operators or workmen, but you'd have never known. They wore suits and ties and their shoes were shined. Maids were just the same. I put on a hat and gloves to post a letter.
>
> It started to change after the blackout . . . 1977—that was it. It seemed as if the people just went crazy! They had trucks ready to crash through store windows. They looted and burned, and police sirens wailed all night long. Decent folks were afraid to come outside of their homes. By then the Theresa had closed as a hotel and had been turned into a residence for old people. There was still a liquor store on the corner, though. All the liquor stores were robbed first. When the next day came, it was over and my Harlem was never the same place again.
>
> One of the reasons that I have this house today is because of a promise that I made to myself back when I was just a little girl. Our place was down by the river, just on the outside of town. Up on the hill above us the Shells' Victorian mansion stood empty. Old Mrs. Shell was widowed and went

to live with her son. The homestead was too big for her. We were crowded in our little cabin. Although allowed to play up there in all twenty rooms, we couldn't live in the Shells' house—it was considered too good a place for colored to live in. I vowed one day to live in my own mansion.

## GRACE WILLIAMS: 118 WEST 120TH STREET

Nothing about the limestone Richardsonian Romanesque facade designed by Neville & Bagge and completed in 1893 prepares the visitor for the unrestrained splendor found on the interior of 118 West 120th Street. Here is an Aladdin's cave of glistening bits of beaded stuff, mirrored mosaics, flowers, lengths of tulle, swathes of silk, and spangles. Shell-encrusted chairs are emblazoned with African images, dolls move unexpectedly, and exotic fragrance and the cooing

of doves appeal to the senses. This rarefied environment is the life work of artist Grace Williams, who is the third generation of her family to live on West 120th Street. It is easy to forget that at the turn of the century the house was occupied by Mr. and Mrs. Joseph Guttenberg (see page 147). In 1902 they celebrated their golden wedding anniversary in the dining room; although it retains many of its original details, the room is nevertheless utterly changed, much as a caterpillar metamorphoses into a butterfly.

## KATHERINE AND ALFRED WILLIAMS: 414 WEST 149TH STREET

Embowered with roses and wisteria, Katherine and Alfred Williams's garden at 414 West 149th Street is also unexpected. It is a city retreat that is wonderfully situated to take in a view of neighboring gardens in an effortless survey. The house, one of a group designed by Christian Steinmetz and completed in 1893, is today a sunny, inviting space, partly because the kitchen was moved into the old pantry and the old kitchen was converted into a dining room. Decorative pieces include custom leaded-glass cabinets, whimsical Sears oak sideboards, and

Neville & Bagge, Mr. and Mrs. Joseph Guttenberg house (now Grace Williams house), 118 West 120th Street, 1893. Parlor

other antiques. On the parlor floor, the former dining room has become the master bedroom; it has a view of the gardens below. Close at hand, a modern movement African-inspired cupboard, designed by Harlem architect Jack Travis, conceals a miniature kitchen—perfect for midnight feasts and parties. The first residents of the house were the family of local real-estate developer Peter J. McCoy. In the 1930s, when the area came to be known as Sugar Hill, number 414 stood directly across from the community's most prestigious institution, the Cosmopolitan Tennis Club at 433 Convent Avenue. Althea Gibson, the international champion and first African-American to compete (and win) at Wimbledon, was a member, as were Mr. and Mrs. Walter White. The courts, replaced in the 1950s by an apartment building, were first laid out in the 1890s for the New York Tennis Club, which later became the Heights Club and then moved to Forest Hills in Queens.

Christian Steinmetz, Peter J. McCoy house (now Katherine and Alfred Williams house), 414 West 149th Street, 1893. Parlor

Peter J. McCoy house (now Katherine and Alfred Williams house). Kitchen (now dining room)

Warren C. Dickerson, Columbia Flats
(Margaret Anderson apartment), 3–5
West 122nd Street, 1901. Entrance

OPPOSITE
Columbia Flats (Margaret Anderson
apartment). Parlor

## MARGARET ANDERSON: 3–5 WEST 122ND STREET

In an upscale development such as Mount Morris Park, every attempt was made to provide the
same spaciousness, fine materials, and careful ornamentation in apartments as was found in area
houses. Erected in 1901, Columbia Flats was designed by Warren C. Dickerson. Originally,
the six-story structure at 3–5 West 122nd Street had just two apartments per floor. Even though
these suites were divided in half during World War II when the building was renamed the Palm
Trees Apartments, they are still quite expansive by current standards—which is apparent in
Margaret Anderson's home. The lobby's onyx wainscoting and tile mosaic floor are a fitting
prelude to the actor's Victorian country retreat in the midst of the city. Quaint floral chintz covers
an overstuffed sofa, oak floors are covered here and there by rag rugs, Bradbury & Bradbury
wallpapers enrich the entrance hallway, and Anderson's own stained-glass designs grace the
transoms and foyer entrance door.

THIS IS MY
WISH
FOR YOU

C. P. H. Gilbert, 458 West 152nd Street (now George Goodwill house), 1889. Sitting room

458 West 152nd Street (now George Goodwill house). Bedroom

## Collectors in Harlem

### MARVIN P. SMITH, GEORGE GOODWILL, VALERIE JO BRADLEY, ALEXA AND BETHANY DONAPHIN, ANN AND DALE DOBSON

Marvin P. Smith is a living landmark of Harlem; through his person he conveys much of the spirit of community that will, if it can be done, preserve Harlem's architectural legacy. He lives in a nondescript tower on Riverside Drive at West 139th Street where he has created an environment that is as much a self-portrait as Grace Williams's unusual surroundings are. He and his twin brother, Morgan, were born to sharecroppers in Nicholasville, a few miles south of Lexington, Kentucky, in 1910. Their artistic gifts were readily apparent, and they realized early on that their opportunities to cultivate such talents in the South would be limited. In 1933 they came to Harlem. Emerging from the subway at West 135th Street, they marveled that this bustling metropolis could be the province of blacks and immediately fell in with the artistic community around them, becoming students of sculptor Augusta Savage. Working as gardeners in Central and Mount Morris Parks, they began to photograph what they saw and soon were able to support themselves as freelance photographers. By 1940, they opened a photography studio at West 125th Street next to the Apollo Theatre. A year later "Marvelous Marvin" joined the Navy and afterward went to Paris on the G.I. Bill, where he and Romare Bearden studied with Fernand Léger. After Marvin returned, the brothers continued to photograph the people of Harlem and beyond: Nat King Cole dancing at his wedding, Josephine Baker handing out candy to children, and Adam Clayton Powell Jr. at his marriage to Hazel Scott in 1945.

Number 458 West 152nd Street was designed by C. P. H. Gilbert as part of a row of three houses in the Queen Anne style; it was completed in 1889 and was originally owned by a ship's chandler. The current owner, George Goodwill, is a retired administrator at Harlem Hospital. He now fills his time with community service; he is also the chairman of Community Planning Board 9 and a trustee of St. Mary's Center (the AIDS hospice run by St. Mary's Church–Manhattanville). An advocate of local historic preservation, Goodwill is a masterful cook and renowned host, with a remarkable collection of Victoriana and African and African-American

George and Edward Blum, Beaumont (Ann and Dale Dobson apartment), 730 Riverside Drive, 1912. Living room

antiques and artworks that is proudly displayed—even in the midst of an extensive renovation. He notes, "I demolished partitions myself. They had made this into a rooming house for eighteen people. I painted all the walls downstairs and put up pictures—even though I knew I'd have to replaster eventually." In the late 1990s, his extensive renovation efforts were undone by termites; all of the main floors and joists had to be replaced.

Valerie Jo Bradley, the director of the Mount Morris Park Community Improvement Association, lives at 144 West 120th Street in a brownstone designed by Andrew Spence (see page 133). Completed in 1887, it was originally owned by Thomas Jacke. Bradley's collections include not only works by Romare Bearden but an 1890s mahogany parlor suite with needlework upholstery.

Architect Alexa Donaphin was drawn to her house at 464 West 144th Street (see pages 94, 124, 126) by the need to accommodate her grandmother's rather large quartered oak suite of dining room furniture. She and her daughter, Bethany, live in one of the incomparable row houses designed by William Mowbray and built by developer William H. De Forest Jr. in 1890. The purchase price of the house included an American Empire sideboard, also oversized, which now dominates a corner of the upstairs sitting room. "The woman who sold us the house was only the third owner. There was no electricity, and she apologized the night we moved in because the men she had hired to bring an ax and 'break up' the sideboard, as well as a Steinway parlor-grand piano, hadn't yet arrived!" recalls Donaphin. A less welcome discovery was a three-foot-long poisonous snake; a specialist at the Bronx Zoo said it might have been living undisturbed in the butlers' pantry cabinetry (now kitchen cabinets) for decades.

Ann Fonteneau Dobson and her daughter Dale Leslie Dobson evidence a shared measure of preservationist zeal in their attempts, assisted by decorator twins Joan and Jane Michaels of English & Michaels, Inc., to reclaim the glory of their top-floor home in the Beaumont (1912) at 730 Riverside Drive, designed by George and Edward Blum (see pages 176, 177). The chair of the rental building's tenants' association, Dale Dobson has spearheaded the reinstatement of the lobby's original finishes. It has been more difficult to persuade the Landmarks Commission to grant landmark designation to this remarkable structure.

265

## Harlem's Hopeful Future

From the historic homes of eighteenth-century American aristocrats to the contemporary enigma of parquet floors and attack dogs, Harlem advances as a site of extraordinary, almost unbelievable transformation. It has changed and it is changing still; very little remains static, except the many happy instances in which old buildings, representing the best of the past, extend a high level of living even to ordinary people. A firm believer in this principle of the accessibility of good architecture is Lana Turner, a graduate of the Lydia F. Wadleigh School and Sarah Lawrence College, who shares a birthday with her film-star namesake. A realtor, Turner states that she is selective in accepting clients from among the many people now interested in Harlem real estate; her criteria is "a sense that I'm helping people who will love Harlem as much as I do."

Frank H. Norton, 270 Convent Avenue
(Lana Turner apartment), 1915

Among this group are long-term residents Robert Van Lierop, who lives at 411 West 148th Street and has his law practice at 420 West 143rd Street (see pages 128, 144–46), and Peggy Shephard and Charles Lovejoy, who live at 465 West 140th Street (see page 131). Newcomers include the family of Beth Venn and Thomas Draplin. The independent curator and commercial illustrator enjoy an authentically detailed space on Hamilton Terrace, which they share with their two children.

### BARRY BERGDOLL AND WILLIAM RYALL: 358 WEST 118TH STREET

A professor of architectural history at Columbia University and author of several acclaimed monographs, Barry Bergdoll knows as well as anyone that it is possible to restore virtually any ruin to pristine authenticity. He is also aware of the cost of such propositions. When architect William Ryall first encountered their 1888 house, designed by William H. Boylan, it was in an advanced state of disrepair. He and Bergdoll had yet to meet, and Ryall began reconstructing a new house within the empty shell of the old one.

"It was an enlightening process," Ryall recalls. "Once the rotten wood and crumbling plaster were cleared away, it was possible to discover all sorts of interesting clues concerning Victorian construction techniques that I had never been taught about at architecture school." For example, a somewhat diminutive blocked archway stands in the painted brick of a party wall. When modern residents discover such arches they soon tell tales of the adjacent house being owned by the sister or parents of the original occupant of their own house. "They are in each house in this row, on every floor," Ryall explains. "They were openings that the workmen constructing the houses used, sealing them when they finished their work." The serene and restful decor of Bergdoll and Ryall's house has been a collaborative effort, as has the small secluded garden, where candytuft grows in the crevices of stone steps. Fruit trees blossom in the spring, showering the emerald patch of grass with a scattering of petals.

Before the Harlem of despair, there was a Harlem of James Baldwin's gleaming cornices, shining windows, and open doors. Earlier still, Harlem was a concentration of extraordinary architecture created for ordinary people by both world-renowned and lesser known architects. Prior to this was the period of immense rural estates and aristocratic mansions; even earlier was indigenous Harlem. The Harlem of today still has to define its relation to the epic adventure of history. But thanks in part to so many incomparable buildings it is unlikely ever to be forgotten.

William H. Boylan, 358 West 118th
Street (now Barry Bergdoll and William
Ryall house), c. 1888. Staircase

358 West 118th Street (now Barry
Bergdoll and William Ryall house).
Living room

William Ström, 37 Hamilton Terrace
(now Yuien Chin house), 1899. View
east over central Harlem from garden

Frederick Law Olmsted and Calvert
Vaux, Morningside Park, preliminary
plan, 1873; revised plan, Olmsted
and Vaux with Jacob Wrey Mould,
1887

Riverside Drive looking north from West
145th Street, 1909

# SELECTED BIBLIOGRAPHY

*American Architect and Building News.* 1876–1938.

*Amsterdam News.* 1909–1919.

Anderson, Jervis. *This Was Harlem: A Cultural Portrait, 1900–1950.* New York: Farrar Straus Giroux, 1982.

Andrews, Wayne. *Architecture in New York: A Photographic History.* New York: Atheneum, 1969.

*Architecture and Building.* 1882–1932.

Binney, Marcus. *Sir Robert Taylor: From Rococo to Neoclassicism.* London and Boston: G. Allen & Unwin, 1984.

Birmingham, Frederic A. *It Was Fun While It Lasted.* Philadelphia: Lippincott, 1960.

Bolton, Reginald Pelham. *Washington Heights, Manhattan: Its Eventful Past.* New York: Dyckman Institute, 1924.

Boyer, M. Christine. *Manhattan Manners: Architecture and Style, 1850–1900.* New York: Rizzoli, 1985.

Brown, Henry Collins, ed. *Valentine's Manual of Old New York.* New York: Valentine's Manual, 1916–28.

Caldwell, A. B. *The History of Harlem: An Historical Narrative Delivered at Harlem Music Hall, April 24th, 1882.* New York, 1882.

Cromley, Elizabeth Collins. *Alone Together: A History of New York's Early Apartments.* Ithaca, N.Y.: Cornell University Press, 1990.

Desmond, Harry W., and Herbert Croly. *Stately Homes in America from Colonial Times to the Present Day.* New York: D. Appleton, 1903.

Dolkart, Andrew S., and Gretchen S. Sorin. *Touring Historic Harlem: Four Walks in Northern Manhattan.* New York: New York Landmarks Conservancy, 1997.

Eastlake, Charles. *Hints on Household Taste in Furniture, Upholstery & Other Details.* London, 1869; American ed., ed. Charles C. Perkins, Boston, 1872.

Grant, Ian, ed. *Great Interiors.* New York: Dutton, 1967.

Hamilton, Allan McLane. *The Intimate Life of Alexander Hamilton.* New York: Scribner's, 1911.

*Harlem Local Reporter/Harlem Local Reporter and Bronx Chronicle/Harlem Reporter and Bronx Chronicle.* 1873–1908.

*Harlem Magazine.* 1912–1934.

Harris, Cyril M., ed. *Illustrated Dictionary of Historic Architecture.* New York: McGraw-Hill, 1977; reprint, New York: Dover Publications, 1983.

Hodges, Graham Russell. *Root & Branch: African Americans in New York and East Jersey, 1613–1863.* Chapel Hill: University of North Carolina Press, 1999.

*In Pursuit of Beauty: Americans and the Aesthetic Movement.* New York: Metropolitan Museum of Art/Rizzoli, 1986.

Jackson, Kenneth T., ed. *The Encyclopedia of New York City.* New Haven: Yale University Press, 1995.

Johnson, James Weldon. *Black Manhattan.* New York: Knopf, 1930; reprint, New York: Atheneum, 1972.

Kennedy, Rose Fitzgerald. *Times to Remember.* Garden City, N.Y.: Doubleday, 1974.

Kimball, Fiske. *Domestic Architecture of the American Colonies and of the Early Republic.* New York: Scribner's, 1922; reprint, New York: Dover Publications, 1966.

Koeppel, Gerard T. *Water for Gotham: A History.* Princeton, N.J.: Princeton University Press, 2000.

Lewis, David Levering. *When Harlem Was in Vogue.* New York: Knopf, 1981.

Lockwood, Charles. *Bricks & Brownstone: The New York Row House, 1783–1929; An Architectural and Social History.* New York: McGraw-Hill, 1972.

Lodge, Henry Cabot, ed. *The Works of Alexander Hamilton*. New York and London, 1885–86.

Lowe, David Garrard. *Stanford White's New York*. New York: Doubleday, 1992.

McKay, Claude. *Harlem: Negro Metropolis*. New York: E. P. Dutton, 1940.

Morris, Robert. *An Essay in Defence of Ancient Architecture; or, A Parallel of the Ancient Buildings with the Modern: Shewing the Beauty and Harmony of the Former and Irregularity of the Latter*. London, 1728.

———. *Lectures on Architecture, Consisting of Rules Founded upon Harmonick and Arithmetical Proportions in Building*. London, 1734–36.

———. *Select Architecture: Being Regular Designs of Plans and Elevations Well Suited to Both Town and Country*. London, 1757.

Osofsky, Gilbert. *Harlem: The Making of a Ghetto; Negro New York, 1890–1930*. New York: Harper & Row, 1966.

Riker, James. *Revised History of Harlem (City of New York): Its Origin and Early Annals*. New York, 1904.

Ruttenbaum, Steven. *Mansions in the Clouds: The Skyscraper Palazzi of Emery Roth*. New York: Balsam Press, 1986.

Schiffman, Jack. *Harlem Heyday: A Pictorial History of Modern Black Show Business and the Apollo Theatre*. Buffalo, N.Y.: Prometheus Books, 1984.

Schuyler, Montgomery. *American Architecture and Other Writings*. Ed. William H. Jordy and Ralph Coe. Cambridge, Mass.: Belknap Press of Harvard University Press, 1961.

Sheldon, George W. *Artistic Houses: Being a Series of Interior Views of a Number of the Most Beautiful and Celebrated Homes in the United States*. New York: D. Appleton, 1883–84.

Silber, William B. *A History of St. James Methodist Episcopal Church at Harlem, New York City, 1830–1880, with Some Facts Relating to the Settlement of Harlem*. New York, 1882.

Sloane, Eric, and Edward Anthony. *Mr. Daniels and the Grange*. New York: Funk & Wagnalls, 1968.

Stern, Robert A. M., Gregory F. Gilmartin, and John Montague Massengale. *New York 1900: Metropolitan Architecture and Urbanism, 1890–1915*. New York: Rizzoli, 1983.

Stern, Robert A. M., Gregory F. Gilmartin, and Thomas Mellins. *New York 1930: Architecture and Urbanism Between the Two World Wars*. New York: Rizzoli, 1987.

Stern, Robert A. M., Thomas Mellins, and David Fishman. *New York 1880: Architecture and Urbanism in the Gilded Age*. New York: The Monacelli Press, 1999.

———. *New York 1960: Architecture and Urbanism Between the Second World War and the Bicentennial*. New York: The Monacelli Press, 1995.

Stokes, I. N. Phelps. *The Iconography of Manhattan Island, 1498–1909*. 6 vols. New York: Robert H. Dodd, 1915–28.

Watson, Steven. *The Harlem Renaissance: Hub of African-American Culture*. New York: Pantheon, 1995.

Wharton, Edith. *A Backward Glance*. New York: D. Appleton, 1934.

White, Norval, and Elliot Willensky. *AIA Guide to New York City*. 4th ed. New York: Crown, 2000.

*Who's Who in Colored America*. New York: Who's Who in Colored America Corp., 1927–1950.

*Who's Who in New York City and State*. New York: Lewis Historical Publishing, 1904.

# INDEX

Architects' and builders' names are in **bold** type.
Illustrations are indicated by *italic* page numbers.

# ILLUSTRATION CREDITS

Numbers refer to page numbers.

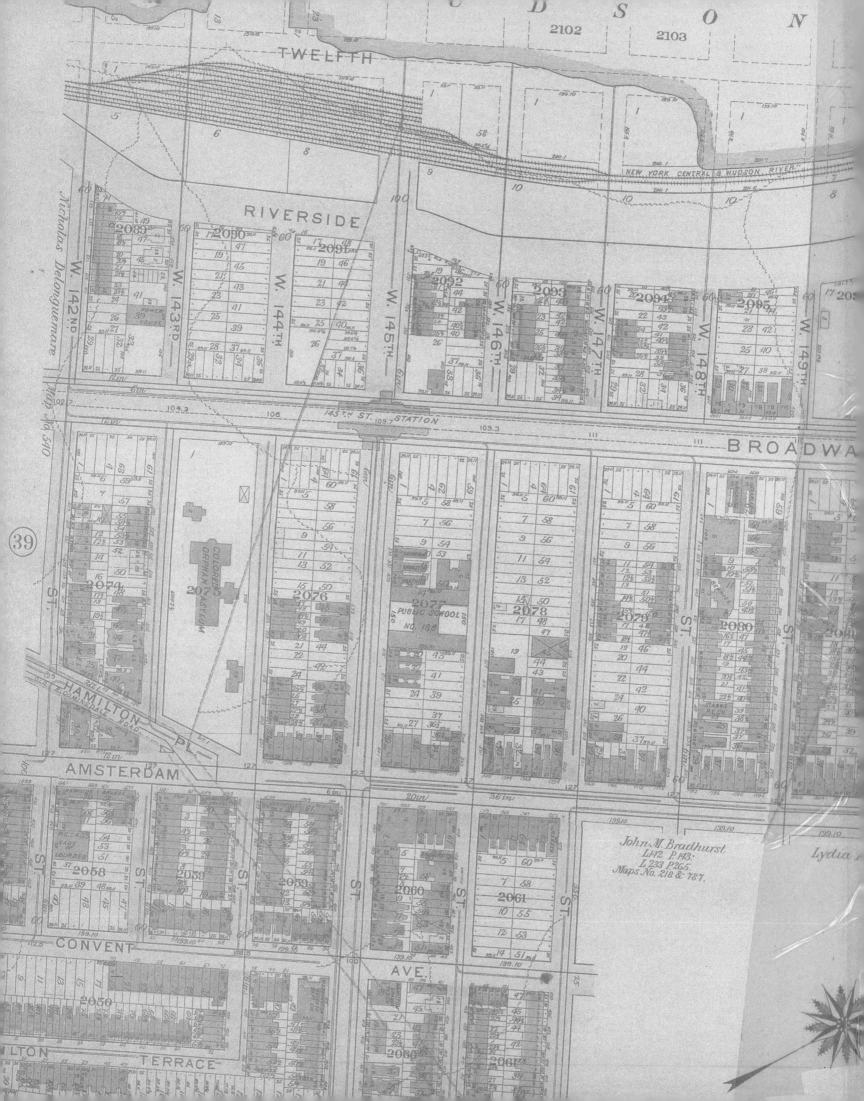